PREMIUM

B2 level | Coursebook

HARROW COLLEGE EFL CENTRE

D0495270

Put it down to experie

Lifestyles

03

06

Science fact, science fiction

07

04

Get away from it all

Entertain me

01

05

Play to win

Richard **Acklam**
Araminta **Crace**

PEARSON
Longman

PREMIUM

Welcome to the **Premium B2 level Coursebook**. This book is part of a course that has been developed to meet the needs of upper-intermediate students who might be considering sitting an international English exam at B2 level.

Premium has been developed both for students who want to take an exam and for those who would like to improve their English but may not wish to take an exam. It provides thorough preparation for exam success as well as comprehensive language development for students who simply want to improve their ability to understand and communicate in English.

Language development

Premium B2 Coursebook offers skills-based development and practice for upper-intermediate level students through engaging topics. These topics have been carefully chosen to generate discussion and provide students with opportunities for expressing their own thoughts.

Each unit contains core skills development in Reading, Writing, Listening and Speaking and practice in the specific functional language needed for Writing and Speaking. There is extensive coverage of Grammar and Vocabulary throughout the book, plus a full reference section at the back. There is also a Writing reference section containing models and tips for a range of different writing genres. Additionally, there are learner tips in each unit to help students maximise their own learning.

The **Exam Reviser** booklet provides a personalised and comprehensive store of vocabulary and functional language. Students can record not only essential words and phrases but also words and phrases that they like and want to use.

The **Premium B2 Workbook** offers plenty of further self-study practice. There is also a **Multi-ROM** with interactive language activities as well as the audio CD for the listening practice.

Exam preparation

For students wishing to maximise their chances of exam success, **Premium B2** develops the key language and exam skills required to achieve success in B2 level skills-based exams. This Coursebook focuses on practice in the First Certificate of English but the exam skills are transferable to other exams at this level. There is also an interactive FCE test on the **iTest CD-ROM** at the back of the coursebook, giving feedback on students' progress and test performance.

The **Exam Reviser** booklet provides students with a record of useful language they will need for a B2 level exam. It includes topic-based vocabulary, phrasal verbs and other useful language chunks. It also contains useful functional language for use in speaking and writing tests at B2 level. Additionally, there are ideas on how to prepare for an exam and specific tips for each paper of the First Certificate of English exam.

Further exam practice can be found in the **Workbook** as well as useful tips and hints on how to tackle exam-style questions.

For students who really want to maximise their chances of exam success, there is the **www.iTests.com** website where you can do more interactive test practice, get feedback on your performance and chart your progress towards exam success.

Whatever your reason for learning English is, we hope you enjoy using this book and wish you every success with your studies.

Richard Acklam
Araminta Crace

Exam information

The Cambridge First Certificate Examination in English consists of five papers. Each paper tests a different area of your ability in English and is worth twenty percent of your total result. After you take the exam you will receive a grade: A, B and C are pass grades; D and E are fail grades.

Paper 1 Reading

This paper contains three parts. Each part has at least one text with a task. There are thirty questions. A variety of types of texts may be used, including newspaper and magazine articles, reports, fiction, and informational material. You will have one hour to answer all the questions.

Part 1: Multiple choice
You choose between four alternatives to answer questions or complete statements about a text. There are eight questions.

Part 2: Gapped text sentences
Seven sentences have been removed from a text. You decide where in the text these sentences should be placed. There is one extra sentence that does not fit any of the gaps.

Part 3: Multiple matching
You read a text divided into sections and then match various prompts to each part of the text. There are fifteen questions. Sometimes more than one part of the text will match to one prompt.

Paper 2 Writing

In this paper you have two tasks. You will have one hour and twenty minutes to complete the two tasks. You will be required to write 120–150 words for Part 1 and 120–180 words for Part 2.

Part 1: this is compulsory and requires you to write a letter or an email based on information and prompts.

Part 2: in this you have a choice from four tasks. These will be a selection from a letter, which could include a 'letter of application', an article, a report, an essay, a review, a story, an article, essay, report or letter on one of the background reading texts.

Paper 3 Use of English

This part contains four parts with a total of forty-two questions. You will have forty-five minutes to answer all the questions.

Part 1: this consists of a multiple-choice lexical cloze. This is a text with twelve gaps, followed by twelve four-option multiple-choice questions.

Part 2: this consists of an open cloze. This is a text with twelve gaps which you must fill with an appropriate word.

Part 3: this consists of a word formation exercise. You will read a text in which there are ten gaps. You are given the stem of the word which you must use to complete each gap.

Part 4: this consists of eight 'key word' transformations. You are required to complete a sentence using a given word, so that it means the same as a previous sentence.

Paper 4 Listening

This paper contains four parts with a total of thirty questions. In each part you will hear the text(s) twice. The texts will be a variety of types, for example, phone messages, news, stories, interviews, advertisements, and conversations, etc. There will be a mixture of native and non-native speaker accents. This will last approximately forty minutes.

Part 1: you will hear eight short unrelated extracts of about thirty seconds each. The extracts could be from monologues or conversations. You have to answer a multiple choice question about each one. For example, you may be asked to decide on the general subject of the text, the relationship of the speakers of the purpose of the conversation.

Part 2: you will hear a monologue or conversation lasting about three minutes. There are ten questions in which you will have to complete the sentences with missing information.

Part 3: you will hear five short related extracts of about thirty seconds each. The extracts could be from monologues or conversations. While you listen you complete a multiple matching task in which you match the speakers to given prompts. There are five extracts to listen to and six prompts. One prompt does not fit any of the extracts.

Part 4: you will hear a monologue or conversation lasting about three minutes. You will have to answer seven multiple choice questions.

Paper 5 Speaking

This paper contains four parts. The standard format involves an interview between two candidates and two examiners. One of the examiners is an interlocutor who speaks to the candidates; the other examiner only assesses the candidates and does not speak. In Parts 1 and 2 of this paper, candidates speak mainly to the interlocutor. In Parts 3 and 4, the candidates speak mainly to each other. This will last approximately fourteen minutes.

Part 1: the interlocutor asks each candidate to say a little about themselves, for example where they come from, what they like doing in their free time, etc. This will last approximately three minutes.

Part 2: candidates compare two photographs they are given by the interlocutor. The interlocutor will ask a question about the photographs and the candidate will talk about them in relation to themselves and their own experience. This will last approximately four minutes.

Part 3: candidates are given visual prompts and are asked to carry out a task together which may involve planning, problem solving, decision making, prioritising or speculating. This will last approximately three minutes.

Part 4: the interlocutor develops the topic covered in Part 3 and asks the candidates to discuss and give opinions on more general questions related to the same theme. This will last approximately four minutes.

Entertain me

live concert

blockbuster

modern art

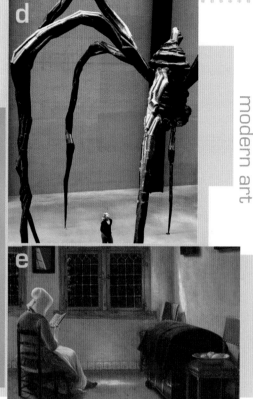

Unit 01

Introduction

1 Match each sentence with the correct picture.
1. It was an absolutely fantastic concert!
2. I saw a really good film.
3. What a brilliant game!
4. I've always loved reading!
5. I went to an interesting modern art exhibition.

2 Describe what you can see in each picture to other students.

3 R.02 ▶ You will hear someone talking about one of the things in Exercise 1. Listen and decide which one he is talking about.

4 Choose two things from Exercise 1 and take turns to tell your partner about them. Encourage your partner to give more details by asking questions.

A: *I saw a really good film yesterday … that new one with Johnny Depp. It's an action adventure film …*

B: *Is that your favourite kind of film?*

Vocabulary | going out

1 Work in pairs and follow these instructions. Then add one more idea to each list.

1 Name five types of music, e.g. *jazz*.
2 Name five types of film, e.g. *horror*.
3 Name five things you can see in a theatre or concert hall, e.g. *a play*.
4 Name five things you can see in a museum or art gallery, e.g. *sculpture*.

exam reviser   p3 | 1.1 ▶

2 Which of the things in your lists do you like? Why?

I really like dance music. I go to clubs regularly where I dance for hours!

3 Work in pairs. Complete the table with the words/phrases in the box. Use a dictionary if necessary.

> a blockbuster   a dance floor
> the dress circle   architecture
> watercolours   a gig   house music
> ceramics   a DJ

film/theatre	art	clubbing
a blockbuster		

4 R.03 ▶ Listen to the words and phrases in Exercise 3. <u>Underline</u> the main stress in each one.

5 Complete the sentences with the correct form of a word/phrase from Exercise 3.

1 I went to a small jazz club last night and saw a great _____ by a new band.
2 We went to a huge club in Ibiza where there are three separate _____ with different types of music.
3 I like most types of dance music. The only one I'm not so keen on is _____.
4 I went to a club last night where the _____ chose really unusual music all night.
5 I've got some great tickets for the musical. They're in the _____, so we'll have a very good view.

6 I generally enjoy low budget films more than the huge Hollywood _____.
7 My favourite kinds of paintings are _____, especially for delicate things like flowers.
8 I've decided to do an evening class in _____ and make a bowl to give my friends as a wedding present.
9 Whenever I visit a foreign city, I like looking at the _____ of the buildings, especially the old ones.

6 Ask each of these questions to different students. Make brief notes of the answers.

- Do you prefer big Hollywood blockbusters or low budget films? Why?
- Would you prefer to go clubbing, to meet friends in a bar or neither? Why?
- Have you been to a show, musical or play? What was it? What was it like?
- Have you been to a gig or concert? Who did you see? What was it like?

7 Choose one of the answers you heard in Exercise 6 and report back to the class. Use your notes if necessary.

premium plus   01

Listening

1 Discuss these questions with other students.

- When and how do you listen to music?
- Do you buy much music? Where do you get it from?

D Sandi Thom

A Abba

B Madonna

C Gnarls Barkley

2 R.04 ▶ You will hear part of a radio interview with a music historian. He talks about some of the changes in popular music in the last fifty years. Listen and answer these questions.

1 What is the connection between pictures A and B?
2 What is the connection between pictures C and D?

LISTENING SKILLS
It will help you understand the interview better if you think about the topic before you listen. Try to predict some of the language you will hear.

3 R.04 ▶ Listen again and complete these sentences by writing one word in each gap.

1 Madonna had to ask _____ from Abba to use their music.
2 Daniel thinks that people became interested in Abba again after the _____ *Mamma Mia* came out.
3 Daniel was inspired to find out about the history of Abba when he went to a concert by an Abba 'tribute' _____.
4 Downloading music from the Internet has become more and more popular – the _____ change took place around 2005 and 2006.
5 *Crazy* by Gnarls Barkley was the first song to get to number one counting download sales _____.
6 Sandi Thom broadcast her _____ to the world in several online concerts using a webcam in her house.
7 About _____ people saw for her first concert.
8 In April 2006, Sony offered her a million-pound _____ contract.

4 Discuss these questions with a partner.
• What music do you enjoy listening to at the moment?
• Do you have any particular singers or groups you have always liked? Who are they?

Speaking

1 R.05 ▶ You will hear four short conversations about these statements. Listen and for each one say which statement they are discussing and whether they have the same opinion.

A It's better to listen to live music than recorded music.
B There's no point in going to see a 'tribute' band because they are not the real thing.
C The average ticket price (€150) for a top band is far too expensive.
D People should pay to download music otherwise the musicians won't get paid enough.

2 R.05 ▶ Listen again and number these phrases in the order you hear them.

Expressing opinions
a I think that … ☐
b I don't think that … ☐
c I've always thought that … ☐
d In my opinion, … ☐
e From my point of view, … ☐
f As far as I'm concerned, … ☐
g I strongly believe that … ☐
h I have my doubts about … ☐

3 R.06 ▶ Listen and <u>underline</u> the words in each sentence which are stressed.

1 I've <u>always</u> thought that the tickets cost <u>far</u> too much.
2 I know what you mean, but from my point of view, it's worth it.
3 I quite like going to concerts but I think that they're often disappointing.
4 I don't think that that's always the case.
5 I strongly believe that people should pay to download music.
6 I agree in a way, but I have my doubts about how it would work.
7 As far as I'm concerned, tribute bands just aren't the same as the real thing.
8 In my opinion, they're still worth seeing.

4 Say the sentences in Exercise 3 to a partner. What effect does stressing these words have?

5 Choose three statements from Exercise 1. Complete the phrases in the Exam Reviser with your opinions about each statement.

exam reviser p19 | 1 ▶

6 Compare your opinions with another student. Do you agree?

7 Work with a different student and discuss these statements. Do you have the same opinions?
• It's better to see a film at the cinema than to watch it on DVD.
• Smoking should not be allowed in any restaurants, bars or clubs.
• The average ticket price (€80) for the most popular musicals is far too expensive.

Writing | review

1 **R.07** ▶ Listen to the song *I wish I was a punk rocker (with flowers in my hair)* by Sandi Thom. Which of these statements do you think best expresses what the song is saying? Compare your ideas with a partner.

- Music should be more easily available on the Internet.
- Music was a more important way of expressing opinions forty years ago.
- The music business is more interesting now because of new technology.

2 Read this review. Do you agree with the writer's opinion of this song?

MUSIC REVIEW OF THE WEEK

Sandi Thom recorded her first album **Smile ... it confuses people** in 2006, and it quickly went to number one in the album charts. The hit single **I wish I was a punk rocker** from the album also got to number one.

I think this is a really fun album with some catchy pop tunes. Sandi is a good singer and her voice is different from most other singers at the moment. My favourite track is **I wish I was a punk rocker**, which is lively and has very interesting lyrics. The only negative thing I would say about the album is that the backing band is a bit weak.

This CD gets better the more you listen to it. I would definitely recommend buying it and watching out for any further albums from this talented artist.

---

3 Read the review again and number three of these paragraph descriptions in the order you read them. (One of them should not be used.)

- A Gives a recommendation about whether to buy the CD or not.
- B Gives some information about the CD and singer.
- C Gives some information about where and when the writer got the CD.
- D Gives the writer's opinion about the CD (both positive and negative).

4 You are going to write a review of a CD. Choose a CD and use the paragraph descriptions from Exercise 3 to write notes about it.

Writing task

You recently saw this notice in an English-speaking magazine called *Music Monthly*.

> **Reviews needed!**
>
> Have you bought any new music recently? If so, could you write us a review of a CD? Include information on the singer (or band) and what the music on the CD is like, and say whether you would recommend the CD to other people.
>
> The best reviews will be published next month.

Write your **review**.

5 Compare your notes with another student. Make any changes that are necessary.

6 Look at the Writing Reference on page 190. Answer these questions.

- Which three tips (around the model answer) do you think are the most useful for you?
- Which expressions from the Useful Language section could you use in your answer?

7 Write your review using between 120 and 180 words. Use the notes you wrote to help you.

Grammar | question forms

1 Look at the question pairs A–H and answer the questions about them with a partner.

1 How is the word order of these two questions different? Why do we use indirect questions?
  - A Direct question: *How did you first get interested in popular music?*
  - B Indirect question: *Could you tell us how you first got interested in popular music?*

2 How do you typically form a *yes/no* question?
  - C Yes/No question: *Does anybody buy singles these days?*
  - D Wh- question: *What was the first single you bought?*

3 What is different about questions which are asking about the subject?
  - E Subject question: *Who are the original members of Abba?*
  - F Object question: *Which song do you prefer?*

4 Which question is *not* natural everyday English? Where in a question do we often put a preposition (if there is one)?
  - G *Where did you get that CD from?*
  - H *From where did you get that CD?*

•• see grammar reference: page 171 ••

2 There is a mistake in each of these questions. Find the mistakes and correct them. Use the information in Exercise 1 to help you.

1 Does she be going to the theatre with us on Friday?
2 You can play the guitar well?
3 What you have been doing all day?
4 What you think of that modern art exhibition yesterday?
5 What did happen at the end of the film?
6 About what are you talking?
7 Could you tell me how much is the entrance fee?
8 Would you mind telling me whether is there a performance this evening?

3 Rewrite these direct questions as indirect questions starting with the words given.

1 What is your favourite type of music?
 I'd like to know _____.
2 Do you like dancing?
 Could you tell me _____?
3 What are you going to do this weekend?
 Would you mind telling me _____?
4 Have you been clubbing recently?
 Could you tell me _____?
5 Did you enjoy the last film you saw?
 I'd like to know _____?
6 What did you do for your last birthday?
 Would you mind telling me _____?

•• see grammar reference: page 172 ••

4 Look at the answers which the pop star Shakira gave in an interview. Write the questions you think the interviewer asked. Write at least six indirect questions. Compare your questions with a partner.

1 It's Shakira Isabel Mebarak Ripoll.
 What's your full name?
2 Yes, I have. My friends call me Shaki.
 I'd like to know if you've got a nickname.
3 My father is from Lebanon and my mother is from Colombia.
4 I was born in Barranquilla in Colombia in South America and I still live there.
5 I've got four brothers and four sisters.
6 I would say I'm a perfectionist and maybe a bit bossy.
7 No, I don't smoke, or drink alcohol or coffee.
8 I'm five foot two inches.
9 I was thirteen.
10 I suppose you would call it Latin/pop-rock.
11 I write all my songs myself.
12 One great moment was when I was given the award for Latin Female Artist of the Year at the World Music Awards in 1998.

5 You are going to interview a partner about his or her free time. First prepare at least six questions you would like to ask. (Use both direct and indirect questions.)

6 Work in pairs. Take turns to interview each other.

7 What was the most interesting question you were asked? Tell other students.

premium plus | 02

Reading

1 Look at the descriptions of different reading skills in the box and discuss these questions.

- Which one or two of the skills would usually be appropriate for reading the following types of texts in everyday life?
 A a newspaper
 B an email from a friend you haven't seen for a long time
 C a train timetable
 D a novel
 E a note or message
 F instructions (e.g. for a DVD player)

- What do you usually do when you find a word or phrase in a text that you don't understand? Why?

- How do you think you could get better at reading in English? Compare your ideas with other students.

READING SKILLS

Skimming: reading quickly to get the general idea of a text

Scanning: picking out specific pieces of information (e.g. numbers)

Detailed reading: reading closely for details contained in a text

2 Look at the pictures of people reading and discuss these questions.

- Where do you think each person is? What do you think each person might be reading?
- Which reading situation in the pictures appeals to you most? Why?

3 Read the first paragraph from Chapter 1 of the novel, *If on a winter's night a traveller* by Italo Calvino. What do you think of the author's unusual style of writing?

4 Now skim the whole extract and choose which of these descriptions 1, 2 or 3 best summarises what the text is about. Spend only two minutes skimming the text and remember not to worry about unknown words at this stage.

1 The reader's position while reading and the author's style of writing
2 The reader's position while reading and the author's sadness at not knowing the reader
3 The author's position while writing and what the reader's expect from the book

Chapter one

You are about to begin reading Italo Calvino's new novel, *If on a winter's night a traveller*. Relax. Concentrate. Dispel[1] every other thought. Best to close the door; the TV is always on in the next room. Tell the others right away, "No, I don't want to watch TV!" Raise your voice – they
5 won't hear you otherwise – "I'm reading! I don't want to be disturbed!" Maybe they haven't heard you; speak louder: "I'm beginning to read Italo Calvino's new novel!" Or if you prefer, don't say anything; just hope they'll leave you alone.

Find the most comfortable position; seated, stretched out, curled
10 up[2], or lying flat. Flat on your back, on your side, on your stomach. In an easy chair, on the sofa, in the deck chair. On top of your bed, of course, or in the bed. You can even stand on your hands, head down, in the yoga position. With the book upside down, naturally. Of course, the ideal position for reading is something that you can never find. In
15 the old days, they used to read standing up. People were accustomed to standing on their feet, without moving. They rested like that when they were tired of horseback riding.

Well, what are you waiting for? Stretch your legs, go ahead and put your feet on a cushion, on two cushions on the arms of the sofa, on
20 the coffee table, on the desk, on the piano. Take your shoes off first. If you want to, put your feet up; if not, put them back. Adjust[3] the light so you won't strain your eyes. Do it now, because once you're absorbed in reading there will be no budging you. Make sure the page isn't in shadow; but be careful that the light doesn't glare[4] on the cruel white of
25 the paper. Try to predict now everything that might make you interrupt your reading.

So here you are now, ready to attack the first lines of the first page. You prepare to recognize the familiar voice of the author. No. You don't recognize it at all. But now that you think about it, who ever said
30 this author had a familiar voice? On the contrary, he is known as an author who changes greatly from one book to the next. You go on and you realize that the book is readable. It's the book itself that makes you curious; in fact, you prefer it this way, confronting[5] something and not quite knowing yet what it is.

5 Read the text again and for questions 1–6, choose the answer A or B which you think best fits according to the text.

1 The writer recommends that if you want to read
  A you should go to a quiet room.
  B you should turn off the TV.

2 He suggests that if you like reading upside down,
  A you could stand on your hands.
  B you could turn the book the other way up.

3 Why does the author say that people used to read standing up?
  A Because they thought it was good for you.
  B Because they needed a change from sitting down.

4 What does the writer say about your feet when reading?
   A You should always take your shoes off and put your feet up.
   B Some people prefer not to put their feet up.
5 What does the word *budging* mean in line 23?
   A moving
   B talking
6 In the last paragraph, it implies that the books of this author
   A are all of a similar style.
   B are all of different styles.

6 Look at the numbered words/phrases in the text and match each one with the correct definition below.
   A lying or sitting comfortably with your legs bent close to your body
   B doing something in order to solve a difficult or unpleasant situation
   C shine with a strong bright light that hurts your eyes
   D change or move something slightly in order to improve it
   E make something go away, especially a belief, idea or feeling

7 Discuss these questions.
   • Does the style of this author make you want to read the rest of the book? Why/Why not?
   • What is your favourite place or position for reading when you're at home (e.g. lying on the sofa)? Why?
   • At what time of day do you prefer to read? Why?
   • In what other situations do you like reading (e.g. on the train)? Why?
   • Do you enjoy reading novels? Why/Why not?
   • Have you ever read a novel or graded reader in English? If so, what did you think of it?

Vocabulary | staying in

1 Work in two groups. Group A look at box A and group B look at box B. Check the meaning and pronunciation of the words and phrases in your box. Use a dictionary to help you if necessary.

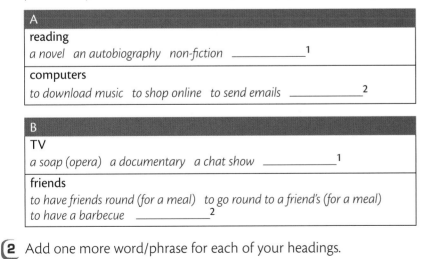

A
reading
a novel   an autobiography   non-fiction _____1
computers
to download music   to shop online   to send emails _____2

B
TV
a soap (opera)   a documentary   a chat show _____1
friends
to have friends round (for a meal)   to go round to a friend's (for a meal)
to have a barbecue _____2

2 Add one more word/phrase for each of your headings.

exam reviser   p3 | 1.2

3 Work in pairs (one from Group A and one from Group B). Tell each other the pronunciation and meaning of the words/phrases in your box.

4 Complete the sentences with the correct form of the words/phrases in Exercise 1.
   A: Have you read *My Side*, David Beckham's book about his life?
   B: No, I don't read many _____1. I prefer _____2, especially books about historical events.
   C: We've done a class survey about what people use their computers for.
   D: What's the most popular thing?
   C: Receiving and _____3 is number one, and second is _____4 onto their iPods.
   E: What's on TV tonight?
   F: Well, there's a _____5 about some kind of medical research, and then at ten there's a _____6 with Shakira as the guest.
   E: That should be good!
   G: Did you have a good weekend?
   H: It was great, thanks. We _____7 a friend's for lunch. She lives in Cambridge, so we didn't have far to go. The weather was good so we _____8 in the garden.

premium plus   03

5 R.08 Listen to four conversations. What answer does each person give to these questions?
   Conversation 1: What kind of programmes do you like watching on TV?
   Conversation 2: Do you prefer reading fiction or non-fiction?
   Conversation 3: What do you use computers for mostly?
   Conversation 4: Do you often socialise with friends at home?

6 Ask and answer the questions in Exercise 5 with a partner. Encourage your partner to give details by asking further questions.

Grammar | prepositional phrases

1 Look at the highlighted prepositional phrases in these sentences. Which one is about time, which about place and which about movement?

1 I like reading with my feet up *on the sofa*.
2 Sometimes I get *into bed* to read a book.
3 *In the old days*, they used to read standing up.

2 Complete each phrase with the appropriate preposition of time: *at*, *in* or *on*.

1 ——— 7.15 a.m.
2 ——— Tuesday
3 ——— 2001
4 ——— the winter
5 ——— New Year
6 ——— March 17th

3 Complete each phrase with the appropriate preposition of place: *at*, *in* or *on*.

1 ——— the bus stop
2 ——— page 56
3 ——— the middle
4 ——— the radio
5 ——— home
6 ——— Germany

4 Complete each sentence with the appropriate preposition of movement: *at*, *to*, *into* or *towards*.

1 We arrived ——— the theatre very late.
2 She got ——— bed and fell asleep.
3 Welcome ——— Australia!
4 A huge dog ran ——— me and I screamed.
5 Throw the ball ——— me and I'll catch it.
6 We're working ——— reaching an agreement.

Grammar note | *at the end/in the end*
Complete each sentence with *at the end* or *in the end*.

1 ———, I found my wallet under the sofa.
2 ——— of the book, they went to live in Canada.
3 There will be time for questions ———.

•• see grammar reference: page 172 ••

---

5 Read Julia's email to Giovanna quickly and answer these questions.

1 What film is she describing?
2 What is her general opinion of it?
3 What did she like most about the film?

Send | Options... | Help

To...
Cc...
Bcc...
Subject:
Attachments:

Normal ▾ A Arial ▾ 10 ▾ A **B** *I* U

Dear Giovanna,

I wanted to tell you about an amazing film I saw *on/at*[1] Friday. It's the second *Pirates of the Caribbean* film, *Dead Man's Chest* – have you seen it? It came out *in/at*[2] 2006, but I missed it then.

Maria and I went to see it *in/on*[3] Friday evening. We nearly missed the beginning because Maria arrived *to/at*[4] the cinema *on/at*[5] 8.00 p.m. – just before it started. When we went *to/into*[6] the cinema, it was all dark and we couldn't see where we were going! But *at/in*[7] the end, we sat right *on/at*[8] the front so we could get the full effect of the big screen.

Anyway, let me tell you about the film itself. It's set *at/on*[9] the same time and *at/in*[10] the same place as the first film and *in/at*[11] the beginning, it continues from where the first film finished. Do you remember Will and Elizabeth were going to get married? Well, something happens *in/at*[12] the middle of the wedding and everything changes! Well, I won't tell you what happens *on/at*[13] the end, because that would spoil it.

At/In[14] one point, I felt that the film was too long and I must say that the plot is a bit weak. But the action is fantastic, especially as you get *at/towards*[15] the end. There are some really good fight scenes and other stunts.

I hope everything is OK with you. I'll write again *at/in*[16] a couple of weeks.

Best wishes,
Julia

6 Complete the email with the correct prepositions.

premium plus 04

7 Think of a film you enjoyed. Prepare to tell your partner about it by writing some brief notes.

8 In pairs, take turns to tell each other about the films you enjoyed. Try to use at least five different prepositional phrases.

Speaking

1 R.09 ▶ Look at the list of questions A–H. Listen to two students talking about themselves and answer these questions.

1 Which question do both students answer?

2 Which other question does the first student, Paola, answer?

3 Which other question does the second student, Antonio, answer?

A What do you like about living here?

B What do you enjoy doing with your friends?

C What do you most enjoy doing when you're at home?

D Where's the best place to spend free time in your town?

E Do you like going to the cinema?

F What are you going to do this weekend?

G How important is TV to you?

H Do you think computers will replace newspapers in the future?

2 R.09 ▶ Listen again. What is the problem with the way Antonio answers his questions?

3 You are going to interview another student. Follow these instructions.

- Choose four questions from Exercise 1 that you would like to talk about.
- Prepare what you might say (refer back to the vocabulary in this unit).
- Say which questions you'd like to talk about.
- Answer the questions that your partner asks. Make sure you answer the actual questions and don't start talking about something else.

FCE close-up | Speaking (Paper 5, part 1)

Exam information

In this part of the exam, you answer some personal information questions that an examiner asks you. There is also a second examiner in the room who listens but doesn't say anything. This part of the exam lasts about three minutes. (The whole Speaking exam lasts about fourteen minutes.)

The examiner starts by asking you where you live (or where you come from) and what you like about it. He or she then asks you two or three more questions. The topics are all connected with personal information about you and your opinions, including some of the following:

1 Homelife (e.g. *What do you most enjoy doing when you're at home?*)

2 Personal experiences (e.g. *What's the most exciting thing you've ever done?*)

3 Education and work (e.g. *Would you prefer to work for a big or a small company? Why?*)

4 Leisure and entertainment (e.g. *Do you normally go out with family or friends?*)

5 The media (e.g. *Do you think computers will replace newspapers in the future?*)

6 Travel (e.g. *What is public transport like in your country?*)

Approach

1 Listen carefully to what the examiner asks you to speak about. If necessary, ask the examiner to repeat anything you don't understand, e.g. *Could you say that again, please?*

2 You don't have to give very long answers, but you do need to try to make them interesting, including a range of vocabulary and structures. For example, *In my opinion, the public transport system in my country is generally very good. The buses and trains are quite frequent and not too expensive …*

3 Make sure you answer the question the examiner asks you. (Don't start talking about something else.)

4 Don't worry if the examiner interrupts you while you are still talking – it does not mean you have done something wrong!

Practice task

R.10 ▶ Work in pairs and decide which of you is Candidate A and which Candidate B. Listen to the recording and follow the instructions.

Go to www.iTests.com or your CD-ROM for interactive exam practice

Grammar

1 Complete the questions with the correct alternative. Ø means no word should be added.

1 Where _____ Linda gone? *have/has/Ø*

2 Is he _____ to come to the party? *going/go/went*

3 Could you tell us _____ what time the swimming pool opens? *does/if/Ø*

4 _____ she play the guitar? *Can/Do/Ø*

5 What _____ happened to him yesterday? *has/did/Ø*

6 Do you know where _____ the butter is? *does/is/Ø*

7 Can you tell me _____ you've finished with that book? *if/what/Ø*

8 When does the film _____? *start/starts/started*

9 I'd like to know whether _____ you're going to the party? *if/are/Ø*

10 Would you mind telling me who _____ gave you this money? *did/have/Ø*

2 There are mistakes in eight of the prepositions in the phrases in *italics*. Find the mistakes and correct them.

1 We went out for a lovely meal *at Valentine's Day*.

2 I spent the whole day lying *at the beach* and reading my book.

3 He stood up and left *in the middle* of the film.

4 I've been *at Rome* twice.

5 We're *working to an agreement* about pay at work at the moment.

6 I'm really looking forward to seeing you all *on New Year*.

7 She arrived *to the party* really late because her train was delayed.

8 Everyone went quiet the minute she *walked to the room*.

9 He's lived *in South Africa* for ten years.

10 It was difficult to get tickets but *at the end*, we got some on the Internet.

Vocabulary

3 Complete this email with the correct form of a word/phrase from the box. Three items cannot be used.

> blockbuster   dress circle   gig   ceramics   architecture
> watercolours   dance floor   DJ   house music

Dear Kate

Sorry I haven't written for so long – I've been so busy!

Last weekend, it was my friend Charlie's birthday and lots of us went out clubbing on Friday night to celebrate. We went to a really good club, which I hadn't been to before where they play fantastic _____[1]! The _____[2] was really good and chose all my favourites – I couldn't stop dancing! In fact, the dancing was amazing and the _____[3] was completely packed the whole evening. Next time you come, I'll definitely take you there.

What else? Oh yes, a couple of weeks ago, I went to see a friend of mine who's in a band. They've just started doing _____[4] in small clubs and bars around here. It was really fun and quite a lot of people turned up.

How's your art course going? I must say I really loved the _____[5] you showed me last time – especially that set of plates you'd made. They were lovely. I think you said you were working on different styles of painting like _____[6] and things now. Is that right?

OK, I'd better go. I'll ring you soon and we'll fix up a weekend for you to come down.

Alex

4 Complete the crossword using the clues.

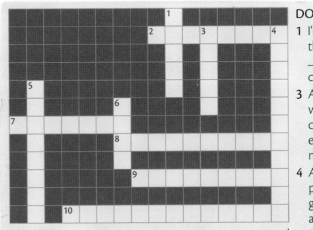

DOWN

1 I'm going to have the neighbours _____ for coffee. (5)

3 A long story written about characters and events that are not real (5)

4 A TV programme that gives information about a subject (11)

5 A TV show in which people are asked questions about themselves (4, 4)

6 I'll _____ you an email tomorrow. (4)

ACROSS

2 Receive information or programme on a computer from the Internet (8)

7 An occasion when you cook and eat food outside (8)

8 Books about real facts or events (3, 7)

9 A TV drama that is on regularly about the same group of people (4, 5)

10 A book that someone writes about their own life (13)

Family and friends

start a family

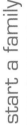

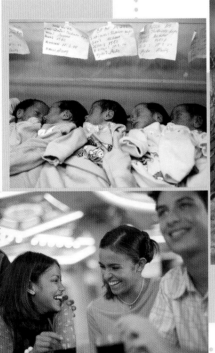

parenthood

friendship

Unit 02

Introduction

1 Look at the pictures. What does each one make you think about?

2 Complete each sentence with a word from the box. Then work in pairs to explain the meaning of each highlighted phrase.

> fallen   close   get   start   distant   touch

1 We're hoping to _____ a family next year after we've moved.
2 We're a very _____ family. We tell each other everything.
3 She's a _____ cousin, but I'm not exactly sure how we're related.
4 Jo is the only one I've stayed in _____ with since leaving university.
5 Dan and Cara have _____ out. Apparently, it was to do with money.
6 I don't really _____ on with Anna's boyfriend, so I see her on her own.

3 Discuss with other students.

- Would you describe your family as close? Why/Why not?
- Who do you get on best with in your family?
- Do you enjoy big family get-togethers? Why/Why not?

exam reviser   p4 | 2.1

premium plus   05

Grammar: present tenses; *quite, a bit* | Vocabulary: relationships; describing people | Writing: an informal letter/email

Unit 02

Reading

1 Look at the pictures and the title of the text. Tell other students what you think it will be about.

> **READING SKILLS**
> Before reading a text, it can often help to look at the title and any associated pictures to get an idea of what it will be about.

2 **R.11** Listen to two friends discussing a TV show called *Family Swap*. What happens in the show? How do they each feel about it?

3 Read the magazine interview with two of the women who appeared on *Family Swap*. Read it quickly to find out whether they each feel positive, negative or neutral about the experience.

Melanie   Margrit

TV Hot Spot – Family Swap

Our media correspondent managed to track down two of the latest participants in the hit show *Family Swap* to find out what they both thought about the experience.

Melanie

Melanie is a British housewife who works two nights a week as a midwife. Her husband, Dave, is the manager of a paint factory. They live together with their children, James (11) and Emily (9).

Q: Why did you want to be on *Family Swap*?

A: When I saw an advert in the newspaper asking for applications, I thought it would be exciting, a bit of of a laugh. When I told Dave, he bet me that I wouldn't do it.

Q: What was it like doing the swap?

A: I enjoyed it – it was very interesting to see what other people's lives are like.

Q: What parts of the experience did you find hardest?

A: The fact that the other family didn't speak English very well was difficult as I don't speak any German. Sometimes they had long conversations in German without trying to include me. I also found that the husband, Franz, spent a lot of time alone in his office and the children would often disappear into their bedrooms to play computer games or read. Eventually, I managed to get the children to watch TV with me after dinner.

Q: How did it affect your relationship with your own family?

A: Dave and I share the housework a lot more now – it's more of a 50:50 relationship and that gives him more time with the kids. I cook a lot more than I did before and that's something I now enjoy doing. We also spend more time together and go out together a lot more.

Q: Would you do it again?

A: Yes, definitely! It was good fun and it really opened my eyes. At first it was difficult for me as Margrit's house was a lot stricter than mine, but they were a really nice family. By doing the swap I found out a lot of things about myself and my own family and I think that's a good thing.

4 Read the article again in more detail. Which of the two women does each of these sentences refer to?

1 She works part-time.
2 Part of the reason she did it was for fun.
3 She wanted to do it because she thought she could learn from it.
4 Language was a bit of a problem.
5 Sometimes she found it hard not being with her family.
6 She wanted the family to spend more time together in the evenings.
7 Sometimes she couldn't help making comparisons.
8 Her husband seems to have done more of the housework before.
9 She's pleased about the way her children respond to her now.
10 Now she allows her children more control over their own rooms.
11 She and her husband go out more since the show.
12 She liked the other family even though there was more discipline.

READING SKILLS
Look for words or phrases in the text which express the same ideas as the key words in the sentences.

5 Discuss these questions with other students.
• What do you think of the way the two women reacted to their experience?
• Have you seen this show or a show like it? If so, what did you think of it? If not, would you be interested in watching it? Why/Why not?
• Would you be interested in being part of another family for a week? Why/Why not?

Melanie

Margrit

Margrit

Margrit is a Swiss housewife, married to Franz, who is a self-employed computer consultant. Their children are Orel (14) and Ueli (7).

Q: Why did you want to be on *Family Swap?*

A: I have always been fascinated by other cultures and other lifestyles. Also, I believe that it is very important to try new experiences. I think we can enjoy good experiences and learn from bad ones.

Q: What was it like doing the swap?

A: I mostly enjoyed the experience. There were bad times as well as good times, as there are with everything, but if you learn from the bad times, then it is a good thing.

Q: What parts of the experience did you find hardest?

A: Above all I missed my family. I found it hard not to compare Melanie's children with my own, especially when they did things I thought were wrong. I found the change in lifestyle difficult, too – I like to watch the news on TV and read newspapers and books, but they weren't interested in things like that.

Q: Do you think you relate to your family differently now?

A: Yes, I think we do relate differently since doing the swap. If I want my kids to do something, I don't have to ask again and again – they just do it! And I think that they appreciate and respect me more than before. I used to tell my kids to tidy their rooms all the time. I'm changing the way I deal with that. Now I just close the door – their rooms are their own and they can do what they want in them. I also learnt a lot of things living Melanie's life for a while. I feel able to say, 'No, I don't like that.' So now I'm doing more things which I want to do.

Grammar | present tenses

1 Look at these examples of present tenses, which relate to the *Family Swap* article on pages 18–19. Match them with the uses A–F.

1 Melanie works two nights a week as a midwife.

2 They live together with their children.

3 If I want my kids to do something, they just do it.

4 I believe that it is very important to try new experiences.

5 We do relate differently since doing the swap.

6 I'm changing the way I deal with their untidy rooms.

A The present continuous is used to describe actions or events going on now or around now.

B The present simple is used to describe permanent (not temporary) situations.

C The simple form is used with verbs that do not have continuous forms.

D The present simple is often used in subordinate clauses which refer to the future.

E *Do* can be used to add emphasis.

F The present simple is used to talk about things that happen regularly or all the time.

2 Choose the correct alternative in these sentences.

1 I usually *go/am going* and visit family in Cyprus, but this summer I *work/am working* as a tour guide to try to make some money.

2 *Do you know/Are you knowing* what 'affection' means?

3 Do *get/getting* in touch with Justin before he *moves/is moving* to Ireland.

4 This cake *tastes/is tasting* delicious. *Does/Is* your brother often *make/making* cakes?

5 I *don't think/'m not thinking* Tina understands exactly what you *want/are wanting* her to do.

6 I hope it *doesn't/isn't* still *rain/raining*./I *'m not wanting/don't want* to get wet on the way to my sister's wedding.

> **Grammar note** | *'State' verbs*
> Which of the following sentences are possible and which are not (or very unlikely)? Why?
>
> 1 A What do you think about?
>   B What are you thinking about?
>
> 2 A Does this fish smell OK?
>   B Is this fish smelling OK?
>
> 3 A I see what you mean.
>   B I'm seeing what you mean.

3 There are mistakes in each of these sentences. Find the mistakes and correct them.

1 I'm seeing my grandmother at least once a month.

2 We'll phone home when we'll get to the hotel.

3 I hate the way his girlfriend often replys for him.

4 Grandparents aren't usually living with their families in this country.

5 Your brother dosen't need to wait for us.

6 I'm really liking Mike's cousin.

7 The average number of children per family falls.

8 He do like you but he's just very shy.

9 I'm promising that I'll try to get on with your parents, but it's not easy.

10 At last my sister is begining to enjoy her new job.

•• see grammar reference: page 173 ••

(premium plus   06)

4 Work in pairs. Find three things you have in common and three differences between you. Tell other students what you found out. Which pair found out the most interesting things?

One thing in common is that both of us are living with our parents. One big difference is that Mario loves computer games but I definitely don't!

Speaking

1 R.12 ▶ Listen to part of a discussion. Which of these statements do the speakers discuss?

1 I think I will stay friends with my best friends forever.
2 I tell my best friend everything.
3 I prefer going out with a group of friends rather than just one friend.
4 My oldest friends are my best friends.
5 I talk to different friends about different things which are important to me.
6 I don't like spending a lot of time on my own.

2 R.12 ▶ Listen again. Which expressions from this box do the speakers use? Which words in the expressions are stressed? What effect does stressing these words have on the meaning of the sentence?

Responding to opinions	
That's more or less what I think.	☐
I'm not quite sure what I think about that.	☐
It depends really.	☐
That's sometimes true for me but not often.	☐
Absolutely not.	☐
That used to be true for me but it isn't any more.	☐
That's never been the case for me.	☐
Definitely.	☐

3 Match the expressions in Exercise 2 with the statements in Exercise 1, according to what is closest to your opinion. (If none of them fits, write sentences of your own.)

4 Work in groups of four. Discuss and explain the reasons for your responses to the statements in Exercise 1. Find the person who has the most similar attitudes to you.

5 Add three of the expressions for responding to opinions to the table in the Exam Reviser.

exam reviser ▸ p19 | 2 ▸

Vocabulary | suffixes

1 Match the words with the suffixes in the box to make nouns. Which combinations need a spelling change?

-ness -ment -ion -ship -hood -ity

friend*ship*   sad_____
child_____   member_____
happy_____   enjoy_____
affect_____   reliable_____
stupid_____   kind_____
excite_____   forgetful_____
father_____   relation_____

2 Complete these sentences with one of the answers from Exercise 1.

1 I had a wonderful _____. We were very close as a family and all got on incredibly well.
2 My gran has aged a lot recently and _____ is becoming a real problem.
3 I think the _____ of the party was all too much for your little cousin. She fell asleep as soon as her head touched the pillow.
4 David's _____ is one of the things I value most about him. If he says he will do something, he does it.
5 I'm afraid the _____ of the local tennis club has fallen to 250 this year.
6 My father isn't very good at showing _____ towards my mother, but I know he adores her.
7 I get a lot of _____ out of playing my guitar even though I'm not very good at it!
8 I'll never forget their _____ to me when I was ill. They were always coming round to see if I was OK or if I needed anything.

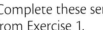 premium plus   07 ▸

3 Choose one of the subjects in the box. Prepare to talk to other students about it for one minute.

friendship   (your) childhood   happiness   parenthood

4 Speak to other students about your subject for one minute. Then answer any questions they have.

FCE close-up | Listening Multiple matching (Paper 4, part 3)

Exam information

In this part of the exam, you hear five short related extracts of approximately thirty seconds each. The extracts can be either about the same topic, e.g. recent holidays, or the speakers will all be doing the same thing, e.g. asking for information.

You match five sentences or phrases to the extracts but there are six options to choose from. You hear all the extracts twice.

Approach

1 Read the instructions to the task. They will tell you the general topic.

2 Read the multiple-matching options before you listen for the first time and mark the key parts.

3 Imagine what you think each person might say.

4 Listen and make brief notes of the main points each person makes.

5 Match the main points in your notes to the most appropriate option.

6 Listen again and check that each option fully matches what each speaker says.

Practice task

R.13 ▶ You will hear five people talking about friends. For questions **1–8** choose from the list **A–F** which statement fits each speaker best. There is one extra letter which you do not need to use.

A He/she is unsure about whether to see his/her best friend.

B His/her best friend is a family member.

C He/she and his/her best friend have spent a lot of time travelling together.

D His/her best friend is someone he/she can rely on in a crisis.

E An experience with friends wasn't what he/she expected.

F He/she doesn't like the idea of having one best friend.

Speaker 1	1
Speaker 2	2
Speaker 3	3
Speaker 4	4
Speaker 5	5

Go to www.iTests.com or your CD-ROM for interactive exam practice

Speaking

1 Look at the Speaking skills box. Then read these sentences and <u>underline</u> the 'fillers'.

1 Some friends have invited me to go with them to Mexico. It's like, you know, an amazing opportunity.

2 You should go and see Kevin Spacey's new film. It's about the breakdown of an ordinary American middle-class family. It's kind of interesting, I guess.

3 'Can you tell me the web address of that site where you can find old school friends?' 'Let me see, I think it's www.friendsreunited.com.'

4 Brian and I, well, you know, have started going out recently.

5 We probably should go to Jim's birthday party. I mean, we haven't seen him for ages.

exam reviser   p20 | 4

SPEAKING SKILLS

There are expressions in English that people use to give themselves time to think as they are speaking. These are often called 'fillers'. They don't have any real meaning on their own.

Be careful. If you use fillers too much, it can become irritating for the person you are speaking to!

2 R.14 ▶ Listen to the last two extracts from the Exam close-up practice task. Make a note of all the 'fillers' that you hear.

3 Tell another student about a special occasion which you spent with a group of good friends. Say what the occasion was, who was there, what happened and how you felt about it.

Grammar | *quite, a bit*, etc.

1 Look at the highlighted words in these sentences. Which three of the words in the box are similar in meaning to *incredibly*? Which two are similar to *quite*? Which one is similar to *bit*?

> pretty   terribly   a little   extremely   fairly   really

1 I'm incredibly close to my best friend.
2 My brother and I are quite similar.
3 My sister is a bit taller than me.

2 There are mistakes in seven of these sentences. Find the mistakes and correct them.

1 She is quite likes Steve but she doesn't know him well.
2 It was terribly freezing in Jill and Dave's new house. They don't have central heating yet.
3 I'm bit thirsty. I think I'll have an orange juice.
4 He was fairly surprised to hear we're getting married.
5 Sam's cousin is quite a nice. I hope he can come to the party tonight.
6 My new car is a little smaller my old one but it's fine.
7 The food's pretty good in that new Thai restaurant. We went there with friends last night.
8 I enjoyed the film but it was a fairly long and a bit sentimental.
9 Tim is a bit clever but he needs to study more.
10 I met quite an interesting guy at the party last night.

•• see grammar reference: page 173 ••

Grammar note | *quite*

Quite often means *fairly*, but it can also mean *completely*. In which of the following sentences does it mean *fairly* and in which does it mean *completely*?

1 You are quite right. We should visit your uncle.
2 Is Paul quite certain that he wants to leave school?
3 Julie is quite amazing the way she runs her own business as well as bringing up three small children.
4 I see my sister a lot as we live quite close.

3 Read this extract from an email message. Which option A, B or C best fits each gap?

Subject:

I went on holiday this summer with my family and it was _____ [1] fantastic! We were staying in this little hotel on the south coast of Turkey. It was _____ [2] close to the sea, ten minutes' walk at the most. It was _____ [3] comfortable and had a great pool. They also did _____ [4] delicious food in the evenings.

A lot of the time we stayed around the hotel and the pool and sunbathed, but I did go paragliding once – off the side of a cliff. It was _____ [5] scary I can tell you! We also spent a couple of days learning to scuba dive, which was good fun and _____ [6] relaxing in comparison.

1 A bit   B very   C really
2 A fairly   B little   C absolutely
3 A completely   B incredibly   C horribly
4 A bit   B fairly   C really
5 A pretty   B bit   C totally
6 A absolutely   B terribly   C quite

premium plus   08

4 Tell another student about the last time you found something:

- really interesting   • fairly dull
- pretty expensive   • incredibly exciting
- a bit annoying

Keeping a learner diary

1 Look at the diary extract on page 170. What different things does this student write about?

2 Discuss with other students. What reasons do people have for keeping a diary? Have you ever kept a diary? If so, what did you write in it? Did you enjoy keeping it?

3 What do you think about the idea of keeping a diary in English? If you did, which of the following things would you like to write in it? Why?

- The things you do on special days, e.g. trips, holidays, birthdays, etc.
- Your feelings at particular times, e.g. when you start living in a new place, at the beginning of a new relationship, etc.
- Quotes/extracts from books you read that you would like to remember
- Your own thoughts about people and life
- Your feelings about learning English
- Ideas for improving your English

learning tip

Vocabulary | describing people

1 Work in groups. Look at the words for describing physical appearance in the Exam Reviser. What other words can you think of to describe:

- hair?
- build?
- general appearance?

exam reviser p4 | 2.2 ▶

2 Look at the words in the box. For the ones you don't know, check these things in a dictionary:

- meaning
- pronunciation
- spoken or written English
- words with similar meanings

> good-looking bright sensible laid-back
> stylish stingy full-of-him/herself reliable
> shy odd stubborn open-minded sensitive

3 Match words from the box in Exercise 2 with each of these sentences.

1 He always tries to get out of paying for drinks when we go out even though I know he's got plenty of money at the moment.

2 Nothing seems to bother him. He's always very relaxed about everything.

3 Once she's made up her mind, it's terribly difficult to get her to change it!

4 Basically, you know that if she says she'll do something, she will definitely do it.

5 Ever since she won a prize for her first novel she's become quite annoyingly arrogant.

6 He doesn't really like social situations where he doesn't know other people. He finds it quite difficult to make polite conversation.

4 Write an example sentence for each of the other words in Exercise 2. Ask another student to identify the matching word.

5 R.15 ▶ You will hear two people describing someone they have met at a party. On a scale of 1–5 (1 is very negative and 5 is very positive), how positive or negative is each speaker about the person they met?

6 Think about three different people that you know well. Make notes of the key words you would use to describe each one.

7 Work in pairs. Take turns listening to your partner describe each of the three different people he or she knows well. Ask questions to find out more about the people. Tell your partner which one you would like to meet and why.

premium plus 09 ▶

Writing | informal email/letter

1 Informal emails and letters can be very similar in style. Which of these statements are true of them both.

1 The writer usually knows the person they are writing to.
2 Contractions (e.g. *isn't*, *there's*, etc.) are used.
3 Exclamation marks are sometimes used.
4 The style is sometimes like spoken language.
5 Informal language is used, e.g. *Can you meet me at 6.00 p.m.?* rather than more formal language, e.g. *Would it be possible for you to meet me at 6.00 p.m.?*
6 They usually end either *Yours faithfully* or *Yours sincerely*.

2 Look at the letter in the Writing Reference on page 192. What is the main subject of each paragraph?

3 Read this email. How many paragraphs do you think it should be divided into? Where would you begin and end each paragraph? (Don't worry about punctuation at this stage.)

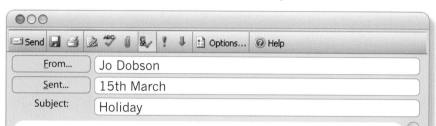

From... Jo Dobson
Sent... 15th March
Subject: Holiday

Hi there!
Thanks for your last email and all your news. You sound like youve been really busy with setting up the new business. I hope lots of orders start coming in soon. Its not long now until the 25th – I cant wait! It seems like ages since I last saw you – and since I had a proper holiday. I know you wont be able to meet me at the airport; its really kind of your brother to say he doesnt mind coming instead. Just so I have some idea of who to look out for, could you give me a rough idea of what he looks like? I dont want to go home with the wrong person! The other thing I wanted to ask you about was your family. Id like to bring them one or two small presents from England, but Im not sure exactly what yet. If you could tell me a little about them and what theyre like, that would be really helpful. I do hope everythings going OK with you. Ill tell you the latest about Silvio when I see you (and theres lots to tell!).
Jo

4 Look at these sentences and discuss with another student when we use the apostrophe (') in English.

1 The dog looks happy. It's just found its bone.
2 I haven't been on my brother's new boat yet. He's very proud of it!
3 My parents' house is very old. Apparently it was built in 1785.

5 Look at the email in Exercise 3. There are thirteen apostrophes missing. Where should each one go?

6 You are going to write a reply to the email in Exercise 3. Follow these instructions.

Be aware that you may not have time to write a first draft in an exam.

Planning
1 <u>Underline</u> the parts in the email/letter which ask you for information.
2 Decide how you are going to organise your reply. How many paragraphs are you going to have? What is going to be the subject of each one?

First draft
3 Write a first draft. Read it through. Does it answer all Jo's questions fully? Does it have a friendly opening and closing paragraph? Are apostrophes used appropriately? Is it written in an informal style?

Final version
4 Exchange your draft with another student. Tell them one thing you think is good about it and one thing you think they could improve.
5 Write your final version. Make sure it is clear and easy to read.

exam reviser   p22 | 9

Grammar

1 Read this email. Put the verbs in brackets into either the present simple or present continuous.

```
○○○
[Send] 🖫 🖨 📄 ✎ 📎 🔖 ! ↓ 📋 Options… ⦿ Help

[To…]    [                                    ]
[Cc…]    [                                    ]
[Bcc…]   [                                    ]
Subject: [                                    ]
```

Dear Jo,

Great to hear from you. I'm very pleased that all the wedding preparations _____¹ (go) well. I _____² (know) how much there is to do, even for a small wedding! I must say I _____³ (look) forward to it so much – I can't wait!

Did I tell you that I _____⁴ (move) out of my flat? The owners have decided to sell it, so I have to find somewhere else. I'm going to stay with Rick and Mary. They _____⁵ (have) a big house in Chorleywood and because their daughter, Meg, moved out in the summer, there's a spare room for me to stay in. Rick _____⁶ (like) to go running every morning, and I've said I'll join him, so hopefully I should get a bit fitter, too!

How's work? _____⁷ (you still have) problems with your boss? I hope not! My job _____⁸ (go) really well and we _____⁹ (open) a new office in Madrid next month. I've been asked to go out and help set it up, which is very exciting!

Do say 'Hi!' to Micky when you _____¹⁰ (see) him. It's hard to imagine him as a new father!

See you very soon now!

Love,
Paula xx

2 Put the word *quite* in the best place in these sentences.

1 It was a surprise to discover a tiny kitten in my bedroom.
2 I couldn't believe how many people were at the concert. It was incredible.
3 He's good at tennis. He plays at least twice a week.
4 I agree with you. We should have a big party for Dad's sixtieth birthday.
5 Why didn't we get our annual bonus. Sales have gone up by twenty percent. It's ridiculous!
6 We enjoyed last night's film, but it should have been half an hour shorter.

Vocabulary

3 Match the words in the box with the dictionary definitions 1–8.

> sensible stingy odd bright laid-back
> sensitive stylish stubborn

1 thinks about how other people will feel about something; easily offended or upset
2 intelligent, clever
3 strange or different from what you expect
4 attractive and fashionable
5 not generous, especially with money
6 refusing to change your mind even when other people criticise you or try to persuade you
7 relaxed and not seeming to worry about anything
8 able to make good and practical decisions

4 Put the word in brackets at the end of each sentence into the correct form.

1 Would you say you had a happy _____? (CHILD)
2 Barry felt great _____ for his grandmother. (AFFECT)
3 I can't believe my _____ last night. I should never have shouted at Fiona. (STUPID)
4 How much does annual _____ of the club cost? (MEMBER)
5 I'm getting very _____. Now I can't find my glasses! (FORGET)
6 I wish Tony was a bit more _____. This is the third time he's not turned up for a game of tennis. (RELIABILITY)
7 In his _____ he had forgotten to switch the camcorder on. (EXCITE)
8 Do you have a good _____ with your sister? (RELATION)

Pronunciation

5 Mark the stress on the correct syllables in these words.

1 _sen_sitive
2 stubborn
3 stylish
4 extremely
5 definitely
6 reliability
7 excitement
8 apostrophe

Lifestyles

lifestyle

urban

upmarket

Unit 03

Introduction

1 Name as many different places that people live in (e.g. cottage) as you can in one minute. Compare your ideas in the Exam Reviser. Then match each word/phrase in the list with the correct definition.

exam reviser p5 | 3.1

2 Look at the places in the pictures and on your list and discuss these questions.
- Which of them most appeals to you as a place to live? Why?
- Which one would you most like to stay in for a short time? Why?

3 R.16 Listen to three people describing their lifestyles. Which two words in the box could you use to describe each one?

sociable   hard   busy   leisurely   high-pressure   lonely

4 Discuss these questions with other students.
- Which of the lifestyles do you think is most like yours now?
- Which is most like the kind of lifestyle you would like to have? Why is that?

Listening

1 Look at the photos and read the text. Write two questions which you would expect to be discussed in the radio interview.

IT'S YOUR LIFE MONDAY

LIFE RADIO, 10.15 A.M. Today's programme is about 'living on the road'. We have an interview with Greg and Marcia Dowling, a couple who have been living, and working, on the road for over ten years. After nearly two years of living a 'normal' life, they swapped their comfortable house for a motorhome, and took to the highways of the United States. Find out about how they feel about the ups and downs of life on the road.

2 R.17 ▶ Listen to the radio interview. Does the interviewer ask the questions you expected?

3 R.17 ▶ Listen again. For each question, choose the best answer A, B or C.

1 What do Greg and Marcia do for a living?
A They are travel writers.
B They are photographers.
C Greg is an explorer and Marcia is a photographer.

2 What does Marcia say about going to bed at night?
A She finds it exciting to sleep in different places all the time.
B She doesn't usually sleep very well in new places.
C She likes sleeping in the same bed each night.

3 What is Marcia's main point about communicating with friends and family?
A She communicates by phone and email but she misses face-to-face contact.
B It isn't a problem because it's easy to contact people using the Internet and mobile phones.
C It's too difficult to stay in touch with people so they don't usually try.

4 Greg says living on the road is hard because
A the van often needs repairing.
B you have to get to know each new place.
C it's stressful not knowing where you're going next.

5 What does Marcia say about washing?
A She misses having a bathroom but she doesn't mind washing clothes without a washing machine.
B She doesn't miss having a washing machine because she likes the simpler life.
C Sometimes she would like a proper bathroom and doesn't like having to wash clothes by hand.

6 Greg says they have to work hard to organise their time because
A there is so much to do in each new place.
B they think it's important to have time on their own sometimes.
C he is not a very organised person by nature.

4 Discuss these questions with a partner.
- How would you describe Greg and Marcia's feelings about their chosen lifestyle?
- Can you imagine ever deciding to live 'on the road' in a similar way to Greg and Marcia? Why/Why not?
- What do you think you would miss most if you lived on the road? Why?

Learning outside the classroom

1 Which of these things have you done or do you do regularly? In what ways do you think they help improve your English? Discuss with a partner.
- Watch news, documentaries or dramas in English on TV.
- Watch films or DVDs in English (with and without subtitles).
- Use CD-ROMs to do grammar or vocabulary exercises.
- Use email, text messaging and computer messaging to chat to other English speakers.
- Use forums on the Internet to discuss issues with other English speakers.
- Use English websites on the Internet to find information.

2 Find other students who have used technology which you haven't used and ask them why they would recommend it.

3 Work in pairs. Tell your partner about one new way of improving your English using technology which you would like to try.

learning tip

Grammar | making comparisons

1 There is a mistake in each of the comparative and superlative forms in these sentences. Find the mistakes and correct them.

1 This lifestyle is more harder work than you might think.
2 We can live a much more flexibler life than before.
3 I certainly have to be tidyer than I was before.
4 Living on the road was most sensible thing to do.
5 Speaking on the phone is not good as having a friend pop round.
6 Is living in a van as exciting than he says?

•• see grammar reference: page 174 ••

2 Read the email quickly and decide how the writer feels about getting a bicycle: completely positive, completely negative or both positive and negative?

```
● ● ●
🖂 Send 🖫 🖨 🖉 ✓ 🖉 🖑 ! ⬇ 🗐 Options... ⓘ Help

  To...     |
  Cc...
  Bcc...
  Subject:
```

Dear Mike,

Just writing to say you must buy that bike you were thinking about! I'm using mine _**more often than**_¹ (often) I thought. I just intended to use it for having fun, but in fact, now I cycle to work every day – and I'm enjoying every minute!

I get to work _____² (quickly) and it's definitely _____³ (cheap) using the car. It's obviously _____⁴ (healthy), too and I'm already feeling _____⁵ (fit) before – especially because I've got two long hills to cycle up! On Fridays, I work in a different office which is _____⁶ (far) away, but it still only takes me half an hour by bike. It's probably _____⁷ (quick) going by car because in a car you often get stuck in traffic all the way.

I was worried about safety at first, but _____⁸ (scary) moment so far was when I rode over a hole in the road. I wobbled a lot and nearly fell off, but managed to keep going! I was a bit concerned, too, that I might get too hot and sweaty but it's _____⁹ (bad) I imagined. I just take some spare clothes and, if necessary, I have a quick shower at work!

I really think getting a bike is _____¹⁰ (good) decision I've made in a long time. You won't regret it I'm sure. Let me know what you decide – I look forward to hearing all about it.

All the best, Sam

3 Complete the email with the correct form of the word in brackets, using comparatives, superlatives or (not) as … as.

4 Look at the information in the box and match these headings with the correct parts A, B or C. Then complete the example sentences 1–7.

1 Describing things which are the same
2 Describing a small difference
3 Describing a big difference

Modifying comparatives and superlatives
A _____
1 *far, much, a lot* + comparative adjective/adverb He's far _____ interested in making money than anything else.
2 *by far, easily* + superlative adjective/adverb This is easily _____ most friendly town I've ever lived in.
3 *not nearly as … as* I'm not nearly as addicted to watching TV _____ you are.
B _____
4 *a bit, a little, slightly* + comparative adjective/adverb You get there slightly _____ quickly by car.
5 *not quite as … as* This neighbourhood isn't quite _____ affordable as it used to be.
6 *nearly as … as* My new flat is _____ as big as my old one.
C _____
7 *(just) as … as* His new house is just as expensive _____ the previous one.

5 Rewrite these sentences using the prompts in brackets to make comparative/superlative forms.

1 I'd be _____ (a bit / interested) in trying to live without technology if I could just keep my phone.
2 I think it would be _____ (much / interesting) to live on a houseboat than in a motorhome.
3 I think _____ (easily / good) thing about living on the road would be meeting different people.
4 I don't think I'd be _____ (quite / willing) to give up my television as other people I know.
5 I'd find it _____ (far / easy) to give up my washing machine than my computer.
6 I think that in the end living on the road would be _____ (just / boring) living in a house.

6 Look at your completed sentences in Exercise 5. Do you agree with them? Find out what other students think. Do you have the same opinions?

premium plus   10 ▶

Vocabulary | at home

1 Add six words or phrases to each of these columns. Compare your ideas with the Exam Reviser.

rooms and places at home	machines and objects at home
living room	*washing machine*

2 You are going to test your partner. First, write definitions for four words/phrases from the lists in the Exam Reviser. Then, take turns to test each other on your words.

A: *A machine that washes cups and plates, etc.*
B: *A dishwasher.*

exam reviser p5 | 3.2

3 Work with a partner and explain the difference in meaning between the verb phrases in *italics* in each pair of sentences. Use a dictionary if necessary.

1 A My brother's just back from Australia so we're having a party to *welcome him home*.
   B Sit down and *make yourself at home* while I make us some dinner.

2 A The living room *overlooks* a lovely square.
   B The kitchen *opens out onto* the garden at the back of the house.

3 A When we *have a loft conversion*, we'll have a spare bedroom for visitors.
   B We're *having an extension built* this year, so the kitchen will be much bigger.

4 A When I moved in, I *did up* the whole house, including putting in a new kitchen.
   B I've decided to *redecorate* all the bedrooms this year.

4 Two different people have written about houses or rooms. Complete each paragraph with the correct form of the words/phrases in Exercise 3.

Author	Message
Janet 120	Posted: 4th August 2007 3.47 p.m.
Member since: Jan 2005	When I was a child, I loved going to my grandmother's house. Nothing had changed for years and I used to hope that she'd never *do it up*[1]. All the paintwork was old and faded – I don't think she ever _____[2] at all. I slept in a tiny bedroom which _____[3] the sea and I loved listening to the waves during the night.

Author	Message
Peter B.	Posted: 17th September 2007 1.12 p.m.
Member since: Feb 2006	Did I tell you that James and Susi have just had a lot of work done on their house? They've had a _____[4] and made a new spare bedroom under the roof. It's great! They've also _____[5] at the back of their house. So now they've got a lovely sunny room to sit in which _____[6] the garden. When I came back from studying abroad last month, they had a party for me to _____[7]. It was lovely weather so we were half-in and half-out. It was very relaxed and everyone just _____[8]!

5 Choose one of these things and tell another student about it. Use at least four of the words/phrases from Exercises 1 and 3.

- A flat/house/room I love
- My flat/house now
- A flat/house/room from my childhood

premium plus 11

Speaking

1 R.18 You will hear someone talking about the pictures. Listen and say which style he prefers and why. Then tell a partner which style you prefer.

2 R.18 ▶ Choose the correct alternative in each sentence. Then listen again and check your answers.

A _____:

1 Both pictures are *connected/connect* to the theme of houses.

2 In both pictures, you can *see/look at* people in their living rooms.

B _____:

3 In this picture, the style they have chosen is very ornate, *where/whereas* in this one, it is a modern, minimal look.

4 The room in the first picture is quite dark and crowded. In *compare/contrast*, the room in the second picture is very airy and light.

C _____:

5 As *long/far* as I can tell, the people in the first picture live there and have chosen that style themselves.

6 I'm not *sure/know* if the people in the second picture live there or not.

D _____:

7 Personally, I much *rather/prefer* the more modern kind of style to this one.

8 I'd *rather/prefer* live in a place that was quite empty than somewhere like that.

9 I'm not very *sure/keen* on that kind of style.

3 Look at the groups of sentences in Exercise 3 again and match them with these headings.

1 Speculating about the pictures
2 Giving a personal comment
3 Talking about differences
4 Talking about similarities

4 Work in pairs and take turns to compare the pictures, giving your own opinions. Use the headings in Exercise 4 to organise what you're going to say.

5 Work in pairs. Student A look at pictures 1 and 2 on page 168. Student B look at pictures 3 and 4 on page 170. Take turns to compare your pictures. Use the headings in Exercise 4 and at least four of the highlighted phrases in Exercise 3.

exam reviser   p20 | 5

premium plus   12

FCE close-up | Writing Informal letter (Paper 2, part 2)

Exam information

In Part 2 of the FCE Writing paper, you need to choose one question from a total of four. The types of tasks that you are asked to choose from include: a letter, a story, a review, an article, a report and an essay. Your answer should be written in an appropriate style in 120–180 words.

There are different types of letters to a friend that you may be asked to write, including: a letter in which you make contact and give news; a letter in which you give advice; a letter in which you write a description (of a person or an object).

Approach

1 Read all the questions in Part 2 and decide which one you think you could do best.

2 If you decide to write a letter, underline the key words in the task and check you know:

- who the reader is (e.g. a penfriend, an organisation);
- what the appropriate style is (formal or informal);
- what the aim/purpose is (e.g. to give news to a friend, to apply for a scholarship).

3 Check that you know what kinds of things you are being asked to do (e.g. give advice, write a description).

4 Spend some time organising your ideas and writing a paragraph plan.

5 When you have finished, take some time to check your writing. Make sure you have:

- organised your writing into paragraphs;
- used an appropriate style (including starting and finishing);
- covered all the points asked for in the task;
- checked any mistakes with grammar and vocabulary;
- checked any mistakes with spelling and punctuation;
- written approximately the correct number of words.

Practice task

You are studying abroad in an English-speaking country. Write a letter to an English-speaking friend, describing the area and the house/flat you are staying in and saying what you like most about it and what you like least.

Write your letter. Do not write any postal addresses.

Go to www.iTests.com or your CD-ROM for interactive exam practice

Reading

1 Look at the pictures and these three pieces of information. They relate to an article you're going to read. Using this information, discuss with another student what you think the article could be about.

- The title of the article is *I will if you will*.
- It's about an organisation called *PledgeBank*.
- The definition of *pledge* is *to make a formal, and usually public, promise to do or give something*.

2 Underline the key words in these questions. (The first one has been done for you.)

1 What is the <u>main purpose</u> of *PledgeBank*?
2 Why are time limits important for *PledgeBank*?
3 Why is text messaging important for *PledgeBank*?
4 Whose idea was *PledgeBank*?

> ### READING SKILLS
> To help you focus on exactly what you need to understand in an article it is a good idea to <u>underline</u> the key words.

3 Read the article and answer the questions in Exercise 2.

I WILL IF YOU WILL

You want to change something in your community – but not on your own. Jane Dunbar finds out about PledgeBank and the power of numbers.

We all know what it is like to feel powerless and to feel that we can't change the things we want to change by ourselves. Many of us live relatively isolated lives without the support of communities. It's sometimes hard to get your opinion heard when you're on your own; it's much easier with the power of numbers behind you. Tom Steinberg, whose company, *mySociety*, sets up websites, wanted to do something about this. Among his most successful websites is *PledgeBank*.

'*PledgeBank* is about connecting you with other people who also want to make a change,' says Steinberg. 'But maybe they don't want the personal risk of being the only person to donate money, or turn up to a meeting, or whatever it is.' The way the website works is simple. **F 1**. For example, if you want to organise a street party, but don't want to do it by yourself, you could organise a pledge which says, 'I'll hold a street party, but only if three people who live in my street will help me to run it.'

It's hardly revolutionary, but even the small things make a huge difference to communities and to people's lives. **2**. If you are a parent, you could say, 'I will help

4 Six sentences have been removed from the article. Match the sentences A–F with the gaps 1–6 (The first one has been done for you.)

A It's free, it's easy to use and it aims to bring communities together to get things done.

B And, as you can see, the applications of *PledgeBank* really are limitless.

C It is essential, however, in order that the pledge creator concentrates properly on finding other people to sign up.

D They've been made so that people can spread messages the old-fashioned way, through post-boxes, on community notice boards, at school gates, and so on.

E There was also a man who encouraged eight people whom he'd never met to bury buckets in their own gardens to make homes for endangered stag beetles.

F You make a public promise, or pledge, which is saying, 'I'll do something, but only if other people will pledge to do the same thing.'

5 Discuss these questions with other students.

• Why do you think *PledgeBank* is so successful?

• Is *PledgeBank* something you would consider doing? Why/Why not? If you would, what kind of pledge do you think you would create?

---

run an after-hours sports club, but only if five other parents will commit one evening a week to doing it.' If you are in a band, you could say, 'I'll hold a gig, but only if forty people will come along.'

The pledges don't just have to be about your local community, either. One pledge creator stated, 'I'll give blood five times this year but only if ten other people will, too.' Someone else promised to 'give £20 to build a block of three classrooms and a dormitory for Bwindi Orphans' Nursery and Primary School in North West Uganda, but only if ten other local people will, too.' **3** . Despite nearly being deleted as a frivolous suggestion, three weeks later the final person signed up, and now there are a series of such buckets buried across the UK.

Once the pledge has been created, people then sign up, and the pledge either succeeds or it runs out of time and expires. The fact that there is a time limit for signing up to the pledge may seem harsh. **4** . And signing up doesn't have to be just via the Internet. Steinberg felt it wasn't a good idea to rely solely

on the Net for something which was trying to create communities.

The site therefore combines modern technology with some well-known approaches. Each new pledge created generates a set of leaflets of various shapes and sizes, designed for printing and distribution. These explain what the pledge creator is trying to do, and how to sign up. **5** . People can then sign up via the website or by a standard rate text message – the details are on the leaflets.

PledgeBank itself came into being as the result of an idea posted by someone on Steinberg's main site, *mySociety*. So it really was created for the people by the people. **6** . So if there's something – anything – you'd like to achieve in your community, in your place of employment, your university, among your friends or in your street, take a look at PledgeBank.com and create a pledge right now.

---

6 You're going to create a pledge in your class. First decide on a pledge you would like to create (or use the pledge below).

I will learn ten new words/phrases every day for a week if six other people will, too.

7 Walk around the room and tell as many students as possible what your pledge is. Encourage them to sign up for it.

8 Discuss these questions.

• Did you get enough people to sign up for your pledge? Why/Why not?

• Which of the pledges you heard about was the most interesting? Why?

Grammar | reflexives

1 Look at these sentences. In which two is the highlighted word necessary for the meaning, and in which one is it just added for emphasis?

1 *PledgeBank* itself was an idea posted on his main website.

2 I forced myself to sign up for a pledge to give up smoking.

3 It's sometimes hard to change things by ourselves.

2 Choose the correct alternatives in these sentences.

1 If you use the automatic timer, the oven turns *it/itself* off.

2 I don't think anybody else is going to help *us/ourselves*.

3 Try to *concentrate/concentrate yourself* on what you really want to do.

4 The idea *itself/oneself* is a good one, but it will be difficult to get enough people interested.

5 We'll see *us/each other* at the meeting later today.

6 John and I email *ourselves/each other* every week.

7 I really don't want to go to the meeting *by/on* myself.

8 I organised the party *by/on* my own, which was tiring.

•• see grammar reference: page 175 ••

3 Read the text quickly and answer these questions.

1 What is unusual about where Louise lives?
2 How are the tasks divided up?
3 How does Louise feel about living there?

Communal living

A HAPPY CO-EXISTENCE OR JUST HARD WORK?

Louise Hackey lives in a community where everyone takes turns to do tasks like cooking and washing up. They grow fruit and vegetables _____ [1] and even have _____ [2] own cows and sheep. She loves the communal aspect of life there, but she _____ [3] admits that it's sometimes hard work.

The group consists of forty-five adults and thirteen children. A large old building in the countryside provides _____ [4] with the chance to live a cooperative, self-sufficient lifestyle. Their intention is not to be isolated from the wider community, however, or to live _____ [5] themselves. Far from it – the group sees _____ [6] as part of the wider community, not separate from it, with the children attending local schools and many people having jobs locally.

Many of the main living areas are communal, although Louise appreciates her _____ [7] private living area, too. 'Sometimes I need to get away and be _____ [8] my own for a while,' she says. Members work for a minimum of 12-15 hours a week. Although they help _____ [9] other with some of the bigger tasks (e.g. the potato harvest), people mostly do individual tasks. You need plenty of commitment for happy co-existence. Louise thinks the hard work is worth it, however, because it gives _____ [10] the kind of lifestyle she believes in.

4 Complete the text in Exercise 3 using the words in the box.

> each own on by her herself itself them
> themselves their

Grammar note | *on your own/alone/lonely*
Look at the phrases in *italics*. Which two mean 'without any other people' and which means 'unhappy because you are without any other people'?

1 I've never lived *on my own* before.
2 I like spending at least one day a week *alone*.
3 I think I would feel *lonely* if I didn't live with people.

> premium plus 13 ▶

5 Ask and answer these questions with a partner. How similar are your opinions?

1 Would you like to live in a community like the one described in Exercise 3? Why/Why not? What would be the best thing and the worst thing about it?
2 What would be your ideal amount of time (e.g. in a day or in a week) to spend on your own and with friends/family?
3 Which of these things do you prefer to do by yourself? Explain why?

- shopping
- studying
- travelling
- cooking
- going to the cinema

Vocabulary | town and country

1 Complete these sentences with the words in the box. There are four words you do not need to use.

> comfortable leafy upmarket fashionable bustling
> quaint inner-city sprawling overcrowded isolated
> supportive historic

1 Manhattan in New York is famous for its expensive shops which are used by _____ people.
2 Parts of Dublin are very beautiful and _____.
3 Boscastle is a lovely old English village which is attractive in a _____ way.
4 Barcelona has a _____ city centre.
5 London is a large _____ city.
6 A lot of money has been spent on the _____ areas of Cardiff to create more parks and green space.
7 There are many _____ islands in Scotland which are difficult to get to.
8 Parts of Tokyo are very busy and _____.

2 How do you pronounce the words in Exercise 1? Say them to a partner and write each word in the correct in this table. Then mark the main stress.

1 syllable	2 syllables	3 syllables	4 syllables
		upmarket	*overcrowded*

3 R.19 ▶ Now listen to the words and check the pronunciation. Say them again with a partner.

> premium plus 14 ▶

4 Work in pairs and take turns to make sentences comparing two places you know. Use the adjectives in Exercise 1.

San Sebastián is a much more picturesque city than Bilbao. It's more overcrowded than it used to be, but ...

> exam reviser p5 | 3.3 ▶

Writing | discursive essay

1 Read this task and answer the questions

Writing task

You have had a class discussion about the following statement:

Life is better without technology.

Your teacher has now asked you to write an essay, discussing points for and against the statement.

1 Who will be reading your essay? What style do you need to use?

2 Which of these two paragraph plans, A or B, do you think is best? Why?

A 1 Introduction (what most people think about the statement)

　2 Positive points about the statement

　3 Negative points about the statement

　4 Conclusion (your opinion based on your arguments)

B 1 Introduction (your opinion about the statement)

　2 Positive points about the statement

　3 Personal opinion about the statement

　4 Conclusion (what you suggest should be done now)

2 Read the essay. Does it follow the best paragraph plan?

Life is better without technology

Many people claim that we rely too much on technology and that it is taking over our lives. I think it is difficult, however, to imagine a life completely without technology.

In my opinion, there are many advantages to reducing the amount of technology we use. Entertainment is a good example. Many people think they would not have any fun without their television or computer. In spite of this belief, people almost always enjoy themselves more by being more active and sociable.

On the other hand, there are some drawbacks to not using technology. Although we might not like it, a lot of communication in the modern world revolves around technology. Emailing and phoning are efficient means of contacting people, whereas writing a letter in the old-fashioned way is not as convenient. Other household equipment, such as fridges and washing machines, also contribute to a comfortable lifestyle.

I strongly believe that there are dangers in having too much technology. Nevertheless, if we are sensible we can enjoy its benefits without it dominating our lives.

3 Underline the six linkers of contrast used in the essay in Exercise 2.

4 Combine the ideas in these two sentences using each of the linkers of contrast. Refer to the essay in Exercise 2 to help you. Be careful about punctuation.

1 The countryside is more peaceful than the city.

2 You can have more fun in the city.

• however

*The countryside is more peaceful than the city. **However, you can have more fun in the city.***

• nevertheless

• although

• in spite of

• whereas

• on the other hand

5 You are going to write an essay about living in the countryside and living in a city. First write some notes in the table.

Advantages of living in the countryside	Disadvantages of living in the countryside
It's peaceful. You're more likely to get to know your neighbours.	There's not much to do.

6 Would you prefer to live in the countryside or in a city? Why? Discuss with other students. Do you agree with each other?

7 Before you write your essay for this task, look at the Writing Reference on page 194. Choose two phrases from the Useful Language box to use in your essay.

You have had a discussion about living in the countryside and in cities. Your teacher has now asked you to write a essay with the following title:

Living in the countryside is boring.

8 Write your essay using an appropriate paragraph plan and at least three of the linkers from the essay in Exercise 2. Write between 120 and 180 words.

Grammar

1 For questions 1–9, read the text and decide which answer A, B or C best fits each gap.

A company in Cornwall is now offering an exciting alternative to the traditional hotel. *The Mighty Oak Tree Climbing Company* now offers 'tree camping' – you don't camp under the trees, but right up in the trees _____¹. Special hammocks or 'tree-boats' are suspended in the branches of oak trees.

Alan and Bethany Stock decided to start their _____² tree camping company in Britain after coming across the idea in the USA. There is no need to feel nervous up in the trees, as everyone attaches _____³ to the hammock with ropes and harnesses. 'I tried _____⁴,' says Mike from London, 'and I enjoyed _____⁵ enormously. It's like being right inside nature. I went with two friends – I don't think I'd like to be there _____⁶ myself all night. At first, we scared _____⁷ other a bit by rocking the tree-boats, but you get used to it!

The instructor _____⁸ stays with you anyway, so you definitely feel safe. In the morning, they bring you breakfast in the trees. It's not cheap – £200 a night if you're on your _____⁹, or £140 per person for a group of up to five – but it's worth the money for such a once-in-a-lifetime experience.'

1	A itself	B himself	C themselves
2	A a	B own	C one
3	A themselves	B them	C it
4	A it	B itself	C them
5	A me	B my	C myself
6	A on	B by	C with
7	A each	B one	C own
8	A itself	B himself	C themselves
9	A own	B himself	C self

2 Complete the second sentence so that it has a similar meaning to the first sentence, using the word given. Do not change the word given. You must use between two and five words, including the word given.

1 Mexico City is more polluted than Tokyo.
as
Tokyo _____ Mexico City.

2 This neighbourhood isn't as friendly as it used to be.
less
This neighbourhood is _____ it used to be.

3 I've never lived in a flat as big as my new flat before.
easily
My new flat is _____ place I've ever lived in.

4 I live a lot nearer work than she does.
lot
She lives _____ away from work than I do.

5 James doesn't play football quite as well as Marco.
footballer
Marco is _____ than James.

6 I've never been to such a bad restaurant as this one.
far
This is _____ restaurant I've ever been to.

7 My sister and I are almost the same height.
tall
I'm _____ my sister.

8 He didn't drive nearly as quickly as he did last time.
than
He drove _____ he did last time.

Vocabulary

3 Complete these sentences with the correct word in the box.

> leafy sprawling upmarket run-down rural
> bustling quaint historic

1 I live in a very _____ area; the nearest town is miles away.

2 There are lots of trees around where I live; it's a very _____ suburb.

3 The city centre was _____ last night – full of people going out and enjoying themselves.

4 The problem with many large, _____ cities is that they are so ugly.

5 I like visiting _____ buildings and finding out about what happened in the past.

6 The local government has put a lot of money into regenerating the _____ areas of the city.

7 We stayed in a _____ little cottage on holiday – it looked like something from a postcard.

8 I love looking in all the _____ shops in Paris, even if I can't afford to buy anything!

Get away from it all

Premium | Unit 04

real adventure

back to nature

paradise

Unit 04

Introduction

1 Look at the pictures. Tell another student which situation appeals to you most and why.

2 Work in pairs to answer these questions. Check any words you are not sure about in a dictionary.

1 What different things are usually included in a *package* holiday?
2 What is the difference between *half-board* and *full-board* accommodation?
3 When do you need to *check in*?
4 What kind of transport can *take off* and *land*?
5 What do you think *ecotourism* is?

3 Discuss these questions with other students.

- Do you prefer to travel by plane, train, car or coach? Why?
- How do you like to pass the time on long journeys?
- Do you have a favourite kind of holiday? If so, what is it?
- Some people say that 'travel broadens the mind'. Do you agree with this? Why/Why not?

Grammar: narrative tenses; time linkers | Vocabulary: travel and transport; synonyms | Writing: a short story

Unit 04

Reading

1 Before reading the article, look at the pictures to predict what it will be about. What do you think is happening? Why? What do you imagine happened in the end?

2 Read the article and check your ideas.

I think the captain's dead

Nigel Ogden had been an air steward for twelve years when the unthinkable happened. Here, he describes how he saved his pilot's life.

I think about what happened every day. It was a beautiful morning and I was up early because I was working on the British Airways 7.30 a.m. flight from Birmingham to Malaga. I was thirty-six, had been an air steward for twelve years and loved my job with a passion. I expected that day to be especially enjoyable. It was a holiday flight, so the eighty-one passengers would be relaxed, and the crew had worked together for years.

It was thirteen minutes after take-off. We had just reached 5,200 metres and everything had been going well. I went through to the cockpit and asked the pilots if they'd like tea. I was just stepping out, with my hand on the door handle, when there was an enormous explosion and the door was blown out of my hands. [1] The whole cabin was filled with mist for a second – then the plane started to plummet.

I whipped round, peering through the mist. I saw that the front windscreen had disappeared and Tim, the captain, was going out through it. I grabbed him round the waist to stop him being sucked out completely. At the same time, somehow, the autopilot had become disconnected and the flight door had landed on the controls. [2]

Everything was being sucked out of the aircraft. I was holding on like grim death but I could feel myself being pulled out, too. John – one of the other stewards – rushed in and grabbed my trouser belt to stop me slipping further.

The aircraft was losing height so quickly, however, that the pressure soon equalised and the wind started rushing in at 620 kph and –17°C. [3] Simon, another steward, came rushing through and, with John, managed to free the controls so that Alistair, the co-pilot, could get the autopilot back on.

I was still holding onto Tim, but the pressure made him weigh the equivalent of 225 kilograms. My arms were getting colder and colder and I could feel them being pulled out of their sockets. I felt my arms weaken and Tim slipping. I thought I was going to lose him, but he ended up bent in a u-shape around the windows, his face banging against the window with blood coming out of his nose and the side of his head. His arms were flailing around and they seemed

3 Sentences A–F come from the article. Look at each one in turn, answer the questions about it and decide where it goes in the text.

A Some of *them* could see Tim out of the window.
- What do you think *them* refers to? Look at the possible gaps and the sentences before them to find something that *them* can refer to.

B *Papers were blowing around everywhere* and it was impossible to hear air-traffic control.
- What caused the papers to blow around everywhere? Find a reason before one of the gaps in the text.

C Fortunately, *his* body had just shut down and *he*'d been in a coma throughout the ordeal.
- Who do you think *his* and *he* refer to? In which paragraph is his physical state after the emergency talked about?

D All I could think was, '*It's a bomb.*'
- Before which gap do we read about things which sound like a bomb?

E I left *him hanging on* and staggered back into the main cabin.
- Before which gap is someone *hanging on* to something? What is he hanging on to?

F *This* meant that the plane was now hurtling down, at nearly 650 kmph, through some of the most congested skies in the world.
- Before which gap are there reasons why the plane would be *hurtling down, at nearly 650 kmph*?

4 Read the article again including the missing sentences. Check that it all makes sense.

5 Discuss these questions with other students.
- What do you think of the air steward's reactions to the crisis? Do you think you would have reacted in a similar or different way?
- Have you ever had to deal with an emergency or crisis situation? If so, what happened?

6 Choose five words from the article that you did not know before and that you would like to remember. Make sure you understand their meaning, pronunciation and what part of speech they are.

to peer (verb) + at/into/through s/thing /pɪə/ to look very carefully, especially because it is difficult to see clearly

7 Tell another student why you chose your five words.

---

about two metres long. I couldn't hold on anymore, so Simon strapped himself into the third pilot's seat and took a hold of Tim's ankles. ☐ **4**

By now, Alistair was in communication with air-traffic control, who were talking him through the landing. He asked for a runway of 2,500 metres because he was worried that the plane was so heavy with fuel, a tyre would burst or it would go off the runway, but all they could give us was 1,800 metres.

Over the intercom, Alistair told the passengers we'd lost the windscreen. ☐ **5** The cabin was silent as the grave as we walked up and down, preparing everyone for an emergency landing. I remember one man at the very back, with a little baby on his knee, saying to me: 'We're going to die,' and I said: 'No, we're not,' lying through my teeth.

It seemed impossible, but Alistair did the most amazing landing – completely smooth and stopping the aircraft only three-quarters of the way down the runway. The entire episode from the explosion to the landing had lasted just eighteen minutes, but it seemed like hours.

The paramedics came on board and put Tim on a stretcher. He was lying there, covered in blood, but to my amazement I heard him say: 'I want to eat.' I just exclaimed: 'Typical pilot!' ☐ **6** I went out onto the front steps, and shouted to the others, 'He's alive!' and then I cried my eyes out.

Using the Exam Reviser

Keep a special page in the Exam Reviser for words/phrases that you especially want to start using actively either in speaking or writing. Check this page regularly and see how often you have managed to use the words.

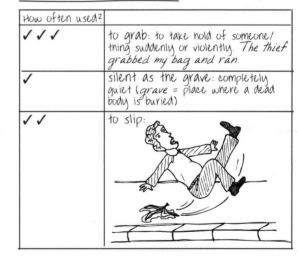

PREMIUM | Notes |

Favourite Words/Phrases

How often used?	
✓✓✓	to grab: to take hold of someone/thing suddenly or violently. *The thief grabbed my bag and ran.*
✓	silent as the grave: completely quiet (grave = place where a dead body is buried)
✓✓	to slip:

Grammar | narrative tenses

1 Work in pairs. Look back at paragraphs 2 and 3 of the article on page 38. Find one example of:

- the past simple
- the past continuous (*was/were* + *-ing*)
- the past perfect simple (*had* + past participle)
- the past perfect continuous (*had been* + *-ing*)

2 Which tense is used to refer to each of these?

1 something which happened before another past action
2 a finished action or situation
3 an action in progress at a definite time in the past
4 something in progress up to the time in the past we are talking about

•• see grammar reference: page 175 ••

3 Read these sentences. Which part in *italics* does each of the letters in the diagram refer to?

1 *At the time of the explosion, Nigel was talking to the pilots.*
2 At the time of the explosion, *the plane had just reached 5,200 metres.*
3 At the time of the explosion, *everything had been going well.*

```
         ———— A ————
    ———— B ————
————————————————— C ——————————— NOW
              X
              D
```

4 Read this text. Put the verbs in brackets into the correct tense.

5 Work in pairs. Look at the pictures. Say what you think these people had been doing or had done before the photos were taken.

premium plus   15

Gambian toad hitches lift

By Patrick Barkham

The smell of shoes in a tourist's suitcase ___was___ [1] (be) just too tempting for a curious creature from Gambia. So the African toad _____ [2] (jump) in and got a lift with a British tourist who _____ [3] (pack) his bags at the end of a winter break in Kotu, in Gambia.

When he _____ [4] (get) home, Farres Powell was more than a little surprised when he opened one of his cases and the globe-trotting amphibian hopped out. 'It looked like he _____ [5] (sleep) inside one of my trainers. I _____ [6] (just take) some souvenirs out of the suitcase and _____ [7] (chat) with my girlfriend about how good the holiday _____ [8] (be) when we heard a noise and _____ [9] (see) this little toad jump out.

'We couldn't believe it! It was the same toad we _____ [10] (see) on the hotel balcony the night before while we _____ [11] (play) cards. At the time we thought that was his home – we didn't think we'd be bringing him back to ours.'

As Terry the toad _____ [12] (try) to make its escape, Mr Powell caught it in a bowl. 'It was 40°C when we left Gambia, so the priority now is to keep him warm. We _____ [13] (get) some advice about his diet and we're feeding him worms from the garden, which he seems to like!'

Vocabulary | travel and transport

1 Work in groups of four. Each choose one of the groups of words 1–4. Explain the meaning and pronunciation of your words to the other members of your group.

1 yacht / canoe / ferry / surfboard
2 jumbo jet / parachute / helicopter / hot-air balloon
3 minibus / scooter / mountain bike / coach
4 wind-surfing / paragliding / water-skiing / white-water rafting

2 Add the words in this box to the correct columns in the Exam Reviser.

> chauffeur cabin crew aisle compartment
> boot runway guard cockpit cruise anchor
> mast bonnet lay-by deck

exam reviser p6 | 4.1 ▶

3 Match each of these words with the correct definition 1–6.

> travel trip journey voyage flight tour

1 the time spent travelling from one place to another
2 a long journey by sea or in space
3 a journey by air
4 a journey for pleasure in which you visit several different towns, areas, etc.
5 a (short) journey to visit a place or for a specific purpose
6 general activity of moving from one place to another

4 Complete the sentences with the words in Exercise 3.

1 Sarah's got an important business _____ to Brussels at the weekend.
2 My _____ to work is quite long and tiring.
3 We went on a fourteen day _____ of all the most famous Egyptian sites.
4 Our _____ to Barcelona was delayed by technical problems with the plane.
5 I think it's very true that '_____ broadens the mind'.
6 She made her transatlantic _____ in a specially designed boat.

5 Read the text about someone's travels after leaving school. Complete each gap with one of the words and phrases from Exercises 1–3.

_____¹ has always been a passion of mine. My first big adventure was to South Africa in the late 1970s. I went out as a young volunteer and got a place as a member of the _____² on a large ship carrying electrical equipment. During the _____³ I spent most of the time on _____⁴, getting a suntan!

While I was in South Africa, I did a lot of hitch-hiking. I remember getting a lift with one elderly man in his 1950s car. We'd gone about one kilometre when smoke and flames started coming out from under the _____⁵. He was very relaxed about it and just stopped and got a fire extinguisher out from the _____⁶. Another time, a beautiful Rolls-Royce picked me up. I couldn't believe my luck. It belonged to the Bishop of Swaziland and was being driven by his personal _____⁷.

At the end of my time, I flew back home. The _____⁸ only took about sixteen hours and was quite full. I was sitting next to a woman called Liz, who told me she didn't like flying. After a few minutes, she got out of her seat and started walking up and down the _____⁹. I think the cabin _____¹⁰ were a little concerned, but after a while Liz sat down and seemed OK. Later on, as we approached our destination, she asked me if she could hold my hand. During the landing, the plane bumped along the _____¹¹ as normal, but I could feel Liz squeezing my hand so tightly I thought my fingers were going to break!

6 Tell another student about any interesting types of transport you have been on. Refer to the words in Exercise 1 and these questions where appropriate:

- When?
- What?
- Where?
- Why?
- Who with?
- Feelings about the experience?

premium plus 16

Listening

1 Look at the pictures and answer these questions.
- Who can you see in the pictures?
- Why do you think they are well-known?

2 R.20 ▶ Listen to a radio interview. What were the main reasons why they wanted to go on this journey?

3 R.20 ▶ Listen again and complete the sentences. You will need no more than three words to complete each gap. The words you need are in the interview.

Professionally, both of Mishal Hussain's guests are _____ [1].

Their journey was _____ [2] miles long.

One of the things they had done on bikes together was to run a small _____ [3].

As a child, Charley grew up in Ireland in the _____ [4].

The first thing that Charley and Ewan talked about was _____ [5].

Ewan says the journey lasted for _____ [6] months.

The journey was difficult for their _____ [7] because they had to look after the children on their own.

They believed they wouldn't do the journey if they waited until their children had _____ [8] and left home.

Charley says they didn't want to do the journey in order to _____ [9] from their family lives.

Charley believes in the expression 'a change is as good as a _____ [10]'.

4 Discuss these questions with other students.
- What do you think about Ewan and Charley's adventure?
- Do you think it would be an exciting thing to do? Why/Why not?

Speaking | travel

1 R.21 ▶ Look at these questions. Then listen to four people responding to them. What do you notice about how each person answers their question?
1 Where did you spend your last holiday? What did you do?
2 What is the longest journey you've ever been on?
3 How do you prefer to travel: by train, plane or car? Why?
4 What is public transport like in your country?

2 Choose either question 1 or question 2 from Exercise 1 and prepare to answer it. Check that you know:
- the main things you want to say;
- the vocabulary you need.

3 Work in pairs. Take turns to answer your question. When you listen to your partner, check that they:
- answer the question directly and don't talk about other things;
- use a good range of vocabulary;
- give a full answer to the question.

4 R.22 ▶ Now listen to two students discussing question 4 from Exercise 1. What expressions do they use to give their opinions? What expressions do they use to respond to the other person's opinions?

5 Work in different pairs. Discuss questions 3 and 4 from Exercise 1. Use expressions for giving opinions and responding to opinions where appropriate.

Grammar | time linkers

1 Complete these explanations with the words in the box.

> then   finally   while   after   when
> by the time   eventually   as soon as
> afterwards   to begin with
> after that   as   at first

after joins two clauses and means when you have done something or something has finished. In a more formal style we can use *after* + *-ing*. *after* is not usually used alone as an adverb. Instead we use other expressions like _____¹ or _____².

_____³, _____⁴ and _____⁵ can introduce a background action or situation which is going on while something else happens.

_____⁶ and _____⁷ mean *in the end*. We use them to say that something happens after a long time or a lot of effort.

_____⁸ and _____⁹ refer to the beginning of a situation, to make a contrast with something different that happens later.

_____¹⁰ and _____¹¹ can be used to talk about two actions or events that happen very quickly, one after the other.

_____¹² is used before a noun/ pronoun + verb and means *not later than*.

Grammar note | *after, afterwards, after that*

Which one of the following sentences is *not* possible?

1 After we arrived at the hotel, we decided to go for a swim.
2 After arriving at the hotel, we decided to go for a swim.
3 Afterwards arriving at the hotel, we decided to go for a swim.
4 We arrived at the hotel and unpacked our bags. Afterwards, we decided to go for a swim.
5 We arrived at the hotel and unpacked our bags. After that, we decided to go for a swim.

2 Match the sentence halves 1–9 with A–I to make one complete holiday story. Notice how the time linkers in *italics* are used to link the text together.

1 *When* Miranda and her brother got to the airport,
2 *Finally,* their plane took off
3 *After* looking for somewhere to stay for several hours,
4 *To begin with* they were quite happy with their hotel,
5 That afternoon they went out to get something to eat,
6 The next morning, *by the time* they had had a shower and some breakfast,
7 They decided to go to the beach, but *as soon as* they got there,
8 They left the beach and went into town, but *while* they were looking around a local museum,
9 *After that,* Miranda and her brother

A but everywhere was closed as it was a public holiday.
B decided it was time to finish their holiday and go home.
C Miranda's bag was stolen.
D they realised it was nearly midday.
E it started to pour with rain.
F but later they realised that there were lots of things wrong with it.
G they *eventually* found a room in a small but cheap hotel.
H and a few hours later they arrived at their holiday destination.
I they were told their plane would be delayed for at least three hours.

3 Which two time linkers are possible in each of these sentences?

1 One day, _____ I was walking to work, I noticed a large group of people coming towards me.
   A after   B when   C as   D by the time

2 I waited in line for nearly an hour and _____ it was my turn.
   A eventually   B finally   C as soon as   D while

3 _____ I got to the party, all the food had been eaten.
   A While   B Afterwards   C By the time   D When

4 I heard a strange noise. _____ I thought it was my cat.
   A Then   B At first   C Suddenly   D To begin with

5 _____ I saw him, I realised I had made a terrible mistake.
   A As soon as   B While   C When   D Finally

•• see grammar reference: page 176 ••

4 Tell other students about a holiday you have had where things didn't go as planned. Explain what happened and why there were problems. Use at least three time linkers.

> premium plus   17 ▶

Vocabulary | synonyms

1 Put three words from the box into each of the columns in the table.

> stunned spellbound expedition shocked fed up
> fascinated quarrel excursion amazed depressed
> intrigued row dispute trip upset

a journey	an argument	interested	unhappy	surprised

2 Check your answers in the Exam Reviser.

 exam reviser p6 | 4.2 ▶

3 Choose the best alternative in each sentence.

1 The hotel has arranged an *excursion/expedition* for us to go and see the volcano on the next island.
2 I was a little *surprised/stunned* when Paul said he was interested in coming on holiday with us.
3 Paula and Ian had a bad *row/dispute* on Friday and they haven't spoken to each other since.
4 When the hotel said we couldn't have a room with a seaview, Mike got quite *upset/depressed*.
5 She was *spellbound/intrigued* to know whether he would take the job.
6 Flights have been cancelled due to a pay *quarrel/row/dispute* between the pilots' union and the airline.

4 Write three true sentences which each include one of the words from Exercise 1.

I have always been fascinated by volcanoes.

I'd love to go on some kind of scientific expedition to the Amazon rainforest.

premium plus 18 ▶

Writing | short story

1 Read this task. You are going to write one of the stories. First think about which one you would prefer to write.

Writing task

You have decided to enter a story competition in an international magazine. The competition rules say that the story must be 120–180 words long and must begin with the following words. Either:

1 We'd been looking forward to this holiday for a long time.

2 It was probably the most unusual type of transport I had ever been on.

2 Read the sentences and say why B would make a better start to Story 1 than A.

A My girlfriend Jenny and I had decided to travel around North Africa.

B My girlfriend Jenny and I had had a secret dream for many years of taking six months off work to explore the North African coastline on my 1,000cc motorbike.

3 Rewrite this sentence to make it a better second sentence for Story 2.

I had always wanted to go up in a hot-air balloon.

4 Work in pairs. Which different past tenses can you see in these sentences? Why are they used?

The first part of our adventure began when we arrived in the magical city of Casablanca. As soon as we had booked into our hotel, we went off in search of the 'medina' or old town. While we were making our way there and enjoying all the new sights and smells of the city, a young man approached us and offered to take us on a special tour of the city. This was when our adventures really began!

5 Look at your sentence from Exercise 3. Add two more sentences to complete the first paragraph of the story.

6 Read the task in the Writing Reference on page 196. Then look at the model answer to this task and answer these questions.

1 How many paragraphs is it divided into? What is the purpose of each paragraph?
2 What different narrative tenses can you see? Why is each one used?
3 Find examples of interesting vocabulary, e.g. *roared*, which is included to help engage the reader.
4 Find examples of time linkers, e.g. *when the second half started*, used to create smooth links between different parts of the story.
5 Does the story have an interesting beginning and ending? If so, what makes them interesting?

7 Write a first draft of your story. Remember you may not have time to write a first draft in the exam.

8 Read another student's first draft and think about the questions in Exercise 6. Tell him or her what you like about the story.

9 Write the final draft of your story. Check for mistakes of grammar, spelling or punctuation. Check that you have written the correct number of words.

FCE close-up | Use of English Lexical cloze (Paper 3, part 1)

Exam information

This part of the exam mainly tests vocabulary. You read a text with twelve gaps. After the text there are four sets of words or phrases for each gap. You must choose the correct option to complete each gap.

This part of the exam can test:

- words with a similar meaning, e.g. *journey, trip, travel*;
- common collocations, e.g. *make a mistake*;
- the grammar of certain words, e.g. *interested in something*;
- phrasal verbs, e.g. *give up something*;
- linking words, e.g. *despite, even if*.

Approach

1 Read the title and then skim the complete text to get the general idea. Don't worry about the gaps or the options below at this stage.

2 Read the text again. Look at each gap and the words before and after it carefully. Think about what word could go in the gap. Remember the word must fit the grammar and meaning of the sentence.

3 Consider the options for each gap. Eliminate the ones you know are wrong. Think about the different reasons why a word might be wrong in the context. In the given example, *voyage* is used for a water–based journey, *flight* for a journey by air, *travel* is uncountable.

4 Read the completed text all the way through to check your ideas. Don't leave any gaps. You do not lose marks for wrong answers.

Go to www.iTests.com or your CD-ROM for interactive exam practice

Practice task

For questions **1–12**, read the text below and decide which answer (**A**, **B**, **C** or **D**) best fits each space. There is an example at the beginning (**0**).

Example:

0 A voyage **B** journey **C** flight **D** travel

Long Way Round
by Ewan McGregor

Long Way Round is the tale of a remarkable **(0)** *journey* made by two men on motorbikes. But these are not **(1)** _____ any two men; Ewan McGregor is one of Britain's most successful actors and Charley Boorman is the son of the well-known film director John Boorman.

McGregor, it seems, is **(2)** _____ about motorbikes. And one day, while **(3)** _____ at a map of the world, it occurred to him that there was no **(4)** _____ why they wouldn't be able to ride by bike all the way round the world. So, he **(5)** _____ the idea over a meal to his best friend, Charley Boorman.

(6) _____ afterwards, they raced through Europe, Russia and then down through Canada and America. But as the miles slipped beneath the tyres of their big BMWs, their troubles started. Exhaustion, injury and accidents **(7)** _____ their strength. Treacherous roads, **(8)** _____ weather and turbulent politics challenged their stamina. And **(9)** _____, despite all the obstacles, they managed to ride more than twenty thousand miles in four months, changing their lives forever in the **(10)** _____. As they travelled, they documented their trip, taking photographs and writing diaries by the campfire.

Long Way Round is the **(11)** _____ of their adventures – a fascinating, frank and highly entertaining travel book about two friends riding round the world together and, against all the odds, **(12)** _____ their dream come true.

1 **A** only	**B** hardly	**C** quite	**D** just
2 **A** keen	**B** mad	**C** insane	**D** infatuated
3 **A** gazing	**B** glaring	**C** watching	**D** noticing
4 **A** purpose	**B** cause	**C** reason	**D** sense
5 **A** considered	**B** encouraged	**C** suggested	**D** raised
6 **A** Quickly	**B** Shortly	**C** Promptly	**D** Instantly
7 **A** tested	**B** evaluated	**C** examined	**D** investigated
8 **A** undecided	**B** uncomfortable	**C** unlikely	**D** unpredictable
9 **A** however	**B** but	**C** yet	**D** even
10 **A** course	**B** practice	**C** method	**D** process
11 **A** result	**B** finish	**C** produce	**D** event
12 **A** making	**B** completing	**C** realising	**D** understanding

Vocabulary

1 Use the clues to complete the crossword.

ACROSS

1 I like catching the _____ across to France. You can get out of your car, have a walk around and then get something to eat and drink. (5)

4 _____ we'd been in the coach all morning, we were very glad to get out and stretch our legs. (5)

6 Let's have a walk on _____ and watch the sun set before we go down below for a drink. (4)

10 We need to go down the river by _____. There is no path from this point. (5)

11 If you _____ through that window you can just see the trees at the end of the garden. (4)

12 Did the boys enjoy their _____ to Florida? (4)

DOWN

2 He loves sailing and last year he bought his own _____. He plans to sail around the Greek islands this summer. (5)

3 This afternoon we're going on a short _____ of the old part of town. Apparently, we'll visit the houses of some famous local artists. (4)

5 James is quite _____ up about breaking his leg on the first day of his skiing holiday. (3)

7 The main problem with the cruise was our _____, which was very small and very hot. (5)

8 Sarah was very _____ when she found out that Simon had lied to her. (5)

9 Did you know that the train _____ is almost double if you leave before 9.30 a.m.? (4)

10 Even today the _____ and the officers don't mix much on board ship. (4)

13 Tim and I had a _____ this morning and now he's not speaking to me. (3)

Grammar

2 There are mistakes in the narrative tenses in these sentences. Find the mistakes and correct them.

1 After he'd checked in his luggage, he was deciding to go and get a coffee.

2 Holly and Mary were out jogging when they had noticed the man on the motorbike.

3 They taken around all the local tourist sites and had a wonderful time.

4 After they found their seats, they had started arguing about who should have the MP3 player.

5 We were just driving into Rome when we were hearing the announcement on the radio.

6 The two brothers had been sat in silence for several minutes before one of them spoke.

7 By the time Derek arrived home, he was being tired, wet and exhausted.

8 James had thought nothing else could go wrong with their holiday, but he had been forgotten one very important thing.

3 Complete the story with these time linkers. There is an extra one that you do not need.

> as soon as   while   to begin with   by the time
> eventually   afterwards

Andy
12:59 p.m. Tue

It's great to be home, but the journey back was terrible! _____[1], just as we were leaving, Flo said she couldn't find her passport. So then we had to turn the flat upside down to find it. _____[2] we discovered it down the back of the sofa. _____[3] we had found it, it was too late to get to the airport by bus. So I tried to call a taxi, but the earliest a taxi could come was in an hour, which would mean missing our flight. _____[4] I kept ringing taxi firms, Carol went next door to see if our neighbours could give us a lift. Amazingly, they could and we raced off to the airport. _____[5] we got to the main airport building, we jumped out of the car and ran for the check-in desk. We needn't have rushed though as the plane was delayed by three hours!

Play to win

Premium | Unit 05

take part

competition

success

Unit 05

Introduction

1 Which of these would you *not* call a sport? Why? Add the words to the table in the Exam Reviser.

> hang-gliding ten-pin bowling snooker ice-hockey skiing golf
> motor-racing tennis archery baseball squash chess snorkelling
> bird-watching boxing badminton rock-climbing jogging yoga

exam reviser p7 | 5.1 ▶

2 Choose the correct alternatives in these sentences.

1 We've got some very good players in our football *band/team* this year.
2 What was the final *score/mark* at the end of the match?
3 Did you *beat/win* your chess match?
4 Tim is an excellent tennis *coach/tutor*.
5 Sandrine is very *competition/competitive*, isn't she?
6 I've just bought some new golf *clubs/rackets*.

3 Find a student who is or has been keen on one of the activities in Exercise 1. Ask them about it using these questions:

- Which one?
- When?
- Where?
- How often?
- What does it involve?
- Why do/did you enjoy it?

Listening

1 Look at this saying. Then discuss the questions with other students.

'It's not the winning, it's the taking part that counts.'

- What do you think the saying means?
- Do you agree with it? Why/Why not?

2 R.23 ▶ Listen to an extract from a radio programme and answer these questions.

1 What is the Scottish Football Association proposing?
2 Is each of the three members of the panel for or against the proposals?

3 R.23 ▶ Listen again and complete the sentences.

1 The name of the programme is _____.
2 The Scottish Football Association is suggesting changes to the football matches which are played by children in _____.
3 One idea is to change the score back to 0–0 if one team is ahead by more than five goals at _____.
4 Another proposal is that a side which is losing badly should be able to add _____ to their team.
5 They also want to stop winning teams receiving _____ at tournaments.
6 Terry's main objection is that these ideas do not reflect the _____.
7 Sarah points out that it is important that children get used to coping with _____ from an early age.
8 She also suggests that these changes could be quite _____ for children who take their sport seriously.
9 Arnold actually thinks the proposals could lead to matches being more _____.
10 He is in favour of _____ of trophies for teams that win tournaments.

4 Discuss these questions with other students.

- What do you think of the proposals in the programme? Are you for them or against them? Why?
- Did you play much sport as a child? Did you enjoy it? Why/Why not?

Grammar | obligation and permission

1 Read the description of a sport. What two names is the sport known by?

article	discussion	edit this page	history

This is a sport played by two teams. A standard match consists of two periods of forty-five minutes each, known as *halves*. The object of the game is to score by getting the ball into the opposing goal. The team that scores the most goals by the end of the match, wins.

Each team consists of eleven players, one of whom **has to** be the goalkeeper. A number of players **can** be replaced by substitutes during a game. Only the goalkeepers **may** touch the ball with their hands or arms but they are only **allowed to** do this in the penalty area in front of their goal.

The basic clothing players are **required to** wear includes a shirt, socks and appropriate footwear. Players are **forbidden to** wear or use anything that is dangerous to other players, e.g. jewellery. The goalkeeper **has to** wear clothing that is clearly different from the other players and the referee.

@ online encyclopaedia @ online encyclopaedia @ online encl

2 Read the text again. Which of the highlighted words and phrases express obligation? Which express prohibition? Which express permission?

3 Discuss these questions with other students.

1 Which sentence is the odd-one-out in these two groups? Why?

   A You can't have any brakes on your bike.

   B You mustn't have any brakes on your bike.

   C You don't have to have any brakes on your bike.

   D You're required to wear special glasses to protect your eyes.

   E You're supposed to wear special glasses to protect your eyes.

   F You ought to wear special glasses to protect your eyes.

2 Which three of these sentences are correct?

   A I have to start doing more sport.

   B I've got to start doing more sport.

   C I often have to train on Saturday evenings.

   D I often have got to train on Saturday evenings.

3 Put these sentences into the past.

   A I *have to* collect my tennis racket on Thursday.

   B I *must* play Tony at golf again because we had such a good time.

   C I've *got to* buy a new cycle helmet.

4 Which sentence is incorrect in each of these groups? Find it and correct it.

   A You don't need to be a member to use the courts.

   B You needn't to be a member to use the courts.

   C It isn't necessary to be a member to use the courts.

   D You can wear protective clothing.

   E You're allowed to wear protective clothing.

   F You're permission to wear protective clothing.

5 In which case, **A** or **B**, was a tennis court definitely booked?

   A We didn't need to book a tennis court as lots of courts were free.

   B We needn't have booked a tennis court as lots of courts were free.

• • see grammar reference: page 176 • •

4 Complete the second sentence so that it has a similar meaning to the first sentence, using the word given. Do not change the word given. You must use between two and five words, including the word given.

1 It's necessary for you to be at the stadium by 11.00 a.m.

   got

   You _____ to be at the stadium by 11.00 a.m.

2 It's fine to get advice in between games.

   allowed

   You _____ to get advice in between games.

3 You cannot stop another player from getting to the ball.

   permitted

   It _____ you to stop another player from getting to the ball.

4 It is not necessary for you to wear any special kind of clothing.

   have

   You _____ to wear any special kind of clothing.

5 We would advise you to stretch well before and after a game.

   should

   You _____ well before and after a game.

6 It's very important to avoid eating a lot before you play.

   must

   You _____ a lot before you play.

7 You're supposed to wear a crash helmet.

   ought

   You _____ wear a crash helmet.

8 It wasn't necessary for me to bring a spare racket.

   have

   I _____ brought a spare racket.

premium plus 19 ▶

5 Think of a sport or game you know. Find another student who doesn't know this sport or game very well. Tell them the basic rules. Explain the aim of the game, how many players there are, what equipment you must use and how you win.

FCE close-up | Reading Multiple matching (Paper 1, part 3)

Exam information

In this part of the exam, you read several short texts or one long text which is divided into sections. You decide which part of the text matches each prompt. (Sometimes more than one part of the text matches a prompt.)

Approach

1 Read the title and sub-headings (if there are any) and skim the text (or sections of text) quickly to get a general idea of what it's about. (Don't read through the multiple-matching prompts at this stage.)

2 Read the prompts carefully. Underline the important words in each one.

3 Go through the text (or sections of text) to find the relevant section of information for each prompt.

4 Underline the part or parts of the text which match the prompt. Look for words or phrases which mean the same as the words in the prompt. These words/phrases will be synonyms rather than the exact same words. (If you can't find the answer to a particular prompt, leave it until the end.)

5 Always choose an answer. You do not lose marks for a wrong answer.

Practice task

You are going to read a magazine article about some different kinds of sports. For questions 1–15, choose from the sections of the article (A–F). The sections may be chosen more than once.

Which section(s) of the article mention(s):

that these are old sports? (1) _____ (2) _____

that you may become addicted to this sport? (3) _____

that these are combinations of other sports? (4) _____ (5) _____ (6) _____

that you can observe or participate in this sport? (7) _____

that this sport is not very enjoyable to watch? (8) _____

the importance of the weather? (9) _____

why some people may not enjoy doing this sport? (10) _____

the enormous physical effect of doing this sport? (11) _____

how you score in competition? (12) _____ (13) _____

that this sport is increasingly popular? (14) _____

possible benefits the sport may have for wildlife? (15) _____

Try something new!

Feeling like you'd like to spice up your life with a new and different kind of activity. Here are a few sports which you may not have tried out yet.

A This is a sport which draws elements from a wide range of activities, but is basically high-speed yachting – without the water. Hence the name '**land-yachting**'. It usually takes place on beaches where you can find the necessary strong wind currents. Rigs closely resemble a canoe on wheels; some have sails attached, while others use huge kites to power them. Many participants come from a sailing background and some of them reach speeds of up to 70 mph, but you don't actually need a great deal of experience to drive one. Activity centres offering equipment and tuition provide an excellent introduction into the sport.

B Crawling on your hands and knees through a dark, damp hole deep underground may not be everybody's idea of having a good time, but if you get the bug, you'll find yourself going back time and time again. **Potholing** is the sport of exploring caves and involves crawling through narrow spaces, climbing with ropes and getting wet! It can be an eerie experience but also great fun. Many centres organise outings to local caves and, in addition to guides, they'll provide you with the all-important mud-repellent clothing.

Go to www.iTests.com or your CD-ROM for interactive exam practice

C Put hockey together with waterpolo and sub aqua, and you have one of the fastest-growing watersports in the UK, and a possible candidate for future Olympics. **Octopush** involves two teams of six attempting to push a heavy lead puck into a goal at either end. Competition bouts last fifteen minutes each way, with frequent surfacing for breaths of air. It's not a great spectator sport, for obvious reasons, but has a growing following among both men and women of all ages.

D We have to go way back in history to find the beginnnings of the art of **falconry**. Its predatory stars attract a wide range of people. Groups can watch while a selection of birds are put through their paces and the braver ones among you can have a go at handling one. Sessions are built around the fact that birds fly for food, usually raw meat. When they have had enough to eat, they sometimes stay in a tree and refuse to return. Many of the birds used are endangered species, so, in addition to being educational, an interest in falconry helps to raise money for research.

E A sport that truly deserves the label 'extreme', **skysurfing** is a cross between skydiving, surfing and gymnastics. Skysurfer pairs jump in tandem; one performs death-defying tricks while his or her team-mate films the manoeuvres. The boards are reinforced snowboards that allow riders to carve through the air. With your feet strapped to the board, the execution of spins and somersaults places a tremendous strain on the body, similar to that experienced by jet pilots.

F The ancient discipline of **fencing** remains as popular as ever, despite the decline in duelling with a foil blade to sort out one's differences! In competition, fencers fight on a special marked area that allows them to move forwards and backwards but restricts sideways movement. You get points when the tip of the foil strikes your opponent's electronic chest guard. Practice to achieve the necessary speed, fitness and lightning reflexes can be done at clubs around the country.

Vocabulary | success

1 Complete the report from a high school headteacher with the words in the box.

> pass   prize   achievement   won   record   successful
> achieved   result   did   success

We are proud to report another _____[1] year in all areas at Headland High. Starting with sports, our football first team, under the expert guidance of Joss Partley, _____[2] the Sussex Schools Trophy for the second year running. And in athletics, Sarah Mayhew broke the junior national 800 metre _____[3].

The end-of-year school concert was also a great _____[4] with over 150 children taking part in various ways and £375 being raised for charity.

In addition, our sixth form students _____[5] extraordinarily well this year. For the first time, 100% managed to _____[6] their A-level exams and nearly 75%_____[7] the necessary grades for them to go to the university of their choice. 35% were awarded 'A' grades, which is a remarkable _____[8].

The Brodie _____[9] for all-round _____[10] goes to Francis Brown. Francis has worked consistently hard at all his academic subjects and has also been active both musically and on the sports field. He is an example to all of us of the fruits of hard work.

2 There is a mistake in each of these sentences. Find the mistakes and correct them.

1 The performance was a great successful and everyone was very pleased.
2 To our surprise, we won the other team 3–0.
3 I think space travel is one of our greatest achieves.
4 She is the most succeeding salesperson in the company.
5 I won first record in a competition – it's a new car!
6 Do you know the achievement of the England versus Italy game?
7 Everyone in our class took the maths exam with an 'A'.
8 Ian beat the 1,500 metres although he isn't really fit.

exam reviser   p7 | 5.2

3 Tell another student about something you were pleased to have achieved or something you won.

> **Vocabulary note** | *win, gain, earn*
> Complete the sentences with the correct form of *win*, *gain* or *earn*.
>
> 1 I _____ nearly twice as much in my new job.
> 2 You can _____ €25m in this week's lottery.
> 3 She _____ a lot of useful experience by working in her father's firm.

Reading

1 Discuss these questions with another student.

1 Have you ever flown a kite? When/ Where? Did you enjoy it?

2 Have you ever heard of/been to a kite-flying tournament?

3 How do you think someone could 'win' a kite-flying tournament?

2 Read the extract from the novel *The Kite Runner* and find the answer to question 3 in Exercise 1.

The Kite Runner

Every winter, districts in Kabul held a kite-flying tournament. And if you were a boy living in Kabul, the day of the tournament was the highlight of the cold season. I never slept the night before the tournament. 5 I'd roll from side to side, make shadow animals on the wall, even sit on the balcony in the dark, a blanket wrapped around me. I felt like a soldier trying to sleep in the trenches the night before a major battle. And that wasn't so far off. In Kabul, fighting kites was a little 10 like going to war.

As with any war, you had to ready yourself for battle. For a while, Hassan and I used to build our own kites. We saved our weekly allowances in the fall and dropped the money in a little porcelain horse Baba had 15 given me. When the winds of winter began to blow and snow fell in chunks, we went to the bazaar and bought bamboo, glue, string and paper. We spent hours every day shaving bamboo for the center and cross pieces, cutting the thin tissue paper which made for easy 20 dipping and recovery. And then, of course, we had to make our own string, or *tar*. If the kite was the gun, then *tar*, the glass-coated cutting line, was the bullet in the chamber. We'd go out in the yard and feed up to five hundred feet of string through a mixture of ground 25 glass and glue. We'd then hang the line between the trees, leave it to dry. The next day, we'd wind the line around a wooden spool. By the time the snow melted and the rains of spring swept in, every boy in Kabul had numerous cuts on his fingers from a whole winter 30 of fighting kites. I remember how my classmates and I used to huddle, compare our battle scars on the first day of school.

The Kite Runner

The kite-fighting tournament was an old winter tradition in Afghanistan. It started early in the morning 35 on the day of the contest and didn't end until only the winning kite flew in the sky – I remember one year the tournament outlasted daylight. People gathered on sidewalks and roofs to cheer for their kids. The streets filled with kite fighters, jerking and tugging on their 40 lines, squinting up to the sky, trying to gain position to cut the opponent's line. Every kite fighter had an assistant – in my case, Hassan – who held the spool and fed the line. The rules were simple: No rules. Fly your kite. Cut the opponents. Good luck.

45 Except that wasn't all. The real fun began when a kite was cut. That was where the kite runners came in, those kids who chased the windblown kite drifting through the neighborhoods until it came spiraling down in a field, dropping in someone's yard, on a tree, 50 or a rooftop. The chase got pretty fierce; hordes of kite runners swarmed the streets, shoved past each other like those people from Spain I'd read about once, the ones who ran from the bulls. And when a kite runner had his hands on a kite, no one could take it from him. 55 That wasn't a rule. That was custom.

For kite runners, the most coveted prize was the last fallen kite of a winter tournament. It was a trophy of honor, something to be displayed on a mantle for guests to admire. When the sky cleared of kites and 60 only the final two remained, every kite runner readied himself for the chance to land this prize. He positioned himself at a spot that he thought would give him a head start. Tense muscles readied themselves to uncoil. Necks craned. Eyes crinkled. Fights broke out. And 65 when the last kite was cut, all hell broke loose.

3 Read the extract again. For questions 1–8, decide which answer A, B, C or D fits best according to the text.

1 How did the narrator feel before the kite-flying tournament?
  A relaxed
  B excited
  C aggressive
  D uncomfortable

2 How did they get the materials to make their kites with?
  A They found them.
  B They were given them.
  C They gambled for them.
  D They used their pocket money to buy them.

3 The cuts on their hands were caused by
  A ground glass.
  B string.
  C knives.
  D wood.

4 The tournament would usually take
  A a morning.
  B all day and all night.
  C most of the day.
  D part of the day and part of the night.

5 *Shoved* (line 51) describes a way of
  A standing.
  B talking.
  C pushing.
  D running.

6 The kite runners
  A started running before the kite had been cut.
  B kept away from others when they ran.
  C fought for the fallen kites when they found them.
  D would follow a fallen kite anywhere.

7 The kite runners wanted the last fallen kite in order to
  A show off to other people.
  B fly it themselves.
  C prove their speed.
  D get a prize.

8 The writer uses the phrase *all hell broke loose* (line 65) to emphasise how
  A much he feared this moment.
  B much noise and activity there suddenly was.
  C hot it was.
  D terrible the fighting was.

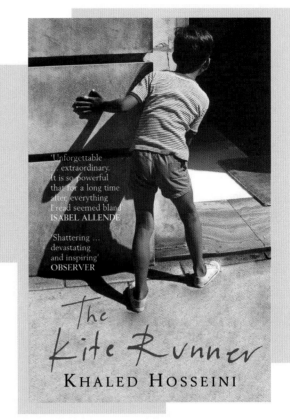

4 Discuss these questions with other students.
  • Would you be interested in watching or taking part in a kite-fighting tournament? Why/Why not?
  • Do you know of any customs or sports that are special to your country? Describe them.
  • Did you like the way the extract above was written? Would you be interested in reading more from this book? Why/Why not?

5 American spelling is sometimes a little different from British spelling. Find the American spelling for these words in the last two paragraphs of the story.

> neighbourhoods spiralling honour

6 Look at these pairs of words. In each pair, which word is American and which is British? (Use a dictionary if necessary.)

1 center – centre
2 theatre – theater
3 color – colour
4 favour – favor
5 catalog – catalogue
6 dialogue – dialog

7 skillful – skilful
8 enrol – enroll
9 travelled – traveled
10 defence – defense
11 paralyze – paralyse

7 Can you see any patterns in the way American spelling is often different to British spelling? Do you know any other examples of American spelling? Discuss your ideas.

Grammar | *would* and *used to*

1 R.24 ▶ Listen to five people talking about their attitude to sports/games as children. Match sentences A–F with the speakers 1–5. Use the letters only once. There is one extra letter which you do not need to use.

A He/she describes a game he/she played.
B He/she is surprised by how things have changed.
C The rules of his/her sport have changed recently.
D He/she misses a past activity.
E Things changed a lot for him/her after leaving school.
F He/she can feel frustrated when playing his/her sport.

2 R.24 ▶ Listen again. Then tell another student which of the five people you have most in common with and why.

3 R.25 ▶ Complete these sentences from Exercise 1. Put one word in each gap. Then listen and check your answers.

1 I never _____ to do much sport.
2 I used _____ love finding a good book.
3 We _____ all get to school really early.
4 I didn't have time for any sport. It took ages to _____ used to that.
5 I _____ to be pretty good in my teens.
6 I'm not as fit as I was . . . I can't really get _____ to that.
7 When I was younger we _____ always be outside.
8 I _____ used to getting up an hour or so before I go to work.

4 Match the structures 1–4 with their uses A–D.

1 *would* + infinitive (without *to*)
2 *used to* + infinitive (without *to*)
3 *be used to* + noun/gerund
4 *get used to* + noun/gerund

A to say you are accustomed to something because you have been doing it for some time
B to say you are becoming accustomed to a new situation
C to talk about past habits and repeated actions but not about past states
D to talk about past habits and states that do not occur now or no longer exist

> **Grammar note | *used to***
> Which of these sentences is not correct? Why?
>
> 1 Did you used to play much sport?
> 2 I'm not used to getting up before 7.00 a.m.
> 3 He used to be the fastest boy in my school.

5 R.26 ▶ Listen and write down the six questions exactly as you hear them.

6 Work in pairs. Decide on a particular age, e.g. ten years old. Take turns to ask and answer questions 1–6 in Exercise 5 in relation to that age.

7 Write a summary of what your partner told you.

When José was ten, he used to play lots of sports including football and tennis. He also used to enjoy going bird-watching with his father in the mountains . . .

learning tip

Practising your English

Research shows that people who learn languages well and quickly:

- use every opportunity to practise speaking.
- make every effort to communicate their ideas.
- don't worry about making mistakes when they are speaking.

Discuss these questions with other students.

1 Do you use every opportunity to practise speaking in English? Do you take an active part in speaking activities in class? What ideas do you have for ways of practising speaking English outside the classroom?
2 If you are having problems communicating an idea in English, do you keep trying and use different words to try to get your ideas across?
3 When you are having a conversation, do you worry about mistakes of grammar or vocabulary or do you focus on getting your meaning across?
4 Following your discussion, are there any ways in which you are going to change your approach to speaking in English?

Speaking

1 Which of these is *not* a correct way of giving an opinion?

1 In my opinion,
2 As far as I'm concerned,
3 From my point of view,
4 According to me,
5 I definitely think that

} young people are a lot less physically active than they used to be.

2 Discuss these questions with another student.

- Which word in each phrase 1–5 is usually stressed?
- What other ways do you know to give an opinion?

exam reviser   p19 | 1 ▶

3 Look at the pictures. What do you think are the two main reasons why young people in some countries are less healthy now than in the past? Discuss your ideas with another student.

4 Discuss these questions with your partner. Prepare to report your opinions to the rest of the class.

- What future consequences might there be for society if young people have increasingly unhealthy lifestyles?
- What different ways can you think of to encourage young people to be more physically active?

5 Tell the class the main points made during your discussion. Then listen to find out which other pair had the most similar opinions to yours.

> premium plus   **21** ▶

Writing | report

1 Read this task and look at the information about writing reports in the Writing Reference page 198.

Writing Task

A recent survey has shown that the fitness and health of young people where you live is suffering because they are not doing enough sport or getting enough exercise. You have been asked to write a report for parents and teachers at local schools which a) summarises the problem, and b) makes some suggestions as to ways of tackling this problem. Write your report in 120–180 words.

2 Read this advice for writing a good report. Which is not a good piece of advice?

1 Highlight key words in the instructions.
2 Think about who you are writing the report for.
3 Plan how many paragraphs you will have.
4 Decide on the purpose of each paragraph.
5 Include an introduction to your report.
6 Decide if you want to use sub-headings.
7 Write in an informal style.

3 Which of the phrases in *italics* do you think could be useful in a report? Discuss with another student.

1 *A recent survey has revealed* serious problems with the local transport system.
2 *The aim of this report is to* look at ways of encouraging more recycling by local people.
3 *I would be very grateful if you would consider* my recent application.
4 *One possible way of approaching this problem is to* provide more litter bins in public places.
5 *Another idea which has been effective elsewhere is to* install CCTV cameras along busy shopping streets.
6 *On the other hand*, many young people are heavily involved in voluntary work with local organisations.
7 *They had been sitting by the side of the road* for several hours before someone gave them a lift.
8 *In conclusion then, I would recommend that* a survey of foreign tourists is carried out to discover exactly which are the most popular local tourist sites.

4 Change the endings of the 'useful' sentences to make them appropriate for *your* report.

5 There is a mistake in each of these sentences. Find the mistakes and correct them.

1 *Not only* should parents play different sports with their children, *but* they should *also* to avoid taking them everywhere by car.
2 *As well as* include sports activities as part of the normal curriculum, schools should organise sports matches with other local schools.
3 *In addition* the effect on the physical health of young people, sport can improve mental alertness.
4 Sport helps prevent many kinds of illness. *Furthermore,* can teach young people to work effectively in teams.

6 Write your report for the task, making sure you follow all the advice for writing a good report in Exercise 1. Try to include one or two appropriate linkers of addition.

> premium plus   **22** ▶

Grammar

1 Read the text and complete the gaps. You have been given the first letter of each missing word.

CELEBRITY SCHOOL DAYS

The school I went to was quite strict in lots of ways. We all h_____[1] to wear a uniform including a school cap which everyone hated. You didn't n_____[2] to be at school until 8.45 a.m., but funnily enough I liked arriving early to play ball games in the playground with friends. Inside the school building there was a special system of stairs and corridors. You were s_____[3] to only go one way up and down certain stairs. If you were caught going the other way, you were punished. Furthermore, you weren't a_____[4] to run in the corridors. At lunchtime most boys had the school lunch, but you were p_____[5] to bring your own packed lunch. However, you had t_____[6] eat it in a special room. After school I often used to go to the library to do my homework. Talking w_____[7] not permitted so we used to pass each other notes. In terms of sports, the worst thing was the annual school run. Everyone was r_____[8] to do it unless you had special written permission to miss it. It was miles long and it always rained.

2 Complete these sentences using the prompts.

1 I / used / do / lots /different sports / I / be / younger.
2 Every Sunday afternoon / my brother and I / would / go / local park / play football.
3 She / gradually get / used / work for / large multi-national corporation.
4 We / still / not used / live / in / country.
5 You / use / enjoy /go /school?
6 My family / would / always spend / summer holidays / south of France.
7 Simon / slowly / get / used / long train journey / his new job.
8 You used / drive / left-hand side / road / yet?

3 Connect the pairs of sentences with the words/phrases in brackets. Change the grammar of the sentences as necessary.

1 She plays a lot of badminton. She is in her school swimming team. (As well as)
2 You must lose some weight. You need to make sure you do regular exercise. (Furthermore)
3 The Olympic Games generates enormous interest in sport. It can have a very important economic effect on the host country. (Not only)
4 He won the European title. He would like to get a medal at the World Championships. (In addition)

Vocabulary

4 Complete these sentences with the words in the box. There are two extra words that you do not need to use.

> beat succeed result competitive prize
> successful record score pass achievement

1 I can't believe that Jan managed to _____ all her exams. It's fantastic.
2 Simon has become quite a _____ salesman. He can be quite persuasive.
3 Do you know what the world _____ is for the 100 metres?
4 She won a _____ of £2,000 for her first novel.
5 I get a real sense of _____ when I know I have taught a class well.
6 This election has been a good _____ for the Green Party.
7 We need to _____ the London Lions by fifteen points if we're going to go through to the next round of the tournament.
8 She's given herself two years to _____ in becoming a published writer.

5 Name the sport which is being described.

1 You play on ice and try to hit a hard flat round object into the other team's goal with special sticks.
2 Two people use long sticks to hit coloured balls into holes at the sides and corners of a table.
3 You hold on to a large frame covered with cloth and fly slowly through the air without an engine.
4 Two people use rackets to hit a small rubber ball against the walls of a square court.
5 You shoot arrows from a bow and attempt to hit the centre of a target.
6 You roll a ball along the floor and try and knock down objects at the other end.
7 You hit a small white ball with a special stick across the course and try to get the ball into the hole.
8 Lots of people drive as fast as they can in special cars around a track.
9 You go very fast down a snowy mountain standing on special long pieces of wood or plastic.
10 You go underwater wearing a special mask and plastic tube to help you breath to look at things living in the sea.

Progress Check 1 Units 1–5

1 There is a mistake in each of these sentences. Find the mistakes and correct them.

1 I put all the bags in the bonnet of the car and drove off.
2 She is a very welcoming host and always makes me feel in home.
3 He is so big-of-himself and always tells everyone how great he is.
4 I went ten-pin boxing with some friends last night.
5 Could you pop me off at the train station on your way to work?
6 We've got tickets for the ballet on Saturday. The seats are at the front of the dress balcony.
7 We don't need any petrol. I made the car up yesterday.
8 They live in a self-centred community where they grow all the food they need.
9 They are always arguing. This is the third time this week they've fallen off.
10 He's a far cousin of mine – the son of someone in my family, but I'm not sure who.
11 I'm doing friends round for dinner tonight so I'd better start the cooking.
12 His car was a white-off, but luckily he escaped the accident completely unhurt.

2 Choose the correct alternative in these sentences.

1 I *listen/I'm listening* to music every morning in the car on my way to work.
2 When I *get up/'ll get up* in the morning, I always feel tired.
3 I *live/I'm living* with my parents until my new flat is ready to move into.
4 He almost always wins his races because he totally *believes/is believing* in himself.
5 I get bored on beach holidays, but my sister really *do loves/does love* them.
6 While we were sitting on the bus, we *heard/had heard* a strange noise.
7 We *had had/had been* looking forward to this day for a long time.
8 I soon realised I'd *left/'d been leaving* my bag at home.
9 I *cycled/was cycling* up the hill when I hit a hole in the road and fell off.
10 When I saw her, I knew she *had done/had been doing* some painting.
11 When I was a child, I *must/had to* wear a green uniform at school.
12 You are not allowed *use/to use* dictionaries in the exam.
13 You often *don't have to/mustn't* pay for downloading music from the Internet.
14 We *didn't need/needn't* have taken any ski equipment because it was possible to hire it in the resort.
15 You really *should/ought* to keep in touch with your parents more.

3 There is a mistake in each of these questions. Find the mistakes and correct them.

1 What you usually do at weekends?
2 Do you know if are the tickets available yet?
3 Who did tell you about the party?
4 Do you can pick me up at about 8 o'clock?
5 To who did you give the letter?
6 Would you mind telling me where is the leisure centre?
7 Where did you used to live when you were a child?
8 You had been worrying about me before I phoned?
9 Are you work at that shop again for the summer?
10 Did you had to do a lot of homework last term?

4 Read the text and decide which answer A, B, C or D best fits each gap.

Cities fascinate me and I have a great interest in the history of urban areas, particularly the transport systems and how they change. It is interesting to see the way small towns of the past have changed into huge, _____¹ cities. I am especially _____² by the history and background of the London Underground.

On one of my first _____³ to London many years ago, I was _____⁴ to discover that some parts of the Underground system are over 140 years old. It is certainly the oldest and also one of the busiest underground railway networks in the world. _____⁵ I have found out more about the 'Tube', as it is known, my _____⁶ for it has grown and grown.

Something which is _____⁷ to me is how much evidence still exists of the many changes that have happened to it over the years. For example, _____⁸ you are travelling on the Central Line _____⁹ Holborn, have a look through the window. You will notice a station which used to be called 'British Museum'. No passengers have _____¹⁰ off here since 1932, but the station is still there.

There are about forty of these _____¹¹ stations – or 'ghost stations' – on the Underground network along its entire 408 km of track. Some have vanished without trace whereas others are almost intact – _____¹² time capsules of a past era.

1 A spreading	B stretching	C sprawling	D crawling
2 A amused	B intrigued	C stunned	D flabbergasted
3 A trips	B voyages	C travels	D treks
4 A entertained	B dazed	C amazed	D confused
5 A As	B When	C While	D Finally
6 A happiness	B desirability	C excitement	D affection
7 A embarrassing	B fascinating	C stunning	D misleading
8 A while	B then	C after	D during
9 A for	B forwards	C towards	D backwards
10 A got	B gone	C walked	D tripped
11 A run-down	B bustling	C abandoned	D isolated
12 A desirable	B quaint	C fashionable	D upmarket

Progress Check 1 Units 1–5

5 Complete the text with one word in each gap.

I'll never forget the first time I went to a football match. It was so different from watching a match on TV. From an early age, I used _____¹ love playing football in the park with my friends and I _____² always asking my dad to take me to a real match. I remember it was a freezing cold day _____³ the middle of winter when he came home from work with two tickets. I couldn't believe it! We _____⁴ to get up early on the day of the match because the stadium was quite far away. As _____⁵ as we got off the train, I was amazed to see huge crowds of fans walking _____⁶ the stadium. I hadn't imagined that there would be so many people. They _____⁷ already making an incredible noise and that was even before the match had started! The crowd went really wild _____⁸ our team scored. That was the highlight of the day for me! Unfortunately, we lost the match _____⁹ the end, but it didn't matter really. The whole experience had been far more exciting _____¹⁰ I had imagined and I had enjoyed _____¹¹ so much. That first match with my dad remains one of the _____¹² special memories of my childhood.

6 Use the word given in capitals at the end of some of the lines of this text to form a word that fits in the gap *in the same line*.

Alfred Adler was a pioneer in the study of birth order. He suggested that social **(0)** *relationships*, especially among siblings and between children and parents, had a significant impact on the **(1)** _____ of children later in their lives.	RELATION PERSONAL
(2) _____, studies have linked first-born children with higher academic **(3)** _____ when compared to later-born children. In general, first-born children have been found to be **(4)** _____, assertive and task-oriented, often rising to **(5)** _____ positions as adults.	TRADITION ACHIEVE RESPONSE LEADER
Second-borns and middle children often feel inferior to older children because they do not have their advanced **(6)** _____. Middle children have been found to **(7)** _____ in team sports, and both they and last-borns have been found to be more **(8)** _____ adjusted if they come from large families.	ABLE SUCCESS SOCIAL
The **(9)** _____ of social skills is often strongest in last-borns from large families. As a group, they have been found to be the most **(10)** _____ in relating to others.	DEVELOP SUCCESS

7 Complete the second sentence so that it has a similar meaning to the first sentence, using the word given. Do not change the word given. You must use between two and five words, including the word given.

I don't want to lose contact with all my old school friends.
touch
I want to stay *in touch with* all my old school friends.

1 I'm not nearly as good at tennis as Debbie.
far
Debbie plays tennis _____.

2 You're supposed to phone the school if you're going to be late.
ought
You _____ phone the school if you're going to be late.

3 When I was a child, I went on holiday to Ireland every year.
used
When I was a child, I _____ on holiday to Ireland every year.

4 I'm quite tired so I think I'll go to bed early tonight.
bit
I'm _____ tired so I think I'll go to bed early tonight.

5 The living room has a door which leads directly to the garden.
opens
The living room has a door which _____ the garden.

6 It's essential not to write more than 180 words in your essay.
must
You _____ more than 180 words in your essay.

7 I am familiar with life in this town now and it doesn't feel strange.
used
I _____ in this town now and it doesn't feel strange.

8 My younger brother and I are the same height.
as
My younger brother _____ me.

Put it down to experience

life stages

growing up

coming of age

Unit 06

Introduction

1 Look at the 'stages of life' in the box and discuss the questions.

> a teenager   an adult   a baby   middle-aged   elderly/old   a child

- What do you think the approximate age range is for each stage of life?
- Which stages are do you think the happiest/most difficult? Why?

2 Describe what you think is happening in the pictures. Use phrases from the Exam Reviser where appropriate.

> **exam reviser**   p8 | 6.1

3 R.27 ▶ Listen and answer these questions about Britain.
1 Between what ages are you legally required to go to school?
2 At what age do people typically have a 'coming-of-age' party?
3 At what age can you legally learn to drive?
4 What is the minimum legal age for getting married?
5 At what age do people typically retire?

4 Work in pairs. Ask and answer the questions in Exercise 3 about your country. Do you think any of the ages in your answers should be changed? Discuss your ideas.

Reading

1 Describe what you can see in the pictures.

2 You are going to read a magazine article about people at different stages of life. Skim the text quickly and match each part to the correct picture. Try to do this in one minute.

It's their age ...

A

A recent survey of the aspirations of under-tens has revealed some interesting results. Parents may be reassured by the answers to some of the questions. Firstly, when the children were asked, 'If you came to power, what would you ban?', 'telling lies' was at the top of the list. And the top four answers to 'What are the worst things in the world?' were: drunk people, smoking, litter and graffiti. Perhaps not so pleasing were the answers to the question: 'What are the best things in the world?' The top five things included football, pop music and animals, but the number one answer was 'money and getting rich', with 'being famous' a close second. When they were asked who the world's most famous people actually were, however, the children came up with what, in my opinion, is an astonishing mixture of people, with Wayne Rooney, Robbie Williams, Harry Potter and Father Christmas all in the top ten!

B

A film set in Bangalore, Southern India: the director Kishan Shrikanth confidently tells the actors what to do. Nothing strange in that, except that Kishan is only ten. Starting at the age of four, he has already acted in twenty-four feature films and has starred in 1,000 episodes of a hit soap opera on television in India. Now, he's directing a full-length feature film about a child who lives on the streets. 'When I was six years old, I saw children selling newspapers at the traffic lights and my dad said they do not have parents. I felt very bad and thought I must do something for them,' Kishan told the BBC. Now he juggles school and filming, and although he misses out on playing with his friends, he has no regrets. He has his critics, however, who believe that he is having to become an adult too quickly, which is ironic, considering the subject matter of his film.

C

An exasperated father has discovered that the Internet is not the ideal place to sort out family arguments. Two weeks ago, Steve Williams became so fed up with complaining about his daughter Claire's messy bedroom that he built a website displaying photographs of it to the world. He wanted to make her feel so ashamed of it that she would tidy it up. But Steve's victory was short-lived because twenty-year-old Claire did indeed tidy up her bedroom, but she also started a revenge campaign. With the help of her father's friends, the twenty-year-old business student built a website on which she displayed photographs of her father's untidy garage and her father in various embarrassing situations. Mr Williams was quoted as saying that the boot was on the other foot now, but that he probably deserved it. Despite the embarrassment, however, Mr Williams said he had no regrets. The pictures had the desired effect and Claire's bedroom is a hundred times tidier than it was!

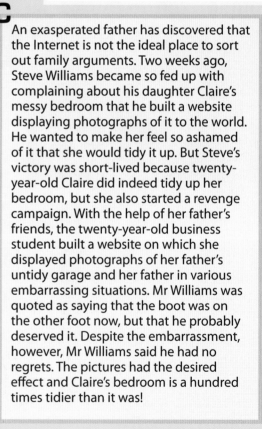

3 Read the text again and for questions 1–12, choose from the parts of the article A–D. The parts may be chosen more than once. <u>Underline</u> the details in the texts which tell you the answers.

Which part(s)
reports on current attitudes? *0* <u>A</u>
talks about a young child/young children? **1**___ **2**___
describes an elderly person's story? **3**___
talks about being humiliated in public? **4**___
mentions someone's father in the story? **5**___ **6**___
describes someone with a regular routine? **7**___
describes someone who did something because he/she was unhappy about something? **8**___ **9**___
mentions that the writer is surprised by something? **10**___
describe someone who has achieved a lot? **11**___ **12**___

4 Discuss these questions.

- How do you feel (e.g. surprised, depressed, pleased) about the survey results in part A? Why?
- In part B, do you agree with the critics (referred to in the last sentence)? Why/Why not?
- How do you feel about what Claire and her father did in part C? Why?
- Can you imagine having the same attitude as Rabbit Kekai in part D when you are in your eighties? Why/Why not? Do you know anyone who is similar to him? In what ways?

Speaking

1 R.28 ▶ You will hear two students and an examiner discussing the question *Do you think teenagers have too much freedom these days*? Listen and say whether you think the students will get good marks? Why/Why not?

2 R.29 ▶ You will hear five students giving full answers to an examiner's questions. Match the questions A–E with the answers 1–5 you hear.

A Do you think teenagers have too much freedom these days?

B What do you think about parents who push talented children into careers at an early age?

C Do you agree that every experience can be a learning experience? Why/Why not?

D How do you feel about the fact that many young people want to be rich and famous?

E At what age should young people be allowed to vote? Why?

3 Work in groups of three and choose three of the questions in Exercise 2 to discuss. Prepare what you are going to say by writing brief notes. Discuss the three questions you chose. Make sure you give full answers with reasons to support what you say.

D

Rabbit Kekai is a top international surfer. He comes from Hawaii and started surfing at the age of four. There are many top surfers from Hawaii, and many of them start young. Not many of them, however, continue surfing and competing in tournaments around the world as long as Rabbit, who is now an incredible eighty-three years old. He and his wife Lynn live in an apartment which is just 200 metres from Waikiki beach, and he gets up at 5.00 a.m. every single day of the year and goes straight down to the beach. He's been surfing virtually every day since the 1920s and still says that he has more to learn. He earns his living by teaching surfing and making commercials, but says, 'I still prefer to compete. I had six or seven first places last year. To be honest, I surf to keep alive.'

Making mistakes and learning from experience

1 Which statement best describes how you feel about making mistakes when you speak in English?

- I'm scared of making mistakes so I often keep quiet even if I've got something to say.
- I try to notice what I get right, not only what I get wrong.
- Sometimes I laugh at myself when I make a mistake. It makes me feel better.
- I focus on trying to communicate what I want to say, so I usually don't worry about making mistakes.
- It annoys me when I make the same mistake again and again.

2 Which attitudes do you think are generally associated with successful language learners?

3 Is there anything you would like to change about your attitude to making mistakes? If so, what is it and how are you going to make that change?

learning tip

Grammar | *so/such; too/enough*

1 Look at these pairs of sentences and answer the questions.

1 In which sentence is the speaker giving new information and in which one is the speaker referring to known information? What tells you this?

A *I had a very good day when I went surfing yesterday.*

B *Oh, really? You didn't think you'd have such a good day, did you?*

2 Which sentence is incorrect? Why?

A *I had such a good time that I've decided to go surfing again.*

B *I had a very good time that I've decided to go surfing again.*

•• see grammar reference: page 178 ••

2 Complete these sentences with *so, such* or *such a/an*. Look at the words in *italics* to help you.

1 Steve Williams was _____ *fed up* with his daughter's bedroom that he put some photos on the Internet.

2 I tidy up my bedroom _____ *rarely* that it's often a complete mess.

3 There were _____ *many people* waiting to vote that I had to queue.

4 It's not right for _____ *young child* to do an adult job like being a film director.

5 I'm _____ *excited* about my wedding next week that I can hardly wait!

6 There's _____ *little time* left before my exam that I have to study every evening.

7 They planned the party _____ *carefully* that it went really well.

8 This is _____ *interesting survey* about the attitudes of young people!

3 Answer these questions. Refer to the Grammar Reference on page 178 if necessary.

1 Which of the words in *italics* in these sentences matches with which explanation **A** or **B**?

1 The law in Britain says you are *too* young to vote at sixteen.

2 Claire is old *enough* to take responsibility for her bedroom.

A as much as is necessary or wanted

B more than is necessary or wanted

2 What is the difference in meaning between these pairs of sentences?

1 A *We arrived at the party very late.*

B *We arrived at the party too late.*

2 A *I haven't got fresh enough vegetables.*

B *I haven't got enough fresh vegetables.*

4 There is a mistake in each of these sentences. Find the mistakes and correct them.

1 These trousers are too much small for me.

2 There's much too salt in this soup.

3 This food is too spicy for me to eat it.

4 Too people tried to board the train and the doors wouldn't close.

5 I'm not enough old to vote.

6 Have you got enough of milk?

7 It's an enough early train to get me there on time.

8 This suitcase is too heavy to me to carry.

•• see grammar reference: page 178 ••

5 Complete the second sentence so that it has a similar meaning to the first sentence, using the word given. Do not change the word given. You must use between two and five words, including the word given.

1 I couldn't reach the shelf because it was too high.
me
The shelf was _____ reach.

2 I haven't seen a film as good as that for ages.
such
It's ages since I've seen _____.

3 This room is too hot to do gymnastics in.
cool
This room _____ to do gymnastics in.

4 I was surprised there wasn't more cheese in the fridge.
so
I didn't think there was _____ in the fridge.

5 The flight was overbooked.
people
There were _____ booked onto the flight.

6 I can't believe you've bought a camera as expensive as this one.
an
I can't believe you've bought _____.

7 Her exam grades were too low for a place at university.
high
Her exam grades weren't _____ her to go to university.

8 The camera instructions were too complicated for me to understand.
that
The camera instructions were _____ I couldn't understand them.

premium plus   23 ▶

6 Do you agree or disagree with these sentences? Discuss with other students and give details to justify your answers.

- My last holiday was full of so many exciting experiences!
- I never have enough time to see my friends.
- My last birthday was such a memorable day that I'll never forget it.
- I often find that I spend too much when I go shopping for clothes.

Vocabulary | prepositions

1 Match the sentence halves 1–12 with A–L to make complete sentences.

1 She was ashamed ...
2 She was depressed ...
3 You should be responsible ...
4 He's famous ...
5 I'm interested ...
6 I'm proud ...
7 Her dad complained ...
8 I succeeded ...
9 We are preparing ...
10 I've decided to apply ...
11 I'm not sure if I believe ...
12 It depends ...

A ... in taking up surfing.
B ... of the state of her bedroom.
C ... for your actions by the time you're twenty.
D ... about the results of the survey.
E ... of passing my exam with an A grade.
F ... for being the oldest surfer competing internationally.
G ... in astrology or not.
H ... about her messy bedroom all the time.
I ... on the weather if we play tennis or not.
J ... for that job I told you about.
K ... for my eighteenth birthday party at the moment.
L ... in passing my driving test the second time I took it.

> **Grammar note** | *Verbs following prepositions*
> Which of these sentences is correct? What is the general rule for the verb form that follows a preposition?
>
> 1 *I'm interested in learn to ski.*
> 2 *I'm interested in to learn to ski.*
> 3 *I'm interested in learning to ski.*

2 Choose six combinations from Exercise 1 that you want to remember and write them in the Exam Reviser. Write complete sentences that have meaning for you.
*I'm **preparing for** the First Certificate exam in June.*

3 Compare your sentences with another student. Add any of your partner's sentences that you particularly like to your list.

exam reviser   p8 | 6.2

4 Complete these questions with the correct prepositions.

1 What's the most difficult exam or test you've ever prepared _____?
2 Have you succeeded _____ doing something difficult recently?
3 Have you ever done anything that you feel particularly proud _____?
4 Do you believe _____ the saying 'Every cloud has a silver lining'?
5 Are you interested _____ taking part in traditional ceremonies and rituals?
6 Would you ever consider applying _____ a job as a driving instructor?
7 If you could be famous, what would you like to be famous _____?
8 When you were a child, did you often complain _____ the food you had to eat?

5 Choose four of the questions to ask and answer with another student. Encourage your partner to give more details by asking more questions.

premium plus   24

FCE close-up | Listening Multiple choice (Paper 4, part 4)

Exam information

In this part of the exam, you hear a monologue or conversation involving two or more speakers, which lasts approximately three minutes. There are seven multiple-choice (A, B or C) questions. You hear the extract twice.

Approach

1 Read the rubric to the task. It will tell you the general topic.

2 Read the questions before you listen for the first time and underline the important parts.

3 Make sure you read the questions very carefully and watch out for extreme words in the options. For

example, the recording could say something like *Some people like X*, whereas one of the options might be *Everybody likes X*, in which case this option would be incorrect.

4 Listen and make brief notes for each question. Don't try to write everything you hear – one or two key words for each question is enough.

5 Go through the questions and choose the option which you think fits best.

6 Listen again and check each option again.

7 Remember that in the exam you should always choose an answer for each question. You do not lose marks for a wrong answer.

Practice task

R.30 ▶ You will hear a radio interview about the coming-of-age ceremony in Japan. For questions **1–7**, choose the best answer (**A**, **B** or **C**).

1 How much does the interviewer know about this ceremony?
   A absolutely nothing
   B hardly anything at all
   C quite a lot about the history

   `1`

2 Why is the interviewer surprised about the age of the people involved in this ceremony?
   A Because he expected them to be younger.
   B Because it happens at a later age for boys than girls.
   C Because they can already vote before the ceremony takes place.

   `2`

3 On which day is the modern-day celebration of adulthood held?
   A any Monday in January
   B the second of January
   C the second Monday of January

   `3`

4 How does the expert describe the special clothes worn by the girls?
   A rather plain and formal
   B very beautiful and striking
   C generally plain but with an impressive belt

   `4`

5 What is the general attitude to the special clothes for girls?
   A They are too expensive so many of them don't wear them.
   B Most families buy them even though they cost a lot.
   C Most girls hire them or use family ones.

   `5`

6 According to the expert, how do the young people feel about the official part of the ceremony?
   A They think it's boring.
   B They like feeling responsible.
   C They find it embarrassing.

   `6`

7 What is the purpose of the ritual of shooting arrows at a target?
   A To ask the gods to stop the young people from going to war.
   B To ask the gods to make the young people strong and successful.
   C To ask the gods to take care of the young people in their adult lives.

   `7`

Go to www.iTests.com or your CD-ROM for interactive exam practice

Grammar | present perfect simple and continuous

1 Read the email and answer the questions.

- How does the writer feel? Why?
- Have you ever been in a similar situation? When? Why?
- How important do you think this type of coming-of-age ceremony is? Why?
- On what occasions do you wear special clothes? What do you wear?

○○○

Send | Options... | Help

To... |

Subject:

I've just tried on the special clothes that I'll be wearing at my coming-of-age ceremony. My suit is amazing and it's definitely the most expensive oufit I've ever worn. I suppose I've always known that I would take part. I mean, it's part of our tradition. I've been to two other ceremonies for other people (my older brothers), but I've never worn the clothes before. This is the first time I've really thought about it for me! My mum has organised everything for the party afterwards. I'm so excited! I really hope you can come.

---

exam reviser p8 | 6.3

2 Look at the highlighted verb phrases in the email in Exercise 1. Match them to these uses of the present perfect simple.

A To talk about an experience or an action in the past when the time is not important or not known. (Often used with *ever* and *never*.)
   I've never worn the clothes before.

B To talk about an action that started in the past and continues to the present. (Often used with *for* and *since*.)
   1 when you're focusing on the finished action
   2 when you're focusing on the number of times the action has been completed up to the time of speaking
   3 with 'state' verbs, e.g. *be, have, like, believe, know*

C To talk about an action that happened in the past but has the result in the present. (Often used with *just, yet* and *already*.)

D To talk about our first/second/etc. experience of something with the phrase *This is the first/second time …*

E When used with the superlative. (Often used with *ever*.)

3 Discuss these questions with a partner.

1 Which of these is correct?
   A ***Have you ever been*** to Japan?
   B ***Have ever you been*** to Japan?

2 Which of these is correct? What's the rule?
   A *I've lived here **for three months**.*
   B *I've lived here **since three months**.*

3 What does each of the following words mean, and what is its usual position in a sentence (at the beginning, at the end or before the main verb)? What is its usual position in a question?
   A *just*
   B *yet*
   C *already*

• • **see grammar reference: page 177** • •

4 Choose the correct alternative.

1 I first *went/have been* on an aeroplane when I was ten.
2 I've been at this school *for/since* more than a year.
3 Have you *yet packed your bag/packed your bag yet*?
4 You'll never guess what *I've just done/I just have done*!
5 He's passed his driving test *yet/already*.
6 This is the first time I *have/'ve had* a place of my own.
7 You're one of the kindest people I *ever met/'ve ever met*.
8 When I *last saw/'ve last seen* Sonia, she was just about to get married.

premium plus 25

5 Answer the questions about these pairs of sentences. They use the present perfect simple and the present perfect continuous.

1 Which sentence is focusing on the finished action and which on the activity itself?
   A *I've read a book about unusual weddings.*
   B *I've been reading a book about unusual weddings.*

2 Match the two sentences 1 and 2 with the attitude each speaker is expressing A and B.
   1 *I've lived in this flat for two months.*
   2 *I've been living in this flat for two months.*

   A I still live here but it's probably temporary.
   B I still live here and I probably won't move.

6 Match the parts of these sentences in *italics* with the correct uses A–C.

1 They*'ve been planning* the party for weeks.
2 I*'ve been writing* the invitations and I posted them today.
3 She's *been looking* for a hat to wear, but she hasn't found one yet.

A to suggest that an action is not complete
B to emphasise how long the action has been going on for
C to describe a recent activity when you can still see the results of that activity

7 R.31 Look again at the verb forms in sentences 1–3 in Exercise 6. How do you think you pronounce them? Listen and check your ideas.

8 Read the email quickly and answer these questions.

1 What has the writer (Sonia) been doing?

2 What does she want Emily to help her with?

◯◯◯

🖂Send 💾 🖨 ✎ ✍ 📎 🖉 ❗ ⬇ 📋 Options... ⚙ Help

To...	Emily
Cc...	
Bcc...	
Subject:	Wedding Plans!

Dear Emily

Just writing to tell you how the wedding plans are going! I've been working[1] so hard to get everything done! It's the first big thing like this that I do[2] and I can tell you, it's the most complicated thing I ever organised[3], for sure! I can't believe that I am thinking[4] about all the arrangements for over three months already … and there's loads more still to do.

I'm pleased though, because one thing I have sorted[5] out is the dress! I loved it the moment I've seen[6] it. I just have tried[7] it on and it's really gorgeous! I'm not going to say more than that because I want it to be a surprise. I didn't decide[8] on the dresses for the two bridesmaids yet. I've been thinking[9] about two different designs and I can't make up my mind. Are you free next week to come up and have a look with me?

By the way, have you received the photos I yet sent you[10]? I'll write again soon.

Sonia xxx

---

9 Look at the highlighted phrases in the email. There are mistakes in seven of them. Find the mistakes and correct them.

> premium plus 26 ▶

10 Look at these topics. Think of one key word which for you relates to each of them.

- Something you feel proud you've done
- Something important that has changed in your life in the last five years
- Something special you've had since you were a child
- A hobby you've been doing for more than a month
- Something exciting you want to do but you haven't done yet
- One of the most memorable places you've visited

11 Compare your key words with a partner. Choose four of your partner's key words and ask him/her to talk about the related topics. Ask questions to encourage your partner to give more details.

Writing | letter/email

1 Read the task and advertisement below. Are these statements true (T) or false (F)?

1 The advertisement is for driving courses.

2 There are five notes about things to ask written on the advert.

3 You don't need to include all the notes in your letter.

4 You should write a maximum of 150 words.

5 You should write your address at the top of the letter.

Writing task

You have seen the following advertisement in a newspaper. You are interested in going, but you would like more information.

Read the advertisement carefully and the notes which you have made for yourself. Then write a letter/email to the *Learner Driver Centre*, using all your notes.

Learn to drive in a week!

Learn to drive at the Learner Driver Centre with highly-trained, professional instructors. You can pass your test in just one week – or take one of the other options. One-to-one practical tuition with all cars and equipment provided. No experience necessary – beginners welcome.

Discounts available in off-peak periods.

Come today and learn an invaluable skill for life!

What? *What times?* *Age?* *When exactly?* *Booking necessary?*

Write a letter/email of between 120 and 150 words in an appropriate style. Do not write any postal addresses.

> exam reviser p23 | 11 ▶

2 Read the two letters/emails written by different students and answer the questions for each one.

1 Are there any language mistakes?
2 Has the student covered all the points in the notes in the task?

A

Dear Sir/Madam,

With reference to your advertisement in *The Times*, I am writing to ask for more information about driving courses at the Learner Driver Centre.

First of all, I'd like to know what times the course starts and finishes each day. Could you also tell me what other possibilities there are, for example, part-time courses? I would be grateful if you could tell me if there is a minimum age for your courses. I will be seventeen next month and I have never driven a car before.

Lastly, could you give me some more information about the available discounts? I'd like to know when the off-peak periods are and how much the courses cost at these times.

I look forward to hearing from you.

Yours faithfully,

M Mendes

Manuel Mendes

B

Dear Sir/Madam,

With referring to your advertisement in *The Times*, I write to ask for more information about driving courses at the Learner Driver Centre.

First of all things, I'd like to know what times do the classes start and finish every day. Could you also say me if you are opened every day? I would be like other options so I would be greatful if you tell me there are part-time courses, etc. Also I would like to know what is the minimum age for your courses.

Could you give me some more information about the different prices? I'd like to know when the off-peak periods is and how much the courses costs.

Finally, could you tell me if it is necessary to book or we can just arrive on the day?

I look forward to hear from you.

Yours faithfully,

Jagoda Rosinska

Jagoda Rosinska

3 Look at these phrases and match them with the best part of the letter/email in the paragraph plan.

1 I'd like to know …
2 Could you tell me …?
3 With reference to your advertisement …
4 I look forward to hearing from you.
5 I would be grateful if you could tell me …
6 I am writing to ask for more information about …
7 Could you give me some more information about …?

Paragraph 1: Introduction (where advert seen/reason for writing)

Paragraphs 2 and 3: Asking for specific information (based on the notes in the task)

Paragraph 4: Finishing the letter (asking for a reply)

4 Read the task and advertisement and underline the key points you must include in your letter/email.

Writing task

You have seen the following advertisement in a newspaper. You are interested in going, but you would like more information.

Read the advertisement carefully and the notes which you have made for yourself. Then write a letter/email to The Job Station, using all your notes.

advice about choosing?

job station

The Job Station will start you on the right track!

Applying for your first job can be a daunting experience. Our courses can help you whatever job you're interested in.

• Completely personalised service – tailored for your specific needs.
• Expert advice on writing a CV which will get you noticed for the right reasons.
• Practical and realistic help with interview techniques.

Day and weekend courses to suit all. Discounts available when you take more than one course.

courses: one-to-one or groups?

computers/ printing facilities?

When exactly?

How much?

Write a letter/email of between 120 and 150 words in an appropriate style. Do not write any postal addresses.

5 Write your letter/email using the paragraph plan and at least four of the phrases in Exercise 3.

6 Read your letter/email and answer these questions.

• Have you included all the points from the task?
• Have you organised your paragraphs appropriately?
• Have you used a formal style with opening and closing paragraphs appropriate for the exam?
• Can you find any mistakes with grammar and spelling?

7 Now rewrite your letter/email, using your answers to the questions in Exercise 6 to improve it.

Vocabulary

1 Complete each sentence with the best word from the box. Four of the words cannot be used.

> off ceremony flatmate partner engaged
> graduated retired primary child teenager

1 We got _____ about eighteen months before we finally got married.

2 I've loved dancing ever since I was a _____, aged about six.

3 In some countries, the coming-of-age _____ is one of the biggest events in a young person's life.

4 My grandfather was bored when he _____ because he liked working and didn't really want to stop.

5 Many young people these days decide to live together with their _____ without getting married.

6 I owed the bank a lot of money at the time I _____ from university.

2 Read the text and choose which answer A, B, C or D best fits each gap.

Bus cleaner retires at 100

A Los Angeles man has just retired from his job at the age of 100. Arthur Winston is proud _____1 the fact that he worked cleaning buses for over seventy-six years. He was so dedicated to his job that he only had one day off – when his wife died in 1988. And in 1996, he succeeded _____2 picking up an award for his hard work and commitment.

Mr Winston's first job was picking cotton at the age of ten. Then after a few years, in 1924, he applied _____3 his first job cleaning the 'buses', which were horses and carts in those days! In recent years, Mr Winston has been responsible _____4 a team of eleven workers, washing dozens of buses every day.

'Some people think I should've retired earlier and enjoyed my old age!' he says. 'But it depends _____5 how you see things. I've never complained _____6 my work. I'd rather be working than lying around the house.' He is now preparing _____7 a different kind of life, but he still wants to work. He is interested _____8 finding some kind of job working with senior citizens.

1 A in	B of	C with	D to
2 A to	B by	C in	D with
3 A for	B to	C at	D with
4 A to	B about	C on	D for
5 A of	B on	C in	D at
6 A about	B with	C for	D to
7 A to	B about	C for	D by
8 A in	B with	C to	D of

Grammar

3 Choose the correct alternatives.

IS SEVENTEEN THE
PERFECT AGE?

I really think seventeen is *such/so*[1] a perfect age! I love being seventeen. I have *so much/too much*[2] freedom – my parents let me do anything I want. I'm still studying at school but I don't have *too many/too much*[3] to do really. Next year will be harder, I think. I'm *enough old/old enough*[4] to learn to drive now, which is really cool. I haven't had lessons yet, though, because I haven't got *enough money/money enough*[5] at the moment. But as soon as I have, I will!

Another thing which is great about being seventeen is that you have *such/so much*[6] to look forward to. There are *such/so*[7] great places to see and *so many/too many*[8] things to do. It's really exciting.

One thing that is a bit frustrating about being seventeen is that you feel *enough responsible/responsible enough*[9] to be an adult but some people treat you like a child. It's *so/such*[10] annoying!

4 Complete the sentences by writing the verb/phrase in brackets in the correct tense.

1 _____ (you / ever / break) your arm or leg?

2 I _____ (know) my best friend since I was five.

3 Tom _____ (phone) me three times yesterday.

4 Oh no! What _____ (you / do) to your hair!

5 She's very upset. She _____ (cry) all morning.

6 It's one of the best songs I _____ (ever / hear).

7 This is the second time he _____ (ask) me to help him.

8 _____ (she / take) her exams yet?

9 I _____ (work) here since May, but I hope to get a better job soon.

10 A lot _____ (happen) in the last couple of weeks.

Science fact, science fiction

Premium | Unit 07

breakthrough

genetics

discovery

Unit 07

Introduction

1 Look at the pictures. What do you think they show? Use these words to help you.

> discover   invention   technology   experiment   analysis

exam reviser p9 | 7.1

2 R.32 You are going to make a list of important inventions. First listen to four people. Which things do they consider?

3 Work in small groups. Make a list of the three most important inventions you know. (Be prepared to justify your choices.) Decide on one invention you wish had never been invented.

4 Explain your choices to the rest of the class. As a class, vote on the three most important inventions and the one thing you wish had never been invented.

premium plus 27

Reading

1 Discuss these questions with other students.
- How did you feel about studying science at school?
- Why do you think a lot of people don't like it?
- Why do you think there is a shortage of science teachers in some countries?

2 Scan the book review quickly and find the answers to these questions.
1 What is the book about?
2 What is the reviewer's general opinion of the book?
3 Do you think you would be interested in reading it?

Craig Brown – *Book of the Week*

A Short History of Nearly Everything by **Bill Bryson**

Like most writers, Bill Bryson has spent most of his life on the 'Arts' side of the 'Arts' and 'Science' divide. While still at school, he found himself captivated by the cover of a science book which showed the Earth with a slice taken out, like a cake, with explanatory arrows pointing to all the different layers in the middle. But when he turned the pages, he found the writing impenetrably[1] boring. It was, he now thinks, as if the writer was trying to keep science secret by making it as hard to understand as possible. And the same applied to all the other science books he tackled.

Giving up on science, Bryson went on to become a hugely[2] successful author of comical travel books, all of which have topped the bestseller lists. Then, three years ago, he set himself the task of writing a popular science book for those who, like him, had been put off the subject at school. 'The idea,' he says, 'was to see if it isn't possible to understand and appreciate the wonder and accomplishments of science at a level that isn't too technical and demanding, but isn't entirely superficial either.' And, as he proved with his brilliantly[3] entertaining histories of the English language, Bill Bryson has an unmatched gift for explaining the most difficult subjects in the clearest possible way.

Like all the best teachers, Bryson knows that stories about people are the best route into any subject. I now realise that one of the troubles – perhaps the key trouble – with my school science textbooks is that they were full of rocks or frogs or atoms, but hopelessly[4] short of people.

Describing the beginnings of the planet, Bryson homes in on the lives of the scientists and explorers who made the first discoveries, and takes it from there. He introduces the idea of gravity, for instance, by telling the story of Isaac Newton, whose quest for knowledge was so insatiable that he once inserted a needle into his eye socket and twizzled it around between the eye and the bone, just to see what would happen. To his disappointment, nothing did.

Unlike most science writers, Bryson has a remarkable nose for the sort of fact that causes people of all ages to open their mouths wide in wonder. Every single page of his book contains three or four utterly[5] extraordinary facts, leading me to spend a large part of last Sunday trying to impress or horrify my children and their friends by shouting them out at regular intervals. Here are a handful:

- If your pillow is six years old, then one tenth of its weight is made up of old skin, living mites, dead mites and mite dung.
- Your heart pumps the equivalent of four Olympic-sized swimming pools of blood a year.
- Crocodiles were once three times as large as they are now, tortoises were the size of a small car, lizards in Western Australia were six metres long, and sloths were big enough to look into an upstairs window.
- There is enough salt in the sea to bury every bit of land on the planet to a depth of 150 m.
- If you could light up all the asteroids in the night sky larger than ten metres,

3 Read the review again and for questions 1–8, choose the answer A, B, C or D which you think fits best according to the text.

1 Bryson found that the science books he looked at as a child were
   A fascinating.
   B over-simplified.
   C inaccessible.
   D overlong.

2 He decided to write a science book because
   A he was bored with writing travel books.
   B he wanted to make more money.
   C he felt sorry for schoolchildren.
   D he wanted to share his excitement for science.

3 The reviewer suggests that Bryson's greatest strength is possibly his
   A clarity.
   B humour.
   C knowledge.
   D enthusiasm.

4 What does the reviewer think of his school science books?
   A They were too complicated.
   B There were too few pictures.
   C They were too serious.
   D They had too few stories about people.

5 The purpose of the story about Sir Isaac Newton is to show
   A how eccentric he was.
   B how gravity was discovered.
   C the extremes to which he would go to learn new things.
   D what a practical scientist he was.

6 *Them* (paragraph 5) refers to
   A children.
   B scientific facts.
   C friends.
   D pages of a scientific book.

7 The reviewer finds some of the facts quoted in the book
   A mildly interesting.
   B fascinating.
   C amusing.
   D ridiculous.

8 The writer uses the phrase *have kept shuttered for too long* (paragraph 7) to show that he thinks
   A it's a shame that people aren't at all interested in science.
   B science teachers are responsible for people's lack of interest in science.
   C many people are worried that science is too complicated for them to understand.
   D more and more people are getting interested in science.

you would see a hundred million randomly moving objects, all capable of colliding with the Earth.

And so on. Some of these facts are bewildering (as the Earth revolves, even as you are reading this article, you are moving at 620 mph) while others are a little depressing (a long human life still only adds up to about 650,000 hours), but they all serve to open windows on a world which many of us have kept shuttered for too long.

A Short History of Nearly Everything has already leapt to the top of the charts, and I'd say it deserves to sell as many copies as there are protons contained in the full stop that ends this review (at least 500,000,000,000).

4 Discuss these questions with other students.
   • Which of the facts quoted at the end of the review do you find most interesting or surprising?
   • Bryson was 'captivated' by a book at school. Are there any books that captivated you at school? If so, what were they and why did you find them so interesting?

Vocabulary | alternatives to *very*

1 Look at the five numbered words in the book review on pages 70–71 and answer these questions.

   1 Can you think of one word with a similar meaning to all of them?

   2 What is the effect of using words like these in this text?

2 Replace all the examples of *very* in this book review with more interesting words from the box. Make sure the word you choose collocates with the adjective. (Use each word once only.)

> notoriously   blissfully   breathtakingly   bitterly
> hilariously   exceedingly   utterly   fabulously

Book Reviews

LOOKING FOR A BOOK FOR THE BEACH? MELANIE WATSON REVIEWS THE PICK OF THE PAPERBACKS.

Michael Hodges' latest title is a science fiction thriller set in the 22nd century. Climate conditions have become quite extreme and most of the action is set in a *very*[1] cold New York City, where temperatures are below freezing for most of the year. Living conditions for most people are *very*[2] harsh as many of the Earth's natural resources have run out.

The story is built around an ex-cop called Krycic and his side-kick, Tnyr, who isn't especially bright but is *very*[3] devoted to Krycic. Krycic has been called back into service by his old boss, Commander Yzeem, after some renegade robots have gone on the run.

Krycic's search takes him all over the galaxy, and some of the descriptions of the landscape that he sees when he goes to nearby planets are *very*[4] beautiful, almost poetic.

While Krycic is looking for the renegade robots, he is *very*[5] unaware of the fact that he is also being hunted by agents of the *very*[6] wealthy corporation that made the robots and doesn't want them destroyed.

As well as being an exciting page-turner, this novel is also *very*[7] funny in places. While it is *very*[8] difficult for science fiction titles to come high up in the bestseller lists, I have no doubt that this will do extremely well. A definite must for holiday reading lists!

exam reviser   p9 | 7.2

Using a dictionary

1 What different information can a good dictionary tell you?

2 Look at this extract from the *Longman Exams Dictionary*. What does it tell you about the meaning, the pronunciation and the grammar of the word?

> **knowl·edge·a·ble** /ˈnɒlɪdʒəbəl $ ˈnɑː-/ *adj*
> knowing a lot: [+about] *Graham's very knowledgeable about wines.* —**knowledgeably** *adv*

3 A good dictionary will often tell you useful collocations with adjectives. What other interesting words do you think can collocate with and intensify *boring* and *successful*?

Grammar | *like* versus *as*

1 Read the grammar rules about *like* and *as* on page 178 of the Grammar Reference. Match each of these examples with *like* or *as* to one of the rules.

   1 *As* you read this article, you are moving at 620 mph.

   2 He wrote a science book for people, *like* him, who had been put off the subject at school.

   3 *As* he proved with his entertaining histories of the English language, Bryson is excellent at explaining difficult subjects clearly.

   4 Some of the new sciences *like* genetic engineering raise difficult ethical questions.

   5 It was *as* if the writer was trying to keep science secret.

   6 She worked *as* a research assistant in a local university for many years.

   7 He ran *like* the wind to get his assignment in on time.

   8 *As* you know, the government's chief science adviser has just resigned.

> •• see grammar reference: page 178 ••

2 Complete each of these sentences with *like* or *as*.

1 My grandfather looks a bit _____ Albert Einstein!

2 I'm not as good at chemistry _____ my friend, Jules.

3 _____ I was waiting to take my maths exam, I tried to remember all the important formulae.

4 Some of the world's greatest scientists, _____ Marie Curie, have died because of their research.

5 _____ I understand it, we still need two main speakers for the conference.

6 _____ we agreed, we will increase funding for experimentation which avoids using live animals.

7 Everyone said she sang _____ an angel at the concert.

8 If you use that knife _____ a screwdriver, you'll break it.

3 Are any of these statements true for you? Change the ones that are not to make them true.

- I am more like my mother than my father.
- I don't think I am as creative as my best friend.
- I'd be quite interested in working as a tour guide for a couple of months.
- I am very keen to visit parts of east Africa like Kenya.

4 Tell another student your sentences and explain in what way they are true for you.

Speaking

1 Discuss these questions with other students.

- Did/Do you study science at school?
- How do you feel about it?
- What did/do you think of the lessons/the teachers?

2 Which of the following sentences apply to picture 1 and picture 2 and which apply to neither?

1 He's holding *what looks like* a plastic bottle.

2 They *seem to be* watching some kind of monitor, but *I'm not quite sure* why.

3 They don't really *look as if* they're working together.

4 There is someone who *might be* a teacher in the background.

5 They're *probably* lab technicians – from the coats they're wearing.

6 They're *all* wearing plastic yellow glasses *of some sort*.

7 *As far as I can tell*, they *could be* working in a university research department.

8 They *must be* in a science class at school.

9 *One of them* seems to be finding something quite funny.

10 There's *some kind of* tube-like thing and plastic containers on the desk.

3 Which of the phrases in *italics* in Exercise 2 are used for speculating about something you are not sure about? Check your answers in the Exam Reviser.

exam reviser p21 | 6

4 R.33 Listen to someone comparing the two pictures. Which of the sentences from Exercise 2 do you hear?

5 Now look at pictures 3 and 4 on page 169. Which of the phrases in *italics* from Exercise 2 could you use to compare them?

6 With another student, take turns to compare pictures 3 and 4. (Where appropriate, use expressions for speculating.)

Picture 1

Picture 2

Listening

1 What major changes do you think there will be to our lives in the next fifty years? (Think about entertainment, transport, holidays, communication, medicine, etc.) Discuss your ideas.

2 R.34 ▶ Listen to part of a radio programme about one man's vision of the future. Make a note of how far into the future he talks about.

3 R.34 ▶ Listen again and complete the sentences.

1 For the last twenty years, Ian Pearson has mainly worked in the field of _____.

2 By 2050 he thinks it will be possible to _____ a person's mind into a machine.

3 It's difficult to imitate consciousness in machine because there are so many _____.

4 He believes there will be conscious computers by the year _____.

5 He would want a computer controlling a plane to do everything possible to stop it crashing because it was more _____ than him.

6 Pearson thinks that you could _____ a lot of ordinary jobs, such as call centre operators.

7 He suggests that there should be a _____ to discuss the implications of the new technology.

8 We will be able to make everyday items, like yoghurt, 'smart' by putting in _____ circuitry.

9 He predicts we will increasingly spend time in _____ space.

10 We will actually feel as if we are with people on the other side of the world because of the connections to our _____.

4 Work with other students.

- Make a list of the main predictions that Ian Pearson makes about the future. Were any of them similar to your predictions in Exercise 1?
- Which word from the box best describes how you find each prediction?

> interesting exciting worrying
> depressing unbelievable

5 Tell other students the words you chose and explain why you chose each one.

> premium plus 28 ▶

Grammar | overview of future forms

1 Look at these extracts from three email messages. What is the main point of each extract?

Send | Options... | Help

To...

Cc...

Bcc...

Subject:

Just wondering if you've started your packing yet? I can't decide what to take … the weather forecast says it's going to rain for the first few days and then clear up. It's never been really cold there – in fact, I think it'll be quite warm. Have you packed any summer clothes?

Email 1

To...
Cc...
Bcc...
Subject:

Jan and I are taking the kids to the new Science Museum exhibition on Saturday. It's all about dinosaurs and we were wondering if Toby would like to come, too. David has just told me he'll join us for some of the day, but I know he's going to visit his mother in the afternoon. Let me know if you're interested.

Email 2

To...
Cc...
Bcc...
Subject:

Bet you didn't know this, but on Friday, next week, Brian in the R and D department will have been here at TechnoCorp for exactly twenty-five years. We'll be celebrating with him on Friday (15th) at a surprise party at Le Polidor restaurant in Ship Street. Please let me know by email if you can come. (The party starts at 8.30 p.m.)

2 Read the messages again and find examples of these future forms.

1 *will* (two examples)
2 *going to* (two examples)
3 present continuous
4 present simple
5 future perfect
6 future continuous

3 Discuss with other students when we use each form to talk about the future.

We can use 'will' to talk about making predictions based on what we know or believe.

•• see grammar reference: page 179 ••

Grammar note | time clauses
What do you notice about each of the verbs in *italics*? What is strange about this?

1 Tell me when the post *arrives*.
2 Before you *go*, remember to shut all the windows.
3 I want you to go to bed as soon as the film *finishes*.

4 Look at these predictions. For each one decide which alternative is more likely and explain why.

1 I don't feel very well. I think I'*m going to be/'ll be* sick.
2 I'm sure she'*ll say/'s saying* yes. She always loves trying out new things.
3 This time next year, I'*ll be working/'ll work* in New York.
4 What on earth is that man doing? I think he's going to *fall/falling*.
5 I think she's *finishing/'ll have finished* her essay by Friday.
6 There's no point in telling them. No one *will believe/is going to believe* me.

5 Work in pairs. Choose one of the sentences in Exercise 4, think about a possible context and make a short dialogue which includes it.

A: *What's the matter? You look terrible.*
B: I don't feel very well. I think I'm going to be sick.
A: *Maybe it was those prawns you had at lunchtime?*
B: *Don't remind me about the prawns! Go and get me some water … please!*

6 Work in pairs. Try to agree on how to complete the following predictions. Then, find other students who agree with your predictions.

• Our prediction for the weather tomorrow is that …
• Our prediction for the biggest change to happen in the next fifty years is that …

7 R.35 ▶ You will hear someone talking about their future plans. Listen and take notes.

8 R.36 ▶ Listen again, section by section and write down exactly what you hear. You will hear each section twice.

9 R.36 ▶ Listen one final time and check what you have written. In particular, check that your grammar and spelling are correct.

premium plus 29 ▶

10 Complete the following sentences to make plans/intentions that are true for you.

1 This evening I'm definitely …
2 This weekend I'm probably going to …
3 By this time next year I hope I will have …
4 At this time on New Year's Day I will be …

11 Find out how other students have completed the sentences. Which student's sentences are most similar to yours?

Grammar note | *due to/about to*
Which of the following sentences is *not* correct? Why?

1 The match is due to start in two hours' time.
2 The match is about to start in two hours' time.

Writing | article

1 This article is based on the interview with Ian Pearson on page 74. Read it and answer these questions.

1 What is the main area *not* referred to that was discussed in the interview?

2 Do you think the journalist views Pearson as: slightly mad, a misunderstood visionary, a serious scientist with thought-provoking ideas or a potential danger to society?

//////// 'Never-say-die' //////// technology!

Head of the 'futurology unit' at British Telecom, Ian Pearson, is well-known for some of his controversial views, but his latest predictions have caused a lot of interest in the scientific community. People take notice of his ideas, partly because his CV is obviously so impressive – including many years in the fields of theoretical physics, missile design and, more recently, cybernetics. I met him last week to try to find out what all the fuss was about.

Pearson is a mild-mannered individual, which seems at odds with the sometimes mind-blowing projections he is making about our future world. To begin with, he is suggesting that by 2050, physical death will not mean the end for an individual person. Basically, he predicts that by then we will have the technological ability to download human minds into machines. So, the individual in us can live on – perhaps indefinitely.

The next area with potentially massive implications is the development of 'conscious' computers. Pearson says this will be possible by 2020, given

the way computer speeds are accelerating. The problem seems to be defining exactly what 'consciousness' is, but Pearson seems sure that computers will have some kind of emotional reactions soon. So, for example, a plane would actually be 'afraid' of crashing into the ground.

'Virtual reality' is something that he believes is just round the corner, too. In practice, he envisages that we will be able to touch and interact with life-size 3D images of people wherever they might actually be in the real world and this will soon be the normal way of communicating with people.

Pearson is certainly not oblivious to the need for public debate about what all these developments may mean. But, at the same time, he has a very clear sense of the way in which technological advances are currently heading. And, if even one-tenth of what he predicts happens, then the world we are going to be living in, in the not-too-distant future, is going to be quite a different one to the one we know now.

2 Think about the article in Exercise 1 and decide which of the following statements are true about a well-written article.

1 It should have an eye-catching title.

2 It should engage and interest the reader.

3 Each paragraph must have a sub-title.

4 It can 'talk' directly to the reader.

5 It should have specific examples to help bring the points to life.

6 It should be divided into paragraphs, each with a different main focus.

7 It must use formal language.

8 You should make a comment or give your opinion at the end of the article.

3 Check your ideas in the Writing Reference on page 202.

4 You are going to write an article on one of these topics. First choose the most interesting topic.

- a clever invention
- a problem that the world will face in the future

5 Decide what invention or what future problem your article is going to be about. Before you plan your paragraphs, brainstorm ideas.

- Think of *any* points and examples you might include in your article. Note down all your ideas. At this stage, include *anything* you can think of.
- Show your ideas to other students and ask them if they have other ideas. Again, include *anything* they can think of.
- Now choose your best ideas and group them into possible paragraphs.

6 Plan your opening and closing paragraphs. How are you going to introduce your article? What comment or opinions are you going to express at the end?

7 Think of a short, eye-catching title. Show it to other students. Ask them if it would make them interested in reading your article.

8 Write your article (using between 120 and 180 words). When you have finished, read it through. Check that:

- you have included all your best ideas;
- it is divided into paragraphs each paragraph with a different focus;
- the language you use is varied and interesting;
- you have avoided basic grammar and spelling mistakes.

 premium plus 30

FCE close-up | Listening Multiple choice (Paper 4, part 1)

Exam information

In this part of the exam, you hear eight short extracts of one or two people talking in different situations, e.g. friends chatting, part of a radio programme, someone buying something by phone. There is one question for each extract. You hear each extract twice. You must choose one from three possible answers. You will usually be asked about:

- the relationship of the speakers, e.g. Are they friends/strangers/work colleagues, etc.?
- the attitude of the speakers, e.g. Are they happy/annoyed/disappointed, etc.?
- the purpose of the extract, e.g. Is the person complaining/asking for information/returning something, etc.?

Approach

1 Read the eight questions and the options *before* you listen for the first time. Underline the important words to help you focus as you listen.

2 The first time you listen, you will hear the question and then the extract. After each one, choose one answer. Remember that you will hear synonyms and paraphrases of the words in the questions – not exactly the same words and phrases.

3 The second time you listen, check that the other options are wrong. Also, listen out for important words/phrases that justify your choice.

4 Always put something for each question – you do not lose marks for a wrong answer.

Practice task

R.37 ▶ You will hear people talking in eight different situations. For questions **1–8** choose the best answer **A**, **B** or **C**.

1 You hear a school student talking about an exam he has taken.

How does the student feel?

A excited
B relieved
C upset

[1]

2 You hear part of a talk on the radio.

What is the man talking about?

A different uses of early computers
B the true inventor of the modern computer
C problems with the world's first computer

[2]

3 You overhear two work colleagues chatting.

What is the woman's reaction to the man's plans?

A She thinks he is joking.
B She is surprised that their plans are the same.
C She feels his plans are overambitious.

[3]

4 You hear this answerphone message.

What is the main purpose of the message?

A to let people know where she will be
B to let people know how she can be contacted
C to let people know who to contact while she is away

[4]

5 You overhear two friends talking.

Where are they?

A at the theatre
B in a university
C in a restaurant

[5]

6 You hear part of a weather forecast on the radio.

The weather conditions tomorrow are going to be:

A a much rainier day and a milder night.
B a less rainy day and a much colder night.
C a slightly rainier day and a much colder night.

[6]

7 You overhear a woman talking to a shop assistant.

What is she doing?

A organising for something to be delivered
B complaining about a faulty washing machine
C complaining that her order didn't arrive on time

[7]

8 You overhear a woman talking on the phone.

Who is she speaking to?

A an estate agent
B a hotel manager
C a landlord

[8]

Go to www.iTests.com or your CD-ROM for interactive exam practice

Grammar

1 Correct the sentences using *like* rather than *as.* where necessary.

1 Simon was late for the science lecture as usual.
2 Her brother is a physics teacher as me.
3 I hate this flat. It's as living in a shoe box.
4 As you know, Sheila and I are thinking of getting married in the spring.
5 We're using the spare room as Mike's office until the extension is finished.
6 Some of our neighbours, as the people at number seven, want to organise a street party.
7 My feet are freezing. They're as blocks of ice.
8 Paris is great as a place to visit but not to live.

2 Complete this description of the picture. Put one word in each gap.

Well, the two men look as _____ ¹ they are in some kind of laboratory. It's obviously a large room. It _____ ² be the basement of a house, it's difficult to tell. It must _____ ³ at the beginning of the 20th century or some time around then because _____ ⁴ the way they're dressed and the furniture in the room. The man in the front _____ ⁵ like he is doing up his tie. He's standing in front of a table _____ ⁶ is completely covered with different scientific instruments and books. The man in the background _____ ⁷ looking at the first man. He seems _____ ⁸ be saying something. He looks _____ ⁹ little concerned.

3 There is a mistake with the future form in five of these sentences. Find the mistake and correct it.

1 What time does this train arrive in Cardiff?
2 Do you think Brazil are winning the next World Cup?
3 We'll be thinking of you at this time tomorrow.
4 What will we have had for dinner this evening?
5 We're going to move to the country next year.
6 It looks like it rains soon.
7 He says he will have finished the report by Friday.
8 If you wait a minute, I'm helping you to the car with those boxes.
9 How long will you have learnt English by the end of this year?

Vocabulary

4 Complete these sentences with the correct word. You have been given the beginning of each word.

1 Is it ever right to do ex_____ on animals?
2 He realised that someone had used his computer without his kn_____.
3 What's the name of the in_____ of the clockwork radio?
4 Our research team are carrying out a detailed an_____ of the test results.
5 Th_____, the crime rate should decrease as employment increases, but that's not always the case.
6 His sister is a hi_____ successful biologist.
7 Put on your gloves. It's bi_____ cold outside.
8 This book is te_____ boring, but I have to read it before I do my next physics assignment.

5 Complete the sentences with the words in the box.

> scientific discover invention technology
> knowledgeable experiment analysis theorectically

1 Scientists are still trying to _____ why dinosaurs became extinct.
2 She's very _____ on the subject of astronomy. You can ask her anything and she'll know the answer!
3 I think it's wrong for scientists to _____ on animals, whatever the circumstances.
4 _____, there's no reason why you can't clone humans, but there are lots of ethical issues to consider.
5 They took some blood samples and sent them to the laboratory for _____.
6 Of course, books had to be written by hand before the _____ of printing.
7 We do keep some records but I'm afraid we're not very _____ about it.
8 Despite advances in modern _____, people don't seem to be any happier.

Language Review

Food for thought

spicy

succulent

mouth-watering

Unit 08

Introduction

1 Look at the pictures. Say what each one makes you think about and why.

2 Work in pairs. Read these sentences and make sure you understand the words/phrases in *italics*. Then ask and answer the questions with your partner.

- How often do you have *fizzy drinks*? Which is your favourite?
- How do you feel about *junk food*? How often do you have it? What, if any, is your favourite?
- What is your favourite thing for *a quick snack*? Why?
- Have you ever had *food poisoning*? What happened?
- When was the last time you had *a slap-up meal*? What was the occasion?
- How often do you get *a takeaway*? Why? What kind?

3 Discuss these questions with another student.

- Do you buy food from a supermarket or from a market stall? Why?
- What was your least favourite vegetable when you were a child? Did your parents make you eat it?

4 Discuss all the questions with other students.

Reading

1 Look at the pictures of two restaurants: *The Carnivore* in Nairobi, Kenya and *Encounter* in Los Angeles, USA. What do you think makes each of these restaurants special or different?

2 Work in two groups, A and B.

Group A   Read the text about *The Carnivore*.

Group B   Read the text on page 168 about *Encounter*.

Read your text quickly and check your ideas from Exercise 1.

THE CARNIVORE, NAIROBI, KENYA

A GREAT PLACE FOR BOTH TOURISTS AND LOCALS, *THE CARNIVORE* – VOTED ONE OF THE TOP FIFTY RESTAURANTS IN THE WORLD – IS AN EXPERIENCE FOR ALL THE SENSES. As you enter the restaurant, the smell of charred meat and fragrant smoke greets you. When you get inside, the first thing you see is a board with a list of what appears to be every African wild animal you can think of. This is your menu. The next thing you see, and hear, is the huge circular stone Masai barbecue with countless spits of roasting meat.

The Masai people of Kenya and Tanzania are a nomadic tribe and are reputed to have the best cattle in the world. Their staple diet is cow blood mixed with milk. Considering that the cow is the very lifeblood of the Masai, you would expect that they know how to cook it superbly – and they do. On the barbecue there are huge joints of meat on Masai spears roasting gently over burning coals. If you look closely, you will see over twenty varieties of meat sizzling away.

The food at *The Carnivore* changes on a daily basis, but the following are among the meats you can expect to try: Crocodile is juicy and well-flavoured. Giraffe is like succulent pork and tastes better if slightly pink. Top of my list was waterbuck which is generally very tender. The smell alone will make your mouth water and you certainly won't be disappointed by the taste, either. Zebra, on the other hand, is slightly tough. Hartebeest, too, requires a substantial amount of chewing that will give you jaw ache for about five minutes. It's tasty but not really worth the effort.

Not only is the food unusual, but the service at *The Carnivore* is, too. When you take your seat, you will be given a plate, napkin, knife and fork, and a flag. The flag is very important. When you are ready to eat, you put your flag upright and the waiters know that

you are ready to be served. They come to your table waving huge Masai spears with hunks of meat spilling their juices on the floor and tables. Your waiter will plonk the end of the spear on your cast iron plate and carve away. When you have eaten your fill, simply lower your flag and the waiter will leave you alone. If, after a pause, you are ready to eat again, simply raise your flag and your waiter will reappear.

The Carnivore is an eat-as-much-as-you-can restaurant, with starters, dessert and coffee, as well as the meat, of course, all included in one price. Also included are an amazingly lively atmosphere, wonderful music and friendly, helpful staff. In my opinion, it really is an experience-as-much-as-you-can restaurant! You won't be disappointed (unless you're a vegetarian, that is).

3 Read your text again and make notes about your restaurant.

	The Carnivore	Encounter
1 Decor and atmosphere		
2 Main feature of the restaurant		
3 Main type of food on the menu		
4 What food is recommended		
5 Waiters and service		
6 Writer's overall opinion of the restaurant		

4 Prepare to tell another student about the restaurant you read about. Look again at the text and the notes you made in Exercise 3. Add any other points you think are interesting.

5 Work in pairs (one from Group A and one from Group B) and tell each other about your restaurant.

6 Discuss these questions.
- Would you be interested in eating in either (or both) of the restaurants described in the texts? Why/Why not?
- What kind of restaurant would you normally choose to eat out in? Why?

exam reviser   p10 | 8.1

Vocabulary | food

1 Work in pairs. Put the words in the box into two groups: *Ways of describing food* and *Ways of preparing food*. Use a dictionary to help you.

> tasty roast slice tough succulent whisk
> juicy mix tender mouth-watering boil
> chop raw spicy well-done bake sweet stir
> sour fry bitter grill grate scramble crunchy
> rare creamy

Ways of describing food	Ways of preparing food
tasty	roast

2 Choose five words from Exercise 1 that you didn't know before and add them to the Exam Reviser.

> **exam reviser** p10 | 8.2

3 Choose the correct alternatives.

1 I've never eaten *rare/raw/well-done* fish. I prefer things cooked.
2 This coffee has a distinctive *succulent/sour/bitter* taste.
3 *Chop/Slice/Mix* the onion into pieces about 1 cm square.
4 You need to *roast/boil/bake* the pasta for about ten minutes in very hot water.
5 This meat has been overcooked and is very *mouth-watering/tender/tough*.
6 *Stir/Whisk/Scramble* all the dry ingredients together slowly with a wooden spoon.
7 Please don't cook the carrots for too long. I prefer them a bit *crunchy/creamy/juicy*.
8 You can either *fry/grill/grate* the cheese or cut it into very small pieces.

> **Vocabulary note** | cook/cooker
> Choose the correct alternative in each sentence:
>
> 1 I've applied for a job to be a *cook/cooker* in an Italian restaurant.
> 2 We need to buy a new *cook/cooker* because the old one doesn't work properly.

4 Look at the Exam Reviser and write down three more types of food for each of the categories.

> **exam reviser** p10 | 8.3

5 Look at the underlined sounds in each of the words in A, B and C. Write the words in the correct columns in the tables.

A

cr<u>u</u>nchy ch<u>o</u>p r<u>oa</u>st t<u>ou</u>gh c<u>oo</u>k well-d<u>o</u>ne
s<u>u</u>cculent c<u>oo</u>ker

1 l<u>u</u>nch	2 l<u>oo</u>k	3 n<u>o</u>t	4 n<u>o</u>te
crunchy			

B

b<u>a</u>ke st<u>ir</u> t<u>a</u>sty r<u>aw</u> gr<u>a</u>te r<u>are</u>

1 m<u>a</u>ke	2 b<u>ir</u>d	3 f<u>our</u>	4 h<u>air</u>
bake			

C

fr<u>y</u> gr<u>i</u>ll wh<u>i</u>sk j<u>ui</u>cy b<u>i</u>tter b<u>oi</u>l sl<u>i</u>ce m<u>i</u>x sp<u>i</u>cy

1 l<u>ie</u>	2 b<u>i</u>t	3 b<u>oo</u>t	4 t<u>oy</u>
fry			

6 R.38 ▶ Listen and check your answers. Then repeat the words.

7 Discuss these questions with a partner.

- How often do you eat meat? What is your favourite kind of meat? How do you like it cooked?
- How often do you eat eggs? What is your favourite way of cooking them?
- Think of a meal you have eaten and/or cooked in the last seven days. What was it? How was it cooked?

> **premium plus** 31 ▶

Grammar | countable and uncountable nouns

1 R.39 ▶ Listen to three short conversations and tick the phrases you hear.

1 a plate	☐	some plate	☐
2 an information	☐	some information	☐
3 a chocolate	☐	some chocolate	☐

2 Which of the phrases in Exercise 1 are not possible? Explain why.

•• see grammar reference: page 179 ••

3 There is a mistake in each of these sentences. Find the mistakes and correct them.

1 I usually have a bread for breakfast.
2 Being a waiter is often a very hard work.
3 Cutting down on sweet things is a good advice.
4 Drinking coffee always gives me terrible headache.
5 I've taken your blood pressure and I'm afraid the news aren't good.
6 I would like a sandwich with a chicken and mayonnaise in it, please.
7 We didn't have any furnitures, so we ate dinner sitting on the floor.

4 Write these words in the correct columns.

plate headache furniture information chicken
news chocolate bread advice work

A Countable nouns	B Uncountable nouns	C Nouns which can be both countable and uncountablee
plate		

5 Add three more words to each column. Then compare your words with a partner. Look at the Grammar Reference on page 179 if necessary.

6 Look again at the nouns in group C in Exercise 4. These can be both countable and uncountable (e.g. *chocolate/a chocolate*). What is the difference in meaning between each pair?

Grammar note | *few/a few* and *little/a little*
What is the difference in meaning between the words/phrases in *italics* in each pair?

1 I've got *a few* biscuits. Would you like one?
There are *few* people who I trust as much as you.

2 I'll just have *a little* milk in my coffee, please.
He's got *little* time now, but he can see you later.

7 Read the information on modifying countable and uncountable nouns on page 180. Then choose the correct alternatives in the text.

My first experience of The *Blind Cow* in Zurich was when I was taken there by a *few/a little*[1] friends for a m̲____ to celebrate passing our exams. *A large amount of/several*[2] people had read good reviews about it and we were all keen to experience this unusual place for ourselves. I must admit, however, that I approached the evening with *a few/a little*[3] nervousness. Why? Well, The Blind Cow isn't like *any/many*[4] other restaurant I know, since you eat your meal in pitch black!

We met in the bar area and spent *little/a little*[5] time getting used to the darkness. I had thought that there would at least be *a few/a small amount of*[6] light somewhere, but there wasn't! There weren't *many/much*[7] other people in the bar, but I still kept thinking I would bump into someone. But it's amazing how quickly it gets easier as you start using your other senses. After *few/a few*[8] drinks in the bar, we went down to the actual restaurant, where already the *plenty of/lack of*[9] light wasn't really bothering me anymore. In fact, I was beginning to enjoy it. There are a *great deal of/a l̲___*[10] waiters and other staff there to help you and I must say, it is one of the most enjoyable meals I've had for *many/a large amount of*[11] years. And also one of the tastiest – somehow because I couldn't see *none/any*[12] of the food, the taste became all the more delicious.

8 How do you think you would feel if you went to *The Blind Cow* restaurant? Why?

9 [R.40] Listen to two people playing 'the shopping trolley memory game' and answer these questions.

1 What are the two rules?
2 What mistake does the man make?

10 Play 'the shopping trolley memory game' in pairs or small groups. Which group got furthest in the alphabet, without making a mistake and naming a type of food for each letter?

premium plus 32

Speaking

1 Discuss with a partner.

- How well can you cook?
- How did you learn?
- How often do you cook?

2 Look at this question and decide with a partner how you would answer it. (Use the three ideas in the box and your own ideas.)

Speaking Task

Schools should provide cookery classes for all students. Do you agree?

- preparing for real life
- learning from parents
- understanding about nutrition

3 R.41 ▶ Listen to someone talking about the question in Exercise 2. How similar are her ideas to yours? Does she start to move away from answering the question at any time, or does she stay on topic?

4 R.41 ▶ Listen again and tick the phrases in the box that you hear.

Organising your ideas

1 *Firstly, …* ☐
2 *First of all, I'd like to say …* ☐
3 *The first point is …* ☐
4 *Secondly, …* ☐
5 *What's more, …* ☐
6 *Another important point is …* ☐
7 *Finally,* ☐
8 *Last but not least, …* ☐
9 *Then, there is the point about …* ☐

5 In pairs, take turns to give your answer to the question in Exercise 2 using three of the phrases in the box.

exam reviser   p23 | 10

Writing | letter/email

1 Discuss these questions.

- What times are meals in your country? When do you have them?
- What is a typical breakfast in your country? What do you have?
- Is there any food that you really don't like or that you are allergic to?
- Have you ever eaten food from any of these countries? What are typical dishes/ingredients from these countries?

> India   Mexico   Japan   China   Thailand   England   France   Turkey

2 Read the task and letter and tick the things which are mentioned.

1	Meal times	☐	4 Trying new restaurants	☐
2	Breakfast	☐	5 Picnics and barbecues	☐
3	Learning to cook	☐	6 Food preferences and allergies	☐

Writing task

An English friend, Alex, has recently invited you to stay and has just sent you a letter. Read Alex's letter and the notes you made on it. Then write a suitable letter/email to Alex, using **all** your notes.

Thank you for your letter telling me about your arrival date in September. I'm looking forward to having you come and stay with me.

I'd really like to make your stay with us as comfortable and happy as possible. Firstly, could you let me know what kinds of food you like and, of course, what you really don't like! It would also be very useful to know if you are allergic to any kind of food.

— Most things but especially pasta

Mushrooms and ...?

— Nuts (serious) and milk (a bit)

You will probably find that eating habits and times are a bit different in Britain from what you're used to. What times do people have their meals in your country? And what do you usually have for breakfast? Do you go out to restaurants very much? Where I live, there are quite a few restaurants with lots of different types of food. I wonder if there is a particular kind of food you would like to try.

Dinner quite late

Coffee – always! And ...

Indian and maybe something else?

Write a **letter/email** of between **120** and **150** words in an appropriate style. Do not write any postal addresses.

exam reviser   p22 | 9

3 The sentence in *italics* in this paragraph is a topic sentence. What is the purpose of a topic sentence?

My friends and I had a really fantastic picnic last week. We were celebrating my friend Sam's birthday and there were about eight of us altogether. The day before it had been raining, but in the end we were really lucky with the weather – it was warm and sunny all day. I took a football and we ended up playing with that all afternoon. It was really good fun.

4 Look again at the letter in Exercise 2. What are the three topic sentences?

5 Write a topic sentence for this paragraph.

_____. I've never really learned how to cook properly so I can only cook very basic things – not very well! Then I saw an advert in the library for some cookery classes. They are every Thursday evening and they are held in the local school. So, don't be surprised if I invite you round for dinner in a few weeks.

6 Look at this possible paragraph plan for the task in Exercise 2 and write a topic sentence for paragraphs 2, 3 and 4.

1 Thanks for letter
2 Describe your food preferences and allergies
3 Describe how meal times/food are different in your country
4 Say what kind of restaurants you like
5 Ending

7 Write your letter or email using the paragraph plan and topic sentences in Exercise 6 to help you. (You could also look at the Writing Reference on page 200.)

8 Read through your letter or email and answer these questions.

1 Have you included all the points from the task?
2 Have you organised it clearly with topic sentences?
3 Have you used an informal style with friendly opening and closing paragraphs?
4 Can you find any mistakes with grammar and spelling?

9 Now rewrite your letter or email, using your answers to the questions to improve it.

Listening

1 All these facts about chewing gum are true. Which one surprises you most? Why?

A Most people prefer the sugar-free varieties of chewing gum.
B Just one company produces most of the world's chewing gum.
C To clean all the chewing gum off the streets in the UK would cost over £150 million.
D A British artist paints tiny pictures on chewing gum stuck to the pavement.
E Scientists are developing a chewing gum which can be destroyed in a way which does not harm the environment.
F It has been known for people to buy chewing gum (which has already been chewed) on an Internet auction site.

2 R.42 You will hear five people talking about chewing gum. Choose from the list A–F in Exercise 1 which of the facts each speaker talks about. Use the letters only once. There is one extra letter which you do not need to use.

Speaker 1: _____
Speaker 2: _____
Speaker 3: _____
Speaker 4: _____
Speaker 5: _____

3 R.42 Listen again and say what these numbers/dates refer to.

1	90%	6	$100
2	1892	7	3,500,000,000
3	£317 million	8	300,000
4	40%	9	41
5	3/4		

4 Discuss these questions with other students.

• Do you chew chewing gum? Why/Why not?
• How do you think the problem of chewing gum litter on pavements could be solved?
• What do you think about the artist who paints on chewing gum stuck to the pavement? Is it a good thing or do you think it is a kind of graffiti and should not be allowed? Why?

Grammar | articles

1 Find the underlined examples of articles in the audioscript on pages 164–165 and match them to the uses in the box.

> **The indefinite article *a/an* is used:**
>
> With singular countable nouns (mentioned for the first time or when it doesn't matter which one), e.g. _____[1]
>
> With jobs, e.g. _____[2]
>
> **The definite article *the* is used:**
>
> With previously mentioned nouns, e.g. _____[3]
>
> With superlatives, e.g. _____[4]
>
> With particular nouns when it is clear what we are referring to, e.g. _____[5]
>
> With national groups (when described as a whole nation), e.g. _____[6]
>
> With inventions and species of animal, e.g. *the computer, the polar bear*
>
> When there is only one of something, e.g. *the moon, the equator*
>
> With rivers, oceans, seas, e.g. *the River Thames, the Atlantic Ocean*
>
> **No article (the zero article) is used:**
>
> With uncountable, plural and abstract nouns used in their general sense, e.g. _____[7], _____[8] and _____[9]
>
> With most streets, villages, towns, cities, countries, lakes, mountains, e.g. _____[10], _____[11] and _____[12] (For countries and groups of islands in the plural, we use *the*, e.g. _____[13].)

2 Complete the texts using *a, an, the* or Ø (zero article) as appropriate.

THE ORIGINAL SANDWICH

Selling sandwiches is __Ø__[1] big business, thought to be worth $50 billion a year globally and growing fast. _____[2] Americans are _____[3] biggest consumers of sandwiches in _____[4] world, including such favourites as the peanut butter and jelly sandwich, as well as _____[5] hamburgers of course.

Its origins are not in the States, however. _____[6] sandwich is said to have been invented in _____[7] England in the 18th century by the 4th Earl of Sandwich. The story goes that he didn't have _____[8] time to eat _____[9] proper meal so he asked for _____[10] meat and cheese to be served between two slices of bread.

THE MOST EXPENSIVE SANDWICH

In Selfridges department store in London you can buy _____[11] sandwich which costs £85. That almost certainly makes it the most expensive sandwich in London, or maybe anywhere. _____[12] gigantic sandwich weighs 600 g, contains 2,500 calories and is made of _____[13] long list of specialised ingredients, including _____[14] Japanese beef, red pepper and paté de foie gras. _____[15] bread is freshly-baked every morning from _____[16] original recipe specially created for the sandwich.

3 Work in small groups. Choose one of these topics. Try to speak for one minute even if you make a mistake.
- sandwiches
- chewing gum
- a recipe you like making
- a restaurant or café you like
- a food shop or market you like

`premium plus` 33 ▸

Vocabulary | compound adjectives

1 Complete these sentences with the compound adjectives in the box.

> sugar-free   never-ending
> mass-produced

1 William Wrigley started making the first _____ gum in 1892.
2 _____ brands are now the most popular.
3 Biodegradable gum may solve the _____ litter problem.

2 Match these words to make compound adjectives.

1	ice-	A	air
2	deep-	B	made
3	home-	C	minute
4	world-	D	famous
5	open-	E	fried
6	last-	F	cold

3 Complete each sentence with the best compound adjective from Exercise 2.

1 All the cakes are _____ in the kitchen behind the shop.
2 We were lucky to get a _____ booking. It's a very popular restaurant.
3 I don't think Jamie Oliver is a _____ cook but he's certainly very well-known in Britain.
4 One of my favourite things is fresh prawns, _____ in very hot oil.
5 I love going to the Mosaica restaurant in warm weather when you can sit in the _____ area at the back.
6 There's nothing like an _____ drink at the end of a hot, busy day.

`premium plus` 34 ▸

FCE close-up | Use of English Word formation (Paper 3, part 3)

Exam information

This part of the exam consists of a text in which there are ten gaps. At the end of some of the lines, there is a word in capital letters. You have to form a new word based on this word which can be correctly put into the gap in the same line.

Approach

1 Read the text quickly before filling in any of the gaps in order to get a general sense of the meaning.

2 Before you fill a gap, decide whether the missing word is an adjective (e.g. *hungry*), an adverb (e.g. *hungrily*), a noun (e.g. *food*) or a verb (e.g. *eat*).

3 Remember that the missing word will sometimes need to be plural (e.g. *children*) and will sometimes need to be negative (e.g. *unfortunately*). Read the whole sentence to check.

4 Remember, too, that sometimes the change will not just be adding a prefix (e.g. *un-*) or a suffix (e.g. *-ness*) but that the whole word will need to change (e.g. *long > lengthen*).

5 For each gap, form words from the word in capitals and see which one you think fits the gap.

6 Check that each word you have written is the right part of speech (noun, verb, etc.) for that sentence and that the whole sentence makes sense. Remember to check that your spelling is correct, too.

7 Remember that in the exam you should always write something in each gap: you do not lose marks for a wrong answer.

Practice task

For questions **1–10**, read the text below. Use the word given in capitals at the end of some of the lines to form a word that fits in the space **in the same line**. There is an example at the beginning (**0**).

Write your answers IN CAPITAL LETTERS **on the separate answer sheet**.

Example: | 0 | B E N E F I C I A L |

The wonders of tea

The first people to realise how **(0)** _____ tea were were the Chinese over 5,000   **BENEFIT**

years ago. The **(1)** _____ of benefits that they identified were helping with pains in   **VARIOUS**

joints, **(2)** _____ blood vessels, increasing mental performance and reducing   **STRONG**

(3) _____ .   **TIRED**

Tea was first brought to Britain in the 16th century. Now, over 70% of the British **(4)** _____   **POPULATE**

drink tea. On average they drink three cups a day each, and 90% of them take milk with their tea.

Nowadays, scientists have made further **(5)** _____ about the benefits to one's   **DISCOVER**

(6) _____ of drinking tea. Firstly, tea can be used as a   **HEALTHY**

(7) _____ measure against tooth decay as it is a natural source of fluoride. The tannin in   **PREVENT**

tea also protects teeth from damaging acid attacks. It is also **(8)** _____ rich in substances   **PARTICULAR**

known as flavenoids, which have properties that help slow down the **(9)** _____ process,   **AGE**

protecting us not only from wrinkles, but also from **(10)** _____ such as cancer and heart   **ILL**

disease.

Grammar

1 <u>Underline</u> the alternative which is *not* possible.

1 Would you like *some/a piece of/a* toast?
2 There are *plenty of/several/much* tickets still available.
3 Have you got *a few/a small amount of/any* good books I could borrow?
4 I saved *a piece of/a few/a little* cake for you.
5 I haven't got *much/a great deal of/a lack of* money left.
6 We saved *a huge amount of/a little/several* time by leaving very early in the morning.
7 Let me give you *a bit of/some/an* advice.
8 It's OK. We've got *a little/little/a bit of* time before we have to go.
9 There are quite *a lot of/a little/a few* plates that need washing up.
10 The show was cancelled because there was *few/not much/a lack of* interest.

2 Choose the correct alternatives (Ø = zero article).

Choose one of these desserts and see what the psychiatrists say about **you!**

• **Chocolate cake** • **Carrot cake**
• **Ice cream** • **Lemon pie**

If you chose chocolate cake, you are *a/an*[1] adventurous type with *Ø/a*[2] clever sense of humour. *The/Ø*[3] people often choose you to be *a/the*[4] leader of *a/the*[5] group as you are usually *Ø/the*[6] best person for the job.

If you chose carrot cake, you are a fun-loving person who likes *the/Ø*[7] laughter. You often choose *a/the*[8] company of people from warmer places like *the/Ø*[9] South America.

If you chose ice cream, you are active and love *the/Ø*[10] sports. *The/Ø*[11] sports you are most interested in are usually competitive ones. You would like nothing better than to sail round *a/the*[12] world as fast as possible.

If you chose lemon pie, you are articulate and intelligent. You are *the/an*[13] excellent speaker and would make *Ø/a*[14] very good teacher. You are also ambitious and have *the/Ø*[15] high standards.

Vocabulary

3 Complete the gaps in the recipe. Each gap shows the first letter and the number of missing letters.

Pasta with spinach, red peppers and halloumi cheese

This is a t _ _ _ _[1], colourful pasta dish with a creamy sauce combining the s _ _ _ _[2] taste of red peppers with the slightly b _ _ _ _ _[3] taste of spinach. The deep-fried haloumi cheese adds extra interest.

• Wash the red peppers and g _ _ _ _[4] them until the skins are blackened. Then s _ _ _ _[5] them into thin strips.
• C _ _ _[6] the halloumi into small cubes and then f _ _[7] in very hot oil, turning once until golden.
• Fry the onion, garlic and chilli in a frying pan for a couple of minutes.
• Wash the spinach and then b _ _ _[8] briefly in very little hot water.
• Cook the pasta in boiling water for about ten minutes.
• Add cream and yoghurt to the onion mixture. Then add the red peppers, halloumi and spinach. Then slowly s _ _ _[9] in the pasta with a wooden spoon.

4 Add the best compound adjective from the box in the correct place in each sentence.

> open-air last-minute never-ending
> ice-cold sugar-free home-made deep-fried

1 I think what we all need are some drinks.
2 I've decided to go on a diet for the next month.
3 I'm not going to eat chicken anymore. I'll grill it instead.
4 He seems to have a lot of complaints at the moment.
5 Do you want to come to the concert next weekend?
6 I'm going to do some revision tonight before my food technology exam tomorrow.
7 My grandmother makes the most delicious apple pie I've ever tasted.

The world around us

dramatic

energy saving

disaster

Unit 09

Introduction

1 Work with another student and answer these questions.
- What can you see in the pictures?
- What thoughts or feelings do you have about each picture?

2 Match the words in the box to the headings.

> lion jungle earthquake pollution elephant flood beach cliff
> mountain volcano drought buffalo greenhouse effect forest stream
> leopard famine ocean ozone layer coast river global warming rhino

- Environmental problems
- Geographical features
- Natural disasters
- Animals

exam reviser p11 | 9.1

3 Discuss these questions with other students.
- What are the main environmental dangers the world faces now?
- In what everyday ways can ordinary people protect the environment?
- Is it important to protect animals that are in danger of extinction? Why/ Why not?

Reading

1 Discuss with other students.
- Do you know of any famous volcanoes or volcanic eruptions? What do you know about them?
- What do you imagine happens before and during a volcanic eruption?

2 Read the article. Tick the topics it refers to.
1 the story of Vesuvius before AD79
2 how prepared for the eruption the people were
3 the action that Pliny's uncle took
4 how Pliny's uncle died
5 what happened during the eruption
6 what happened to Pliny after the eruption ended

Pompeii:
A disaster waiting to happen

POMPEII: A DISASTER WAITING TO HAPPEN

On August 24, AD79 Mount Vesuvius erupted, throwing tons of molten rock and sulphuric gas miles into the atmosphere. A firestorm suffocated the people of the neighbouring Roman cities of Pompeii,
5 Herculaneum and Stabiae. Tons of falling debris filled the streets until nothing remained to be seen. Buried for almost 1,700 years, the cities were more or less forgotten until excavation began in 1748.

It is certain that on the morning of August 24, AD79, the
10 people of Pompeii were totally unprepared for the eruption of Vesuvius – they were getting on with their busy lives, in total ignorance of what was to come. It is mainly thanks to the letters of Pliny (a Roman administrator and poet) that we have an extraordinary eyewitness account of what
15 happened.

Staying with his uncle nearby, Pliny wrote a number of letters which describe in detail his experience during the eruption. The elder Pliny was in charge of the fleet in the Bay of Naples. When the eruption began, the population of the
20 towns and villas that circled the bay could only respond with panic. However, Pliny describes his uncle as calmly sailing directly into the danger zone.

'My uncle was stationed at Misenum. On August 24, in the early afternoon, my mother drew his attention
25 to a column of smoke of unusual size and appearance. Seeing at once that it was important enough for a closer inspection, my uncle ordered a boat to be made ready.

As he was leaving the house, he was handed a message from Rectina, whose house was at the foot of
30 the mountain, so that escape was impossible except by boat. She was terrified by the danger threatening her and begged him to rescue her from her fate. He changed his plans and hurried to the place which everyone else was leaving, steering his course straight for the danger zone.
35 Ashes were already falling, hotter and thicker as the ships drew near.

For a moment my uncle wondered whether to turn back, but then decided they must make for his friend, Pomponianus, at Stabiae. When they arrived,
40 Pomponianus had already put his belongings on board ship, intending to escape but then the wind changed direction. My uncle embraced his terrified friend and tried to encourage him. Thinking he could calm his fears by showing his own calmness, he gave orders that he
45 was to be carried to the bathroom. After his bath he lay down and dined; he was quite cheerful, or at any rate he pretended he was, which was no less courageous.

Meanwhile on Mount Vesuvius great sheets of fire and flames blazed at several points, emphasising the darkness
50 of night. My uncle and Pomponianus debated whether to stay indoors or go outside, for the buildings were now shaking with violent shocks, and felt as if they would be torn from their foundations.

Having gone down to the shore to investigate the
55 possibility of any escape by sea, my uncle found that the waves were still wild and dangerous. At this point it seems that the flames and smell of sulphur which gave warning of the approaching fire were too much for him and he suddenly collapsed. When daylight returned on the 26th
60 – two days after the last day he had been seen – his body was found intact and uninjured, still fully clothed and looking more like sleep than death.'

Like his uncle, the young Pliny also stayed calm, but his mother wept and begged him to leave with her. By the

3 Read the article again. Explain the significance of these words/phrases in the story.

August 24, AD79 – the day Vesuvius erupted

1 Pompeii, Herculaneum and Stabiae
2 1748
3 an eyewitness account
4 a column of smoke
5 Misenum
6 the wind changed direction
7 a bath
8 wild and dangerous waves
9 a rain of ash
10 midnight
11 an exceptional catastrophe

4 Work with a partner and find these things.:
1 The opposites of these words?
possible prepared injured
2 The nouns from these words?
possible dead survive
3 The adjectives from these words? (there may be more than one):
courage danger calmness

5 Check your answers to Exercise 4 by finding the words in the article.

6 Discuss these questions.
- How do you think you would have reacted if you had been living in Pompeii in AD79?
- Do you know any films or stories about natural disasters? If so, what happened?
- When one country suffers a natural disaster, how do you think the rest of the world should respond?

65 time they set out to escape northwards, a dense black cloud of ash had blotted out the light and there were crowds of screaming people fleeing around them in terror.

The eruption lasted for more than twenty-four hours from its start on the morning of 24 August. Those who fled at once, leaving behind 70 their possessions, had a chance of survival, for the rain of ash that descended for several hours was not necessarily lethal.

It was not until around midnight that the first pyroclastic flows happened. (A pyroclastic flow is an avalanche of hot ash, pumice, rock fragments and volcanic gas, which rushes down the side of a volcano 75 at 100 km/hour or more.) These meant certain death for the people of the region. It is impossible to tell what proportion of the inhabitants died, but the Romans were accustomed to losses mounting to tens of thousands in battle, and even they regarded this catastrophe as exceptional.

80 The corpses found by archaeologists in Pompeii or Herculaneum should be regarded as only a small sample: the destruction encompassed the entire landscape south of Vesuvius. As many died in the countryside or at sea as in the cities. Even as far north as Misenum, the ash lay deep in drifts.

Practising reading

1 One of the best ways to improve your reading skills and increase your vocabulary is by reading. How many different ways of practising reading in English can you name?

follow the subtitles of films

2 Which of the following tips do you think could help you to increase the amount you read in English? Tell another student.
- Read things that interest you.
- Read little and often.
- Read for pleasure not for study.
- Read things you know about (e.g. articles in the news) so your world knowledge can help you.
- Read graded readers of classic or modern stories.

Do you have any other tips to encourage other students to read more in English?

3 Decide on one thing that you are going to do to increase the amount you read in English.

learning tip

Vesuvius

Misenum
Herculaneum
Pompeii
Stabiae
BAY OF NAPLES

Grammar | participle clauses

1 Look at the examples of participle clauses in *italics*. How could you express the sentences with additional words to show the meaning?

After being *buried for almost 1,700 years,* . . .

1 *Buried* for almost 1,700 years, the cities were more or less forgotten until excavation began in 1748.
2 *Staying* with his uncle nearby, Pliny wrote letters which describe his experience during the eruption.
3 *Seeing* at once that it was important enough for a closer inspection, my uncle ordered a boat to be made ready.
4 *Having gone* down to the shore to try to escape by sea, he found that the waves were still dangerous.

•• **see grammar reference: page 181** ••

2 Complete the story with the participles from the box. There are more participles than you need.

> looking named starting behaving taken wanting
> finding given being having separated

_____¹ from his mother after a recent flood, a baby hippo in Kenya was close to death. _____² the one-year-old hippo alone and dehydrated, rangers took him to a sanctuary in Mombasa. _____³ 'Owen' by the staff at the sanctuary, he quickly became a firm favourite, despite _____⁴ quite nervous and shy at first.
After a few days, _____⁵ to get his confidence back, Owen tried to make friends with a 100-year-old tortoise called 'Mzee' (meaning 'Old Man'). Despite _____⁶ in quite an unfriendly way to begin with, Mzee now refuses to be apart from Owen.

3 Imagine you are writing a dramatic story. Complete these sentences.

1 Walking through the dense jungle, they suddenly ...
2 Having woken up to find he was a prisoner in a small room, Terry ...
3 Washed up on a small island after the plane crash, Sue ...
4 Knowing how hot it could get in the desert, they ...

4 Compare your sentences with another student. Who had the most dramatic endings?

premium plus 35

5 Rewrite this story using participle clauses.

On a warm spring day three years ago, Aron Ralston was just another young outdoor enthusiast. **Wanting a new challenge, he was attempting to be** . . .

On a warm spring day three years ago, Aron Ralston was just another young outdoor enthusiast. He wanted a new challenge. He was attempting to be the first person to climb all fifty-nine of Colorado's 14,000-foot-plus peaks in winter by himself. However, he went into a Utah canyon where an 800-pound boulder broke free and rolled onto his right hand, trapping him. He repeatedly tried to lift and break the rock but he couldn't move it. After six days, a dehydrated and desperate Ralston bent his arm against the rock and broke it. He used his penknife to cut through his arm and managed to free himself. He stumbled out of the canyon and remembers thinking that his story would amaze his friends. It did ... and the rest of the world.

Listening

1 R.43 ▶ You will hear people talking in five different situations. For questions 1–5, choose the best answer A, B or C.

1 You overhear a woman talking on the phone. Who is she speaking to?
   A a builder
   B a friend
   C her boss

2 You hear part of a news programme. What is the reporter doing?
   A criticising international aid agencies
   B explaining the cause of a difficult situation
   C asking for help

3 You overhear a man talking to a friend. What was the main activity on this man's holiday supposed to be?
   A learning to sail
   B sunbathing
   C sightseeing

4 You overhear a woman talking to a friend. How does the woman feel about her experience of the weather where she lives now?
   A surprised
   B disappointed
   C frustrated

5 You hear part of a radio weather forecast. The weather forecaster is warning motorists about a problem. When is this problem going to occur?
   A this afternoon
   B this evening
   C tomorrow morning

3 Have you ever had an experience similar to those in Exercise 1? If so, tell other students.

I remember my dad driving me to the airport really early in the morning last winter. It was freezing and the roads were really icy. We saw at least two or three accidents on the way.

Vocabulary | weather

1 Look at these extracts from postcards about the weather. Put the words/phrases in **bold** in the correct column in the table.

1 I can't believe it - it's been **pouring with rain** all week long!

2 Most days it's been fairly **cloudy** with a **light drizzle** - I wish it would decide if it's going to rain properly or not!

3 Yesterday there was a **strong wind**, which was great for windsurfing.

4 It's quite **warm** and **humid** during the day, but it can get **freezing cold** at night.

5 When we went outside the tent this morning, there was **frost** on the ground and a **thick fog** - we could hardly see the other tents!

6 The weather's been lovely - blue skies and **unbroken sunshine** but with a **gentle breeze** to keep us cool!

7 Last night there was the most amazing storm with some really dramatic **thunder and lightning**.

8 It's been quite **chilly** for September and we've had quite a **few showers**, too, which hasn't been great.

rain	wind	temperature	snow/ice	other
pouring with rain	strong wind			

eHam reviser p11 | 9.2

2 Look again at the types of weather in Exercise 1. Answer these questions.

- Which do you hate?
- Which do you not mind?
- Which do you love?
- Which have you never experienced?

3 Talk to other students. Find the person who has the most similar answers to you.

4 Read the story. Complete each gap with one of the words from the box. There are three extra words that you do not need to use.

> warmth chilly shone shady cloud breeze power
> hot shivered harder poured blew icy stronger

The Wind and the Sun were arguing about their strength.

'I have the strongest _____¹ that ever was,' said the Sun. 'Nothing can stand against me.'

'Nothing except me,' said the Wind. 'I am far _____² than you.'

'We shall find out,' said the Sun. 'I know a way to settle the argument. Do you see that man coming down the road? Well, whichever one of us makes him take off his coat, he must be considered the strongest. You try first.'

The Sun hid himself behind a _____³ while the Wind began. The Wind _____⁴. The man bent his head. The Wind whistled. The man _____⁵. The Wind roared and raged and sent _____⁶ blasts against the man. But the _____⁷ the Wind blew, the closer the man wrapped his coat about him.

'My turn now,' said the Sun as it came out from behind the cloud.

At first the Sun _____⁸ gently, and the man unbuttoned his coat and let it hang loosely from his shoulders. Then the Sun covered the whole Earth with _____⁹. Within a few minutes the man was so _____¹⁰ he was glad to take off his coat and find a _____¹¹ place.

premium plus 36

5 Discuss with other students.

- What do you think the moral of this story is? (The original moral is given on page 169.)
- Do you agree with it?

Listening

1 Discuss with other students. What do you know about Emperor penguins?

2 R.44 Listen to an interview with a film critic. What possible reasons are mentioned to explain the success of the film *March of the Penguins*?

3 R.44 Listen again. For questions 1–6, choose the best answer A, B or C.

1 Why is Steven Jacobs (the film critic) very surprised?
   A *March of the Penguins* has made a lot of money.
   B A lot of people have been trying to see *March of the Penguins*.
   C He thought more people would have been to see the new Batman film.

2 What is the main theme of *March of the Penguins*?
   A the hostile environment of Antarctica
   B the dedication of the penguins to their families
   C how many human characteristics penguins have

3 What was the reaction of the audience in the cinema that Steven Jacobs was in?
   A They were mainly amused.
   B They were mainly frightened.
   C They had a mixture of reactions.

4 What is director Luc Jacquet's reaction to the success of the film?
   A He is somewhat surprised by it.
   B He knew that the film would do well.
   C He is shocked that the film has done so well.

5 Why did Luc Jacquet want to make the film?
   A Because Emperor penguins face extinction.
   B He had been emotionally affected by learning about the penguins.
   C He wanted to make a film for children.

6 What happened to Luc Jacquet's cameramen?
   A They lost parts of their hands.
   B They fell through the ice
   C They were taken by surprise by a snowstorm.

4 Discuss these questions with other students.
   • Have you seen the film *March of the Penguins*? If so, what did you think of it? If not, would you be interested in seeing it? Why/Why not?
   • Do you ever watch wildlife programmes on TV? Why do you like/dislike them?

Writing | review

1 Read the review. What is one negative point that the reviewer mentions about the film?

March of the Penguins

RELEASED: 30 MARCH 2005, CERT PG
WILDLIFE BASED ANIMAL ADVENTURE STORY

Made in 2005, *March of the Penguins* is now firmly established as a wildlife classic, thanks to the amazing efforts of French filmmaker Luc Jacquet and his devoted team. Together they endured a year of extreme conditions in Antarctica to track the extraordinary life cycle of Emperor penguins on film.

The film is remarkable in its story, which is beautifully narrated by Morgan Freeman. But even more incredible is its photography. Hundreds of penguins are seen returning, in a single-file march of seventy miles or more, to their frozen breeding ground. At times dramatic and at times just plain funny, the film follows their treacherous task of protecting eggs and hatchlings in temperatures as low as 128 degrees below zero. This unique film perfectly balances fascinating scientific information with highly entertaining visuals.

A story of love and survival, *March of the Penguins* is an eye-opening and educational experience. Although some will criticise it for being sentimental at times, it certainly is a must for anyone interested in wildlife.

2 To write effective reviews that will interest the reader, it is important to use a good range of vocabulary. Put the words in the box in the correct columns in the table, according to their meaning.

> extraordinary amusing fascinating gripping
> unbelievable dull hilarious intriguing
> nail-biting tedious

funny	exciting	interesting	surprising	boring

exam reviser p11 | 9.3

3 Choose the correct alternative in these sentences.

1 Last night's party was incredibly *gripping/tedious/amazing*. I didn't know anybody and they were all talking about the weather.

2 Your brother is absolutely *hilarious/nail-biting/exciting*. His story about his boss made me laugh until I cried!

3 There was a *dull/funny/fascinating* programme on TV last night about global warming. It made me want to find out a lot more about the subject.

4 Did Sarah tell you the *extraordinary/boring/dull* story about how her dog saved her from drowning?

5 The end of the race was absolutely *nail-biting/amusing/tedious*, but in the end Pierre won by half a second.

4 You are going to write a review of a film you have seen. Follow these instructions.

1 Decide on the film that you would like to review.

2 Make notes about:

• information about the film you would like to include

• your opinions of the film

• recommendations you have for people who might be interested in seeing the film

3 Refer to the Writing Reference on page 190 for 'Dos and don'ts' and 'Useful language' for writing reviews.

4 Write your review in 120–180 words, using a range of interesting vocabulary.

Speaking

1 Work in pairs. Look at the pictures which show different types of films. What can you see in each one?

2 R.45 ▶ Listen and follow the instructions. Allow about three minutes to do the task.

3 Discuss with your partner how well you did the task. What could you have done better?

4 Now work with a different partner and do the task again. Try to improve in the areas you discussed with your first partner.

Vocabulary | animals

1 R.46 ▶ Listen to three people playing the 'Animal alphabet' game and answer these questions.

1 How do you play the game?

2 Why does one person say *Challenge!*?

2 Work in groups of three. Play the 'Animal alphabet' game. Which group got furthest in the alphabet without making a mistake?

3 In your groups, look at the pictures. Can you name the different parts of each animal? Which group can name the most parts?

premium plus 37 ▶

4 Discuss with other students. Which animals are often considered to be:

1 loyal?   4 intelligent?

2 cunning?   5 hard-working?

3 brave?   6 independent?

5 If you were an animal, what would you choose to be and why?

Speaking

1 R.47 ▶ Listen to Charlotte and decide which of these subjects she talks about.

1 Her experience of being a vegetarian
2 The responsibility we have towards animals
3 What she believes governments should do
4 What action she has taken personally
5 Her ideas for a new kind of zoo

2 R.47 ▶ Listen again. Which statements are true?

1 She was surrounded by a lot of animals as a child.
2 She didn't have an easy time when she was at school because of her views.
3 She thinks that every country has a duty to protect its animals.
4 She started getting interested in animal rights after she left college.
5 She has appeared on television to publicise her views.
6 She is against all zoos.

3 Read these statements. Which ones do you think Charlotte would agree with and which would she disagree with?

1 I think animals should have the same rights as people.
2 Certain animals becoming extinct is just part of nature.
3 A pet can be like another member of the family.
4 Zoos can be useful places for teaching people about wild animals.
5 I think people who eat meat should see the conditions in which the animals they eat are kept.
6 It's OK to test new products (e.g. shampoo) on animals if it protects people from possible bad reactions.

4 Work in groups and choose four of the statements in Exercise 3. Prepare to give your opinions about them. Look at the language for expressing opinions, responding to opinions and agreeing/disagreeing in the Exam Reviser.

exam reviser p19 | 2 ▶

5 Discuss your opinions of the statements you chose with other students. Which ones (if any) do you all agree about?

Grammar | expressing purpose

1 The expressions in *italics* in sentences A–C are all used to express purpose, i.e. to say why someone does something. Answer the questions.

1 What do you notice about the grammar of the underlined part of each sentence?
2 What is the difference in meaning between **A** and **B**?
3 Which expression in *italics* in **C** is the least formal?

A I'm going to take a camera *in case we see* any animals.
B I'm going to take a camera *so that we can take* photos of the animals.
C I'm going to take a camera *to/so as to/in order to take* photos of any animals we see.

2 Choose the best alternative in these sentences.

1 It's important to get plenty of publicity *in case/so as to* put pressure on the government to change the law.
2 Showing children animals in zoos *so that/in order to* teach them about life in the wild doesn't make sense.
3 I think I'll make a vegetable curry *in case/so that* either of them are vegetarians.
4 We need to be more active in the community *to/so that* ordinary people understand the kinds of tests that some of these drug companies are carrying out on animals.
5 We're making this advertisement *in case/in order to* remind people that when they buy an animal as a pet, it is a responsibility for life.

•• see grammar reference: page 181 ••

Grammar note | infinitive of purpose
Which of the following sentences are not grammatically correct?

1 She stopped to admire the view.
2 He went to the information desk for to find out the time of the next train.
3 I left some soup for them to have when they got home from the match.
4 I got up early for packing for my holiday.
5 She moved to a new flat so as be near her new job.

---

3 For questions 1–5, complete the second sentence so that it has a similar meaning to the first sentence, using the word given. Do not change the word given. You must use between two and five words, including the word given.

1 I'd like to save the discussion about zoos until next week so as to be able to finish the meeting by 5.00 p.m.
order
I'd like to save the discussion about zoos until next week _____ be able to finish the meeting by 5.00 p.m.

2 You should read this book in order to know how to look after your pet rabbit.

so

You should read this book _____ know how to look after your pet rabbit.

3 Suki decided to work late because she wanted to finish her monthly report.

as

Suki decided to work late _____ finish her monthly report.

4 Could you arrive early to help us organise the banners for the demonstration?

that

Could you arrive early _____ help us organise the banners for the demonstration?

5 Take this compass to help you if you get lost.

in

Take this compass to help you _____ get lost.

---

premium plus 38 ▶

4 Write sentences using each of the phrases in the box. Make sentences which are true or meaningful for you.

> so that   in order to   in case   so as not to

*I'm learning English **so that** I'll be able to apply for a place to study veterinary science at an Australian university.*

5 Tell other students your sentences. Make a note of the most interesting sentence you hear.

FCE close-up | Writing Essay (Paper 2, part 2)

Exam information

Part 2 of the Writing paper consists of a choice of questions; you need to choose one question from a total of four. The types of tasks that you will be asked to choose from include: a letter (formal or informal), a story, an article, a report, a review and an essay. The essay will usually be written for your teacher, perhaps as a follow-up to a class activity, and will probably include some opinions and suggestions on the subject. Your answer should be written in an appropriately formal/neutral style in between 120 and 180 words.

Approach

1 <u>Underline</u> the key words in the task and check that you know:

- who it is written for
- the aim/purpose of the essay
- if it asks a) for your opinion b) for both sides of an argument

2 Spend some time thinking of all the ideas/arguments to support your opinion and against your opinion.

Practice task

You have had a class discussion on animal rights. Your teacher has now asked you to write an essay giving your opinion on the following statement.

Experiments which cause suffering to animals can never be justified.

Write your **essay** in 120–180 words.

Then organise these ideas and write a paragraph plan. A typical plan will be either:

1) Introduction 2) Your opinion 3) The other side of the argument 4) Conclusion (+ Recommendation)
or
1) Introduction 2) Arguments for 3) Arguments against 4) Conclusion (+ Your opinion)

3 It is important that you only write about the statement in the question. Make sure the points you make are clear and give examples where appropriate. Be careful not to include irrelevant information which is not asked for.

4 When you have finished writing your essay, take some time to check your work. Make sure you have:

- organised your essay into paragraphs;
- used an appropriate style;
- responded to the statement in the question and nothing else;
- checked any mistakes with grammar and vocabulary;
- checked any mistakes with spelling and punctuation;
- written approximately the correct number of words.

Go to www.iTests.com or your CD-ROM for interactive exam practice

Grammar

1 There are mistakes in some of these sentences. Find the mistakes and correct them.

1 Remembering it was Sally's birthday, he decided to give her a call.

2 Anyone arrived after the performance starts will not be permitted to take their seats until the interval.

3 Not have a garden of his own, he likes to go and sit in the park nearby.

4 Because being from a large family, he enjoyed big meals with lots of talk and laughter.

5 He just sat on the sofa, watching TV.

6 Smiled to herself, she put the Sunday newspaper on Simon's desk.

7 Knowing how much she liked flowers, he bought her a large bunch of white roses.

8 When noticing that the front door was open, he went inside to investigate.

9 Having so much money didn't always make him particularly happy.

10 As soon as realising he had left his umbrella at home, he decided to go back and get it.

2 Combine these pairs of sentences into one sentence using the expression in brackets.

1 I'd like to take a map of the area. I don't want to get lost. (so that)

2 We should take a first-aid kit. It's possible someone might have an accident. (in case)

3 We need to start packing this evening. This will mean we can leave by 9.00 a.m. tomorrow. (in order to)

4 We must keep very quiet. We don't want to disturb any of the animals. (so as not to)

5 Shall I pick you up from the airport? Then you won't need to worry about getting a taxi. (so that)

6 Let me give you my mobile number. You could call me if there are any problems. (in case)

7 He made this film. He wanted people to know that these animals are nearly extinct. (to)

8 We took a taxi. We wanted to be sure we arrived on time. (so as to)

9 I think I'll take a book. It's possible that I will have to wait a long time for a doctor to see me. (in case)

10 It's important that we look at alternative forms of energy. We must protect the environment in the future. (in order to)

Vocabulary

3 Choose the correct alternatives in these sentences.

1 You don't really need an umbrella – it's just a light *drizzle/storm/rain*.

2 I wish it wasn't so *humid/chilly/cloudy* today. I can't stop shivering.

3 There's a really *strong/heavy/rough* wind. We should go and fly our kite.

4 The *fog/cloud/frost* was so bad we couldn't find the car for ages.

5 I got caught in a heavy *shower/sunshine/lightning* on the way home and got soaked to the skin!

6 Apparently, this little thing on my penknife is for getting stones out of horses' *hooves/feet/claws*.

7 I think that little bird has broken its *fin/wing/arm*. It doesn't seem to be able to fly.

8 *Whales/dolphins/sharks* are actually mammals not fish and can grow up to 90 m long.

4 Complete these sentence with the correct word. You have been given the beginning of each word and the exact number of missing letters.

1 I saw a h_ _ _ _ _ _ _ _ comedy film on TV last night about a dog that could talk.

2 There's an i_ _ _ _ _ _ _ _ _ story behind the strange disappearance of Agatha Christie in 1926. Nobody seems to know the real truth.

3 Long parts of the book are very t_ _ _ _ _ _ with nothing much of interest, but the final chapter is excellent.

4 Simon made us all smile last night when he told us quite a f_ _ _ _ story about how he got his first job.

5 There's a n_ _ _ - _ _ _ _ _ _ end to the film. Honestly, I was on the edge of my seat with excitement.

6 The traffic was u_ _ _ _ _ _ _ _ _ _ _ last night. It took me four hours to get home!

7 I don't find his jokes at all a_ _ _ _ _ _.

8 She could never understand how he could find geology to be such a f_ _ _ _ _ _ _ _ _ subject.

9 This book I am reading about outer space is absolutely g_ _ _ _ _ _ _. I really don't want to put it down!

10 Her boyfriend is so d_ _ _. All he ever wants to talk about is cars and computers!

Talk, don't talk

Premium | Unit 10

whisper

now you're talking!

chat show

speak up!

Unit 10

Introduction

1 What can you see in each picture? What do they have in common?

2 Work in pairs. Check you understand the phrases in *italics* and answer the questions.

- How do you feel about *making small talk* in English?
- How much experience of *public speaking* do you have? How do you feel about it? Why?
- What do you think of TV *chat shows*? Do you have any favourites?
- Do you have experience of any *English-speaking* countries? What did you think of them?

3 **R.48** ▶ All the numbers, dates and times in the box refer to facts about text messaging. Listen and say what each one refers to.

> **fcts abt txts**
> 1992   85%   10   10.30 p.m.   11 p.m.   New Year's Day 2006   43.2 seconds

4 Discuss these questions with other students.

- Which of the facts in Exercise 3 surprised you most? Why?
- How often do you send text messages? How fast are you at writing texts?
- Who do you mostly send texts to? What are they typically about?

Song

1 R.49 ▶ Listen to the song and read the lyrics. Which of these statements do you think best describes why the singer feels so frustrated and lonely?

A He is lost and isolated in a foreign country.

B He wants to write more songs but he hasn't got the inspiration.

C He can't find anyone who really understands him.

D He is worried about what his brother will do in the future.

Talk by Coldplay

Oh brother I can't, I can't _____¹ through

I've been trying hard to reach you, cause I don't know what to do

Oh brother I can't _____² it's true

I'm so scared about the future and I want to talk to you

Oh I want to talk to you

Chorus

You can take a picture of something you _____³

In the future where will I be?

You can climb a ladder up to the sun

Or _____⁴ a song nobody has sung

Or do something that's never been done

Are you lost or incomplete?

Do you feel like a puzzle, you can't find your missing piece?

Tell me how do you feel?

Well I feel like they're talking in a language I don't _____⁵

And they're talking it to me

(Repeat chorus)

So you don't know where you're going, and you want to talk

And you feel like you're going where you've been before

You _____⁶ anyone who'll listen but you feel ignored

Nothing's really making any sense at all

Let's talk, let's talk

Let's talk, let's talk

2 Complete the song lyrics with the verbs in the box. Two of the verbs cannot be used.

> talk   tell   say   speak   see   write   believe   get

3 R.49 ▶ Listen again and check your answers.

4 Discuss with other students.

1 What do you think these two lines from the song mean?

- *I feel like they're talking in a language I don't speak*
- *You tell anyone who'll listen but you feel ignored*

2 What do you think about the ideas expressed in the chorus? Choose one of the interpretations below or use your own ideas, giving reasons for your opinion.

A The ideas in the chorus don't fit at all with the rest of the song – they don't really mean anything.

B The chorus is about the fact that doing interesting things in your life is not as important as finding someone whom you can really talk to.

C The chorus is about wanting to share the future with someone special who understands you.

5 Do you have someone that you would talk to if you felt like the singer in the song? Who is it? Why would you choose him/her?

Vocabulary | phrasal verbs (speaking)

1 R.50 ▶ Listen to eight dialogues and match each one with the correct phrasal verb.

A to get through (to someone)

B to get (your point/message) across

C to speak up

D to speak out (about something)

E to talk down (to someone)

F to pick up (a new language)

G to pass on (a message/greetings/congratulations/etc.)

H to bring up (a point/the subject)

2 Look at the audioscript on page 165. Rewrite the underlined parts using the correct phrasal verb.

It's a big room so you'll need to <u>speak loudly</u>. → It's a big room so you'll need to speak up.

3 R.51 ▶ Listen and check your answers to Exercise 2.

exam reviser   p12 | 10.1 ▶

premium plus   39 ▶

4 Discuss these questions with other students.

- Do you find it more difficult getting your message across in English on the phone than in person? Why/Why not?
- Generally, do you prefer speaking to people face to face or on the phone? Why?
- How do you feel when you get through to a company's electronic answering system (e.g. when you hear 'Press 1 for ...' and/or music while you wait to be connected)?
- What kind of issues have you spoken out/might you speak out about, e.g. at a public meeting?
- How long do you think you need to live in a country before you pick the language up? Do you think it's important to have lessons as well? Why/Why not?
- How do you feel about bringing up the subject of money with your boss? How about with your friends (e.g. when deciding who pays for a meal)? Why?

learning tip

Practising speaking

1 Have you ever taken part in any of the following?

- A 'conversation club' with other students (e.g. you all commit to speaking English for an hour a week together);
- A 'conversation exchange' with a native English speaker who wants to practise speaking your language (e.g. you speak for thirty minutes in English and thirty minutes in your language);
- An 'Internet conversation exchange' with other speakers of English (using the 'speak' facility on your computer, e.g. with headphones);
- An 'email conversation exchange' with other speakers of English (practising the informal 'spoken' style of English often used in emails).

2 Which one(s) would you like to take part in?

3 Do you think you (and some friends) could set any of them up yourself?

Writing | report

1 Read this task and answer the questions 1–5. Refer to the Writing Reference on page 198 if necessary.

Writing task

Your company/school has been given a large sum of money to spend on either a new Internet café or a new garden area. You have been asked to write a report for the director, describing the advantages of each plan. Say which one you think should be chosen and why.

Write your **report** (120–180 words).

1 Which of these would be most appropriate to include in your introductory paragraph?

A state the purpose of the report

B give your personal opinion about which option is best

C recommend your preferred option

2 What will the two main paragraphs be about?

3 Which of these would be most appropriate to include in your concluding paragraph?

A state the purpose of the report

B give your personal opinion about which option is best

C recommend your preferred option

4 What four subheadings could you use?

5 Who are you writing the report for? What does that tell you about the style of your writing?

2 Complete these sentences about advantages and recommendations with the words in the box.

> benefit benefits beneficial valuable points
> difference recommend offer appeal

1 More webcams would be extremely **_beneficial_** as the present facilities are too limited.

2 A new Internet café would offer many _____ to the company.

3 There are a number of good _____ about the existing computer suite.

4 A new garden area would be a _____ addition to the existing outdoor area.

5 Spending the money on networking the computers would _____ the company in two main ways.

6 A DVD player in every classroom would _____ to many students.

7 A larger covered patio area would _____ the following advantages.

8 A new Internet café would make a big _____ to the school.

9 I would strongly _____ spending the money on a new Internet café.

3 Check your answers in the Exam Reviser.

exam reviser p24 | 14 ▶

4 Before you write your report, look again at the Writing Reference on page 198. Which three of the tips are most relevant to you?

5 Write your report. Use some of the language from Exercise 2 as appropriate and start with these words: *The purpose of this report is to recommend which project would ...*

6 Read your report and answer these questions.

- Have you organised your report clearly, using paragraphs and subheadings?
- Have you used an appropriate style?
- Have you used a range of appropriate vocabulary to talk about advantages?
- Have you made any mistakes with grammar?

7 Make changes to your report as necessary.

Reading

1 Discuss with other students.

1 What is a polite way of responding in each of these situations in Britain?

A You can't hear what someone says.
Pardon? / Can you say that again, please? / Sorry, what did you say?

B Someone holds a door open for you.

C Someone thanks you for holding a door open.

D Another driver allows you into a queue of traffic.

E You step on a stranger's foot on a crowded bus.

F You want to attract the attention of a waiter.

G You want to get past someone on a crowded commuter train.

H You want to read a newspaper left on a seat in a bus next to someone else.

I You sneeze.

J Someone else sneezes.

K You greet a colleague on arriving at work.

L You are introduced to someone you don't know.

2 How are the ways of responding to these situations similar to or different from polite responses in the same situations in your country?

3 Do you think people are more or less polite than they were twenty years ago? Why do you think this is?

2 Read the extracts from a book about politeness and manners called *Talk to the Hand*. Which of these sentences 1, 2 or 3 best summarises the main point of the text?

1 Good manners in Britain are excessive and people waste a lot of time being too polite to strangers.

2 Good manners are important because they provide a social framework which makes people feel comfortable with each other.

3 Good manners are almost non-existent these days because not enough parents take time to teach them to their children.

Was that so hard to say?

A The trouble with traditional good manners is judging where to draw the line. Politeness is, after all, a ritual of tennis-like exchange and can go on and on with seemingly no end. 'Thank you,' says one polite person to another. 'No, thank YOU,' comes the response.

'No, thank YOU.'

'No, really the gratitude is all mine.'

'No, please, I insist.'

But although these polite exchanges can get out of hand, the principle is a good one. It is therefore staggering that good manners appear to be on their way out. These days, in many cases the words remain unspoken. You hold a door open for someone and he just walks through it. You let a car join traffic, and its driver fails to wave.

B In this book about manners, the decline of polite words seems a good place to start because the saying of such words appears quite a simple matter. Unfortunately, however, it is not quite as simple as it looks. These words are a necessary part of life's transactions. They are passwords which make it easier to get what we want. But politeness is itself a complicated matter. Surely if we hold doors open, we are thinking about the effect on other people? Yet our furious reaction when we are not thanked shows that we hold doors open mostly in order to know that other people are pleased with *us*.

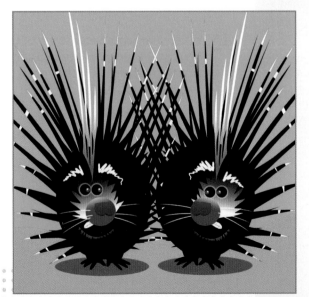

C So, what can we learn about the function of polite words? Let's imagine that you hold the door open and everything goes to plan: the person says, 'Thank you' and you say, 'You're welcome' and the whole episode is successfully closed. When that perfect scene unfolds, how do you feel? Well, **1** relieved that they weren't rude. On the personal level, you feel **2** vindicated[A], **3** validated[B], and **4** virtuous[C]. What is interesting is that you also feel **5** completely indifferent to the person who has thanked you, because no personal relationship has been established between you. All that happens is that a small obligation is raised, then quickly cancelled, and normal life is immediately resumed.

◆ ◆ ◆

D So, what happens when the 'thank you' does not come? The reverse reactions apply.
1 In place of feeling relieved, you are exasperated – but not surprised. Oh no, you are definitely not surprised. 'Typical!' you say.
2 Instead of feeling vindicated, you are dismayed. You feel that the world is laughing at you for holding this door open.
3 Far from feeling validated, you feel obliterated. Are you invisible, then? Have you disappeared?
4 Instead of feeling coolly virtuous, you feel indignant. A good deed has been thrown back in your face.
5 Finally, you HATE the person who did not say thank you. Indifference is no longer an option. The whole incident has now become intensely personal.

◆ ◆ ◆

E Politeness both brings society together, and keeps other people safely at arm's length, and that is why it's so frightening to think about losing it. Suddenly, the world seems threatening – and all because someone's mother never taught him to say 'Excuse me' or 'Please'. There is a German fable about porcupines who need to get close to each other for warmth, but are in danger of hurting each other with their spines. They need to find the best distance to share each other's warmth without putting each other's eyes out. When you respond to each other people politely, you're basically saying, 'I'm here. You're here. I'm staying here. You're staying there. Aren't we both glad we sorted that out?'

◆ ◆ ◆

Glossary:
[A] proven that what someone said or did was right
[B] made to feel that your ideas and feelings are respected
[C] behaving in a way that is morally good

3 Read the text again and for each question, choose the most appropriate section A–E. There is an example at the beginning (0).

In which section does the writer say that

nowadays people don't say 'thank you' when she thinks they should?	**(0)** _A_
being polite is sometimes like a game?	**(1)** __
good manners is a complex issue?	**(2)** __
people have very strong feelings about people who are rude?	**(3)** __
there are two main reasons why being polite is socially important?	**(4)** __
when a stranger is polite to you, you feel good about yourself?	**(5)** __
she is surprised people are not as polite as they used to be?	**(6)** __
if someone is rude to you, you feel very upset?	**(7)** __
we are often polite to people in order to gain their approval?	**(8)** __
thanking a stranger for doing something can happen very quickly?	**(9)** __
good manners are an important way of finding social distance between people?	**(10)** __

4 How do you feel when you do something especially polite and someone responds well? How do you feel if someone responds badly? Give a recent example if you can.

5 What do you think of the author's analysis in sections C and D?

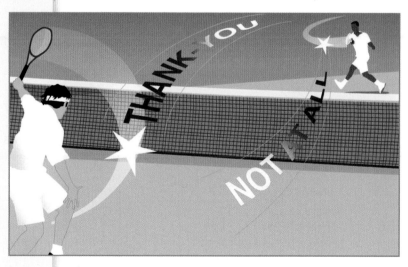

Grammar | adverbs

1 Look at these sentences. What makes the second one more interesting?

A *He spoke to me.*

B *Surprisingly, he spoke to me quite rudely.*

2 Write each of the adverbs highlighted in the text on pages 102–103 in the correct place in the table.

Adverbs of manner	politely, rudely, angrily, well, in a friendly way, _____ 1
Adverbs of place	at the bus stop, in the corner, there, _____ 2
Adverbs of time	today, afterwards, in May, _____ 3
Adverbs of frequency	usually, sometimes, ever, always, rarely, once a week, _____ 4
Adverbs of certainty	perhaps, probably, certainly, _____ 5
Adverbs of completeness	practically, nearly, quite, rather, _____ 6
Emphasising adverbs	very, extremely, terribly, _____ 7
Connecting adverbs	then, next, suddenly, however, anyway, _____ 8
Comment adverbs	surprisingly, stupidly, _____ 9

Grammar note | *adverbs with two forms*

Some adverbs have two different forms with different meanings.

1 Complete these pairs of sentences with the correct adverb. (The meanings of the adverbs are in brackets.)

1 *fine/finely*

A First, add some _____ chopped onions. (= small, carefully-done)

B He's doing _____ in all his subjects at school. (= well)

2 *high/highly*

A She can jump incredibly _____. (= referring to height)

B This restaurant is _____ recommended. (= very much)

3 *late/lately*

A I'm sorry I was _____ yesterday. (= after the expected time)

B He's been working very hard _____. (= recently)

2 Can you think of three more examples of adverbs like this?

premium plus 40

3 There are mistakes in these sentences. Find the mistakes and correct them.

1 He asked me if politely he could borrow €10.

2 The shop assistant spoke to me friendlily.

3 I waited at home all morning patiently.

4 I'll easly finish reading this book by Friday.

5 Always I say hello to shop assistants.

6 She sang beautifully the whole song.

7 I'd rather you didn't drive so fastly.

8 I think he is a truely great singer.

9 At the bus stop I've been waiting for thirty minutes.

10 He always does his homework very carefuly.

•• see grammar reference: page 181 ••

4 Write the adverbs from these adjectives, paying attention to correct spelling. Check in a dictionary if necessary.

> slow secret happy nervous angry loving
> gentle violent quick shy careful automatic
> silly noisy excited

Vocabulary | ways of speaking

1 Match the verb phrases 1–8 with the definitions A–H.

1 boast about something	A to say that you do not like or approve of something
2 exaggerate about something	B to say that you are not satisfied with or not happy about something
3 grumble about something	C to say something very quietly and in a way that is difficult to understand
4 moan about something	
5 mumble about something	D to say something quietly, especially because you are annoyed or do not want someone to hear
6 mutter about something	E to talk too much about your own abilities and achievements in a way that annoys other people
7 insist on something	F to demand that something should happen
8 object to something	G to complain about something in an annoying way
	H to make something seem better, larger, worse, etc. than it really is

2 Choose the correct alternative in each sentence.

1 I *object to/boast about* holding the door open for people when they don't even say 'thank you'.

2 My mother *insisted on/objected to* good manners when I was a child. We always had to say 'please', 'thank you' and 'excuse me'.

3 Nobody will hear you if you *moan/mumble* like that. You'll have to speak louder and more clearly.

4 I couldn't hear what he said because he *grumbled/ muttered* under his breath, but he was clearly angry.

5 My flatmate is never satisfied. It's so annoying because she *moans/exaggerates* about absolutely everything.

6 My brother's so full-of-himself. He's always *boasting/ mumbling* about how clever he is and what good marks he gets in his exams.

7 I heard someone on the bus *mumbling/grumbling* about the weather. She said it was too cold and wet.

8 I'm sure he's *insisting on/exaggerating about* his illness. He's really not very ill – he's only got a bit of a cold.

3 Tell a partner about two situations. For each one you should use one of the verbs from Exercise 1.

A good friend of mine is always exaggerating about things. Recently he told me about an accident he'd had and …

exam reviser p12 | 10.2

premium plus 41

Listening

1 Read the description of a blog and discuss these questions.

- Do you ever read blogs on the Internet? Why/Why not?
- Do you write a blog (or a diary)? Would you consider starting one? Why/Why not?

Blog = The word 'blog' comes from 'web log' and is like a diary on a webpage. People write their thoughts and opinions and other people can add to them.

2 You are going to listen to part of a radio interview with a woman who is doing research into blogging. Before you listen, read the sentences and discuss with a partner how they *could* be completed, using between one and three words.

Globally, there are probably more than _____ [1] blogs now.

The interviewer describes some blogs as _____ [2], but very public, diaries.

Ros compares the importance of blogs today with the impact of when the _____ [3] was invented.

She thinks the best blogs allow both the reader and the writer to exchange _____ [4].

One of the BBC's main aims has always been to _____ [5] its audience.

Before blogs, giving feedback to the BBC or to newspapers was _____ [6].

Anya Peters wrote a blog about her life when she was _____ [7].

Her blog proved to be life-changing when she was offered a _____ [8].

Julie Powell was the first person to _____ [9] for her blog.

Her blog is mainly concerned with _____ [10].

3 R.52 ▶ Listen to the interview and complete the sentences in Exercise 2.

Speaking

1 R.53 ▶ Listen to two pairs of students. Which two questions are they talking about?

1 Which, if any, of the three blogs mentioned in the listening above would you like to read?

2 Do you ever read blogs on the Internet?

3 Do you write a blog (or a diary)? Would you consider starting one?

4 Do you enjoy reading the diaries of famous people?

5 What, if anything, do you mainly use the Internet for?

2 R.53 ▶ Listen again. How do you think they could make what they are saying sound more interesting?

3 Look at the audioscript and replace the words in brackets with more interesting and varied words or phrases.

A: Well, I'm not sure but I think the one about that woman is (interesting) _____ [1] because it would be (interesting) _____ [2] to hear about her life. I want to know about her and why she was living in a car. What do you think? Which one are you interested in?

B: Well, I'd like to look at the news one actually, because I think that sounds (interesting) _____ [3]. Sometimes I hear something on the news and I want to give my opinion.

C: I can't understand why people write blogs. I think it's very strange for people to write about normal things and put it on the Internet for other people to read. And why do people read these blogs? It's (strange) _____ [4]. Do you agree?

D: I suppose you're right. And also it's (strange) _____ [5] that people write things like this and they don't know who will read it. I certainly wouldn't write one.

4 Work in pairs. Choose two questions from Exercise 1 to discuss. Before you start talking, make notes about a range of words and phrases you could use.

5 Discuss the two questions you chose, making sure you use a range of interesting vocabulary.

Grammar | causative *have* and *get*

1 R.54 ▶ Listen to a short phone message. What was the problem? What was the solution?

2 Look at these pairs of sentences. What are the differences in form and in meaning?

1 A *I repaired my computer.*
   B *I had my computer repaired.*

2 A *I had my computer repaired.*
   B *I got my computer repaired.*

3 Match the words in *italics* in 1–4 with the correct uses A–D.

1 She *got her blog noticed* by a publisher.

2 I can't *get this computer to work.*

3 I'll *get this letter finished*, and then I'll help you.

4 We recommend you *get your eyes tested* every two years.

A to talk about when somebody else does something for you (often when you arrange and pay them to do so)

B to talk about an experience or something that happens to you (often something you have no control over)

C to talk about completing work on something

D to talk about when you make somebody/something do something (often with the idea of difficulty)

•• see grammar reference: page 182 ••

4 Look at the words in *italics* in Exercise 3 again and answer these questions.

1 In which two examples can you keep the same meaning by using *have/had* in place of *get/got*?

2 Which three uses have this form: *have/get* + object + past participle?

3 Which one has this form: *get* + object + *to*-infinitive?

5 Read the text and answer these questions.

1 Where do you think you might read this text?

2 How would you summarise the writer's attitude to his trip to the hairdresser: irritated, embarrassed, amused or surprised?

HOME | ABOUT ME | PICTURES | RECENT ENTRIES | ARCHIVE

DAVECORKEYdotCOM

16th January ...

CUT THE CHAT

• •

This is a picture of me – I (just / my hair / cut) _____[1]. My entry today is about (your hair / cut) _____[2] in a trendy ladies' salon – alien territory for a man like me. The cut is fine … it's the chat I object to. My usual barber has gone, so when I went along to this salon, I wasn't quite sure what to expect.

I was greeted by a stylist, Debbie, who (me / put on) _____[3] a robe and sit in front of the mirror. I then had to try to explain what I wanted, which is not something I'm used to doing and I felt terribly awkward. Then, I (my hair / wash) _____[4] and the real chatting started. I really feel that talking to someone who is behind you, while (your head / massage) _____[5] and with your neck at a funny angle, is not all that pleasant. But I tried to listen and mumble some sort of polite reply.

Then the proper hair cutting started. And the chatting stepped up a gear, too.

I thought perhaps I could (her / stop) _____[6] asking me questions by closing my eyes – but no, that didn't stop her. Debbie seemed to continue quite happily with a rather one-sided conversation, however. She told me about (a new kitchen / fit) _____[7], grumbled about her noisy neighbours and talked about (her wallet / steal) _____[8] on the bus last week. I got all the details.

And although she clearly didn't really expect much response from me, I still felt guilty for not wanting to join in. Far from just relaxing, all I could think about was (the whole thing / finish) _____[9], and escaping. Is it just me? Or does everyone feel like this?

• •

***Comments** [2]*

6 Match each gap in the text with the uses in Exercise 3. Can you use *have* or *get* (or both)? Complete the text using the prompts.

7 Correct the mistakes in *italics* in each question 1–5. Then discuss the questions with other students.

1 How do you feel about *having cut your hair*? Do you like chatting to the hairdresser? Why/Why not?

2 How do you feel if you *can't get a machine worked* (e.g. your computer, your car, your TV, your phone, etc.)? What do you usually do?

3 If you won a lot of money, what (if anything) *would you have do* to the place you live in?

4 When was the last time *you taken your photo*? What was it for?

5 *Have you ever had stolen* anything? What was it? What happened?

8 Discuss the questions in Exercise 7 with other students.

premium plus 42 ▶

FCE close-up | Speaking Collaborative discussion (Paper 5, parts 3 and 4)

Exam information

In Part 3 of the Speaking exam, you talk to the other candidate about some photos or pictures. You will be asked to do a task, e.g. put things in order, say which things are the most important, plan something (e.g. a meal) or find a solution to a problem.

In Part 4, you, the other candidate and the examiner discuss your opinions about a topic connected to the task you did in Part 3. You will be expected to give your opinion and to ask and respond to the opinions of others.

You will be able to read both the questions you are asked to talk about (on the same page as the photos/pictures).

Part 3 lasts about three minutes and Part 4 lasts about four minutes. (The whole Speaking exam lasts about fourteen minutes.)

Approach

1 Make sure you have revised the language of:

- expressing and responding to opinions;
- involving other people/asking for someones opinion;
- agreeing and disagreeing;

- starting, moving on and finishing a discussion;
- justifying your choices/giving reasons.

(See Exam Reviser pages 19, 20 and 22.)

2 You can get marks for good interaction, so don't try to dominate or interrupt the other candidate. Let the other person finish what he/she is saying and encourage him/her to speak by asking for his/her opinion, making suggestions, etc.

3 Make full use of the pictures that the examiner shows you. He/she will ask you to '*First talk about … then decide …*'. Only move on to the decision-making part after you have discussed the pictures fully.

4 Don't worry if the examiner stops you before you have completed the task or reached an agreement in the discussion. There is no 'right' or 'wrong' answer; the examiner just wants to hear you speak and respond to the other candidate.

Practice task

R.55 ▶ Work in pairs, listen to the recording and follow the instructions.

- How successful might these suggestions be?
- Which two would attract most people?

Grammar

1 Write the adverbs/adverbial phrases in brackets in the best place in each sentence. (Sometimes there may be more than one correct answer.)

1 I watch chat shows on TV. (never)
2 I'm bad at making small talk at parties. (really)
3 We go to Spanish conversation classes. (every week)
4 I'll meet you at the library later. (probably)
5 She's finished the whole book. (nearly)
6 He started shouting at me. (suddenly)
7 I've been waiting for over half an hour. (here)
8 I couldn't remember how to say 'thank you' in French. (unfortunately)

2 Put the words in the correct order to form sentences.

1 A: Hey! Your hair looks lovely.
  B: Oh, thanks. _____
  (had morning cut it I this)

2 A: Oh dear. You look upset. What's happened?
  B: _____
  (just my had stolen think purse I've I)

3 A: Why are you angry with Monica?
  B: _____
  (can't her to I anything do ask I get)

4 A: Why haven't you got your car today?
  B: _____
  (broke repaired and having It it down I'm)

5 A: Why don't you come out with us tonight?
  B: _____
  (get and I'll I'll done first then my you join homework)

6 A: What's the matter with your eyes?
  B: _____
  (headaches I I to get getting them because keep tested need)

7 A: Why isn't the TV working?
  B: _____
  (can't work not but I'm I sure get the switch to volume)

8 A: Oh dear. I've spilt wine on your jacket.
  B: _____
  (doesn't It I can it later have matter drycleaned because)

Vocabulary

3 Complete the second sentence so that it has a similar meaning to the first sentence, using the word given. Do not change the word given. You must use between two and five words, including the word given.

1 You'll have to talk more loudly because she's a bit deaf.
  up
  You'll have to _____ because she's a bit deaf.

2 I've been trying to contact her about the job.
  get
  I've been trying to _____ her about the job.

3 I'm hoping to learn a bit of Chinese when I go there.
  up
  I'm hoping to _____ a bit of Chinese when I go there.

4 Will you give my best wishes to Maria when you see her?
  pass
  Will you _____ my best wishes to Maria when you see her?

5 I'm not sure how to make people understand my point.
  across
  I'm not sure how to _____ to people.

6 I admire her for saying what she feels in public about testing on animals.
  speaking
  I admire her for _____ about testing on animals.

7 My flatmate really annoys me when he talks to me as if I'm stupid all the time.
  down
  My flatmate really annoys me when he _____ all the time.

8 I'd like to start discussing my promotion prospects.
  up
  I'd like to _____ my promotion prospects.

4 There is a mistake in each of these sentences. Find the mistakes and correct them.

1 She told me she's got hundreds of pairs of shoes, but I'm sure she's examining about it.
2 He's intruding on not coming with us and I can't persuade him to change his mind.
3 He spends all his time saying how great he is and boosting about his achievements.
4 It's not that I obsess to what he's saying; it's just the way he says it.
5 I wish she wasn't so negative. Nothing is ever right with her; she mows about absolutely everything.
6 My teenage son muffles about things all the time and I can't understand a word he says.

Progress Check 2 Units 6–10

1 Complete the sentences with the correct word. The first two letters have been given to help you.

1 I'm not keen on sc_____ eggs, but I do like them fr_____.
2 I wish he would speak more clearly and stop mu_____ – I can't hear a thing he says.
3 Many children these days live on a ne_____-en_____ diet of TV programmes, computer games and ma_____ junk food.
4 I like looking down from the top of the cl_____ when you can see the sandy be_____ below and the co_____ stretching for miles.
5 There was a light dr_____ in the morning, but then the skies cleared and it was warm and just a bit hu_____ in the afternoon.
6 She told me that there were over a hundred people at the party but I think she was ex_____.
7 She's got a very sw_____ tooth and loves all kinds of cakes, biscuits and de_____.
8 My favorite dish at my local restaurant is steak, which I like cooked ra_____, with a mo_____-wa_____ onion sauce they make to go with it.
9 The change in weather patterns means that there are more dr_____ due to too little rain and also more fl_____ due to a lot of rain in a short space of time.
10 It's been po_____ with rain here for too long so I decided to have a short break in Spain. I managed to get a really good last-mi_____ deal.

2 There are mistakes with six of the verbs in these dialogues. Find the mistakes and correct them.

1 A: Why isn't Tina here today?
   B: She'll go to the dentist this afternoon.
2 A: Is Pete coming to the party?
   B: I'm not sure. I'll ask him as soon as I'm going to see him.
3 A: I'm so worried about my driving test tomorrow.
   B: It's OK – you'll be fine. You've done lots of practice.
4 A: I don't feel like cooking at all tonight. I'm too tired.
   B: Oh, don't worry. In that case, I'm making you something.
5 A: Have you decided what to do on your eighteenth birthday?
   B: Yes definitely. I have a big party, but I'm not sure exactly when yet.
6 A: What time is your train tomorrow?
   B: I'd like to catch the one that leaving at 9.25 a.m.
7 A: What time shall I phone you tonight?
   B: After 9 o'clock, because I'll be watching the football until then.
8 A: How long have you lived here?
   B: Well, by the end of this year, I live here for six years.

3 Read the text and decide which answer A, B, C or D best fits each gap.

RAY MEARS – SURVIVALIST

Over the last decade, Ray Mears has become world-famous as an authority on the subject of survival in the wilderness. _____[1] people throughout the world have seen his television programmes in which he _____[2] on his knowledge of survival. He has a down-to-earth approach, showing an obvious love for his subject and a _____[3] deal of respect for the land and people he comes across.

_____[4] up in England, Ray discovered that the countryside around him was full of wildlife and he was _____[5] drawn to learning more about it. His interest in _____[6] survival was further inspired by a teacher, who said to Ray 'In _____[7] to survive in the wild, you don't need equipment, you need knowledge.'

So, Ray digested every _____[8] of information relating to survival that he could find, and then started practising these ancient skills around the world. He met local people who showed him how to build shelters, hunt for food, survive in _____[9] cold conditions. And in 1983, he founded The Woodlore School of Wilderness Bushcraft, _____[10] that others could also learn these skills.

Now, after many years of success, Ray's love of the outdoors remains the same. He is still a modest man and not someone to _____[11] about his extensive knowledge or dwell on his fame and fortune. Instead, he prefers to roll up his _____[12] and get his hands dirty, and show others the joys of survival outdoors.

	A	B	C	D
1	Many	Much	Plenty	Lots
2	gets	brings	passes	takes
3	big	large	great	plenty
4	Bringing	Growing	Getting	Living
5	once	almost	firstly	immediately
6	open-air	inside-out	out-and-about	over-the-top
7	case	that	order	so
8	lots	piece	deal	amount
9	chilly	utterly	bitterly	notoriously
10	so	if	and	but
11	grumble	mumble	moan	boast
12	buttons	zips	sleeves	clothes

4 Choose the correct alternative.

1 I'd like to complain *of/for/about* the poor service.
2 She's preparing *for/with/about* her driving test.
3 Please speak *out/up/across* – I can't hear you.
4 Stop grumbling *for/of/about* the work and just do it.
5 I've tried to get *up/over/through* to her but she won't listen.
6 He succeeded *of/in/with* organising the whole trip himself.
7 The school insists *on/with/for* a strict uniform policy.
8 She tried very hard to get her point *through/across/out*.

Progress Check 2 Units 6–10

5 Complete the text with one word in each gap.

My pet snake

When I was young, I loved exotic animals and wanted a pet shark. Obviously, that wasn't possible so I got interested _____¹ snakes. I bought Sidney at a pet shop ten years ago, when I was twelve years old. I was really proud _____² my new pet and determined to be responsible _____³ looking after him. He was about 70 cm long, very good-natured, not at all poisonous and, in my opinion, _____⁴ best pet in the world. His diet consisted of a mouse once _____⁵ week – depending _____⁶ the time of year.

One day, a _____⁷ years ago, Sidney disappeared. After several weeks I lost all hope of finding him _____⁸ these snakes are famous _____⁹ travelling many kilometres a night. Eleven months later, while I was away on holiday, my dad heard that _____¹⁰ black-and-yellow snake _____¹¹ mine had been seen in a neighbour's garden. We knew it could only be Sidney, and three days later my brother spotted him just sitting by the garden door. He had come back to _____¹² exact spot he had disappeared from.

6 Use the word given in capitals at the end of some of the lines to form a word that fits in the gap *in the same line*.

In 1932, Ole Kirk Christiansen from Denmark set up a business (0) *manufacturing* ladders, ironing boards and wooden toys. The company was called Lego, (1) _____ 'play well' in Danish.	MANUFACTURE MEAN
For the next two decades, there was a lot of (2) _____ within the company with different ways of developing Lego. They used the latest (3) _____ ideas and materials which many scientists at that time were working on, especially the (4) _____ of different plastics. In 1947, the company moved forward hugely with the (5) _____ of the first plastic bricks that fitted together. This was the start of the 'Lego System of Play', (6) _____ in 1955.	EXPERIMENT TECHNOLOGY DEVELOP INVENT LAUNCH
Lego (7) _____ promised that its bricks would 'develop the child's critical judgement and ability to think for himself.' (8) _____ quickly, the company's sales were further increased with the (9) _____ of Lego kits in the mid-1960s, with which children could make all sorts of buildings, trucks, planes and ships.	CONFIDENT EXPAND INTRODUCE
Over fifty years on, these plastic bricks are still a firm (10) _____ with kids, parents and teachers.	FAVOUR

7 Complete the second sentence so that it has a similar meaning to the first sentence, using the word given. Do not change the word given. You must use between two and five words, including the word given.

I can't eat my soup at the moment because it isn't cool enough.
hot
My soup is *too hot to eat* at the moment.

1 Why don't you get the optician to test your eyes?
have
Why don't you _____ by the optician?

2 It was a really sunny day so we took a picnic to the park.
such
It was _____ we took a picnic to the park.

3 We have booked the taxi to pick us up at 10 o'clock.
due
The taxi _____ us up at 10 o'clock.

4 The weather was too cold for us to stay out for long.
so
The weather was _____ we couldn't stay out for long.

5 He annoys me by talking to me as if I'm stupid.
down
He annoys me by _____ me.

6 Eating out in restaurants all the time is too expensive for me.
enough
I haven't got _____ out in restaurants all the time.

7 You might need to phone me so I'll give you my number.
case
I'll give you my number _____ phone me.

8 The strong winds last night blew part of the roof off.
got
Part of the roof _____ in the strong winds last night.

8 Choose the correct alternative.

1 *I've had/ve been having* my pet rabbits for over two years.
2 This is the first time I *ever went/ve ever been* to a wedding.
3 He's been studying science at university *for/since* about a year and a half.
4 *I've just been/I just have been* to my cousin's wedding.
5 He's *sent/'s been sending* over ten text messages in the last ten minutes.
6 She's *bought already/already bought* a really lovely new skirt for the party.
7 When was the last time you *cooked/have cooked* a meal for friends?
8 Have you ever *read/been reading* someone's 'blog' on the Internet?

Cash in hand

inflation

wealth

Hard cash

Unit 11

Introduction

1 Look at the pictures and discuss these questions.
- What traditional symbols of money and wealth do you have in your country?
- In your country, is it common for people to give money as a present?

2 Look at these questions. With a partner, check the meaning of the verbs.

Who is talking about:

A ... inheriting money? E ... raising money?
B ... investing money? F ... squandering money?
C ... owing someone money? G ... haggling over the price?
D ... donating money?

3 R.56 ▶ Listen and match the people to the questions in Exercise 2.

4 Discuss these questions with other students.
- Have you or anyone you know ever raised money for a good cause? How did you do it? What was the money for?
- How do you feel about lending money to, or borrowing money from friends or family?
- How do you feel about haggling over the price of something?

Reading

1 Look at the pictures and discuss these questions.

1 What can you see in picture **A**?
2 What do you think is the aim of the website in picture **B**?

2 Read the text quickly. What does the article say about these things?

1 the writer's out-of-date computer
2 the main aim of *Freecycle*
3 dishonest 'bidders'
4 giving something in return
5 freecycle's need for money

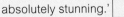

The temptation to buy, buy, buy is hard to resist. A new outfit, a gadget, an item of furniture – someone is buying one right now. Now, guilty shoppers who are keen to get rid of a no-longer-needed purchase have a radical new option – simply giving it away.

Second-hand technology is notoriously difficult to offload. So, I never thought that my sluggish, ageing computer would generate much interest when I put it up for offer online. I was wrong. **1** On a conventional auction site, such as eBay, I doubt there would be any takers. But I'm advertising on its philanthropic cousin, *freecycle.org*. As the name suggests, everything advertised on *Freecycle* must be free – whether it's an old sofa, unwanted CDs or even a few hours' help in the garden. Anyone who is interested simply replies by email: deal done.

Freecycle is one of a number of websites that aim to reduce the amount of rubbish sent to landfill sites by encouraging one of the most efficient forms of recycling – simply giving things to people who want them. **2** Today, *Freecycle* has 1.2 million members and is a cross between an Internet auction house and a global chain of charity shops. Mr Beal says his chief aim is to cut waste and help the environment. He recently told reporters, 'I live in the Sonora Desert in Arizona. It's a place where the landscape is absolutely stunning.' **3** On the London site, interest in my decrepit computer is led by Tung, who wants to get his sixty-seven-year-old mum on the net. Then there's Kate, whose son wants it for his schoolwork. There's also John, who wants it for his daughter, a nurse on a low wage. **4** My inclination is to give it to someone in need, but I have to make a difficult choice between several 'bidders'. Some people may suggest that dishonest individuals could make up heart-tugging stories in order to get freebies, or even to make a profit by selling them on. But my requests seem genuine. **5**

Freecycle embodies some of that old charitable Internet spirit by asking that before members accept a freebie, they put something up for offer. And it's by no means all junk; there are nearly-new toys, furniture, electrical goods, even bikes and cars. **6** She says it reflects the fact people are buying more than ever, but don't want to simply throw things away when they replace them. 'People want to feel a bit better about consuming, and so they're happy to give things away,' she says. Clive Brown, who won my auction, agrees: 'I was given a bed and didn't need the brand-new mattress, so I put it on the site and it was gone in minutes. I was delighted someone wanted it.'

Freecycle has grown rapidly around the world in countries as diverse as Mexico, Nepal, France and Romania and it seems to be on the cusp of breaking through into the mainstream. **7** Mr Beal says he needs the funds to help spread the ethos even further. In the end, it would be better if people simply stopped buying so much. But realistically, until people change their ways, green groups, guilty consumers and those with an eye for the ultimate bargain seem more than happy to make the most of *Freecycle*.

B freecycle™
changing the world one gift at a time
Home Finder FAQ Groups Sponsors Store About Us

Make a Donation!
Tell a friend!

Find your local Freecycle™ Group:

○ Groups in your local area

National Websites:
United Kingdom
France
Deutschland

THE COUNTER:
Number of Freecycle™ Communities: 4,041
Number of Freecycle™ Members: 3,540,995

Welcome!
The Freecycle Network™ is made up of many individual groups across the globe. It's a grassroots and entirely nonprofit movement of people who are giving (& getting) stuff for free in their own towns. Each local group is moderated by a local volunteer (them's good people). Membership is free. To sign up, find your community by clicking on the region on the left. You may then go directly to your local group by clicking on "Go To" or you may immediately join by clicking on "Join." It will generate an automatic

freecycle finder
If your local group is signed up for the Freecycle Finder, enter the name of something you are looking for and your location (zip code) below and click on the button. (More info)

Item:

City, ST:

Find it!

Freecycle Newswire
Freecycle.org: Internet curbside - Features
Plum Telluride | Time to Drop By the Free Box
Web Site Swapping

freecycle

3 Seven sentences have been removed from the article. Read the article again and choose from sentences A–H the one that fits each gap 1–7. There is one extra sentence which you do not need.

A That such high-quality goods are on offer does not surprise Friends of the Earth campaigner Georgina Bloomfield.

B And right in the middle of this desert, you've got this hideous landfill, half of which is full of perfectly good reusable stuff.

C The site is the creation of Deron Beal, an environmentalist from the US, who started it in mid-2003 as an automated email list.

D Money isn't involved, but a kind of auction is taking place to see whose situation most deserves a free PC.

E Controversially, perhaps, it has recently signed up a corporate sponsor.

F Elsewhere on the site, someone is trying to shift a manual for a 1980s Ford Escort, and another has two bags of party clothes.

G I eventually choose Clive Brown, a project worker, who wants it for a client with learning disabilities.

H A bidding war quickly begins for the five-year-old machine, which is 'past its best' and a printer, which only 'probably works'.

4 Discuss these questions.
- What are the three main reasons for *Freecycle's* success?
- Does *Freecycle's* success surprise you? Why/Why not?
- How would you feel about using this website? Why?

Grammar | relative clauses

1 Look at the sentences A–F and answer these questions. Read the grammar rules about relative clauses in the Grammar Reference page 183.

1 Which of the sentences contain defining relative clauses and which non-defining relative clauses?

2 In which sentence could you leave out the relative pronoun? Why?

3 Which sentence sounds quite formal? How could you make it more informal?

A Clive Brown, who won my auction, agrees.

B One of the bidders is Kate, whose son wants the computer for his schoolwork.

C It's a place where the landscape is absolutely stunning.

D *Freecycle* is a website which aims to reduce the amount of rubbish in landfill sites.

E The reason why people like *Freecycle* is it makes them feel better about consuming so much.

F The person to whom I made the complaint was extremely unhelpful.

•• see grammar reference: page 183 ••

Grammar note | *which* versus *that*

In which of these sentences could you not replace *which* by *that*? Why?

1 *The computer, which I bought, was a bargain.*

2 *The computer which I bought was a bargain.*

2 There are seven mistakes with relative clauses in this text. Find the mistakes and correct them.

eBay

eBay is a hugely successful company, which it was founded in 1995. The person what founded eBay was a man called Pierre Omidyar. At first, it was a place which people could sell goods, particularly collectable items. Then in 1998, Pierre brought in Meg Whitman who job was to sustain eBay's success by bringing in new managers. The new vision that she created it was an image of connecting people not of selling things. The items for sale are arranged by topics, that are then sub-divided into smaller categories. People who they want to sell things on eBay pay a small fee, but it is free to buy.

3 Choose the correct relative pronoun for each of these sentences.

1 One thing *what/that* makes me angry is …

2 One place *which/where* I'd love to go is …

3 One person *who/which* I really admire is …

4 One charity *which/what* I donate to is …

5 One person *who/whose* lifestyle I'd like to have is …

6 One reason *what/why* I'd like to have more money is …

4 Complete each sentence to make it true for you. Compare your sentences with other students.

premium plus   43 ▶

Vocabulary | money

1 Work in pairs. Check that you understand the meaning of the verb phrases in *italics* in these sentences. Then discuss the questions.

- Have you ever *bid for something in an auction* (online or traditional)? If so, what was it? If not, would you consider doing so?
- When was the last time you *got a bargain*? Do you know anyone who is good at finding bargains?
- What's the difference between: *pay a fee, pay a fare* and *pay a fine*? What do you think of the cost of bus and train fares in your country/another country you know?

2 Work in two groups, A and B. Look at the words in your box and check their meaning and pronunciation. Use a dictionary if necessary.

A

> get a freebie   pay a deposit
> pay the balance   get a receipt
> get a refund   pay rent

B

> get a discount   get paid overtime
> be in debt   pay tax
> take out insurance   leave a tip

3 Now work in pairs (one from group A and one from B). Tell each other the meaning and pronunciation of the words in your box.

4 Choose the correct alternatives in each sentence.

1 You can often save money by buying a lot of things at the same time and getting a *discount/freebie*.

2 I'm working long hours at the moment so that I get paid quite a lot of *tip/overtime* – I'm saving up for my holiday.

3 If you decide not to go ahead with the booking, you will lose the £100 *balance/deposit* you've already paid.

4 I'm sorry, but we can only give you your money back if you keep the *receipt/refund* as proof of purchase.

5 You are advised to take out *tax/insurance* for all members of the family before you travel.

6 I would never borrow from friends because I never want to be in *rent/debt*.

5 Look at the Exam Reviser. Choose six words/phrases and write a question for each to ask other students.

1 *Do you like going to the sales? Why/Why not?*

2 *Do you think you should always leave a tip in restaurants? Why/Why not?*

> **exam reviser** p13 | 11.1 ▶

6 Ask and answer your questions with other students.

> **premium plus** 44 ▶

Writing | letter/email

1 Discuss these questions with other students.

- Do you ever shop online? If so, what for? If not, why not?
- What do you think are the advantages and disadvantages of online shopping over ordinary shopping?
- What do you think are some of the most common reasons for complaining to a department store or a shopping website?
- Have you ever complained about something you bought (either in a shop or through a website)? What weren't you happy about? What did you do? What was the response? Were you satisfied in the end?

CUSTOMER SERVICES

2 Read the task and advert on page 115 and answer these questions.

1 Which two of the following do you need to do in your letter/email?

A suggest something

B complain about something

C request something

D give information about something

2 How many of the notes written on the advert are about the product you bought and how many are about the service you received?

You bought a camera from the company in the advert below and you were disappointed with both the product and the service you received.

Read the advert carefully and the notes you have made. Then, using all your notes, write a letter/email to the company complaining about the various points and asking the company to do something.

DISCOUNT DIGITAL

We are offering 1,000s of digital cameras at bargain prices. Hurry to take advantage of this amazing offer!

We have all the major brands, including Canon, Sony, Nikon, Fuji, Olympus, Samsung and many more.

All the cameras are this year's models with all the latest, up-to-date features. They are all at discount prices, with up to 50% off on some models. *— I was sent the wrong model – not the one I ordered.*

Every camera comes with all the necessary accessories (e.g. battery pack, battery charger, AV cable, AC cable, 16MB memory card, USB cable, user guide). *— USB cable wasn't in the box.*

Guaranteed low prices if you order before 31st May. Hurry – don't miss the deadline! This is an offer you can't afford to miss. *— It took two weeks to arrive – with no apology or explanation.*

Free post and packing on orders over £100. Guaranteed delivery within 7 working days of placing your order.

You can shop online at www.discountdigital.com or speak to one of our sales staff on 08457 464533. Our friendly customer services team are available from 8.00 a.m. to 6.30 p.m. every day to answer your queries and take your orders. *— When I tried to sort it out, the people I spoke to weren't very helpful.*

Write a **letter/email** of between **120** and **150** words in an appropriate style. Do not write any postal addresses.

3 Which order should these paragraphs go in your letter/email?
  A complaining about the two problems with the product
  B saying what you want the company to do
  C making two further complaints about the service
  D saying the reason for your letter/email

4 Look at the phrases in list A for the opening paragraph of your letter/email and those in list B for the closing paragraph. Decide which of the phrases are appropriate and which are not. Why?
  A 1 I am writing to complain about …
    2 I want to say that I'm not happy about …
    3 I am writing to express my dissatisfaction with …
    4 This letter is to say how cross I am about …
    5 I would like to request that …
  B 6 I must insist that you refund my money immediately.
    7 Please can you assure me that you will replace the … as soon as possible.
    8 I think you should give me my money back now.
    9 I really think you should listen to me and give me another …
    10 I would be grateful if you would give me a refund.

exam reviser p23 | 12

5 Look at these phrases for paragraphs 2 and 3 of your letter/email. Complete each one in a way which you could use.
  1 I was very disappointed by …
  2 I would like to point out that …
  3 The advertisement stated that …, but in fact …
  4 I was assured that …, whereas actually …
  5 When I received the product, to my surprise …
  6 Even more worrying is the fact that …

6 Write your letter/email using the paragraph plan in Exercise 3 and at least three of the phrases in Exercises 4 and 5 to help you.

exam reviser p22 | 9

Checking and correcting your writing

Discuss these questions.
1 How often do you check and correct your writing when you have finished: always, sometimes, rarely or never? Why?
2 What kind of things is it useful to check? Do you find this easy or difficult?

7 Read your letter/email and check these things.
  1 Have you included all the notes from the task?
  2 Have you made a suggestion at the end of your letter?
  3 Have you started and finished your letter in an appropriate way?
  4 Have you written the correct number of words?

learning tip

Vocabulary | numbers

1 Look again at the advert in Exercise 2 on page 115. How many numbers and dates can you find? How do you say them?

2 R.57 ▶ Listen and check your answers.

> ### Vocabulary note | commas and full stops in numbers
>
> How do you write each of these numbers in figures? Think carefully about the correct position of the commas and full stops (and refer to the Exam Reviser if necessary).
>
> 1 Two point five
> 2 Six pounds twenty-five
> 3 One thousand five hundred
> 4 Five million three hundred thousand
> 5 Two thousand, three hundred and forty-nine pounds fifty pence
>
> Repeat these numbers with a partner.

exam reviser p13 | 11.2 ▶

3 Match each question 1–12 with the correct number A–L.

1	What's your date of birth?	A	3.2%
2	What time did you get up today?	B	65 kg
3	How much did your bag cost?	C	07739 456997
4	What's your phone number?	D	27°C
5	What's the speed limit in this country?	E	2 litres
6	How much do you weigh?	F	120 kph
7	What's another way of writing 0.5?	G	17 km
8	What's another way of writing 1/4?	H	1/2
9	How far is your home from here?	I	20.05.83
10	What's the interest rate at the moment?	J	0.25
11	How much water do you drink a day?	K	£5.50
12	What's the temperature today?	L	7.15 a.m.

4 R.58 ▶ Listen and check your answers.

5 Take turns asking and answering each question in Exercise 2 with another student. Make sure you say the numbers correctly.

6 Write down the following numbers. Make sure you know how to write and say them in English.

- An important date
- A four-digit number which is important to you
- An important phone number

7 Tell another student why each number is important to you.

premium plus 45 ▶

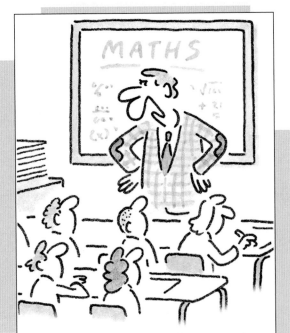

'Half of you got the homework right, half didn't do it and the other half got it wrong'

FCE close-up | Use of English
Open cloze (Paper 3, part 2)

Exam information

This part of the exam consists of a text in which there are twelve gaps (plus one gap as an example). The answer will always be a single word (never a phrase) with the focus on grammar and grammatical vocabulary. In some cases, there may be more than one possible answer. It is important that your spelling is correct.

Approach

1 Read the text quickly before filling in any of the gaps in order to get a general sense of the meaning.

2 Before trying to decide on the correct word, read the words which follow the gap as well as those which come before it.

3 Think about collocations (e.g. **make a mistake**) and prepositions (e.g. **spend on**) which will help you find links between words. Make sure any verb you write in agrees with its subject (e.g. **he spends**).

4 Only use one word to fill each of the gaps. Do not fill any of the gaps with a contraction (e.g. **didn't**, **he'll**) and never use abbreviations (e.g. **T.V.**, etc.)

5 Remember that in the exam you should always write something in each gap: you do not lose marks for a wrong answer.

Go to www.iTests.com or your CD-ROM for interactive exam practice

Listening

1 The people in the pictures have decided, for different reasons, *not* to give their teenage and grown-up children a lot of their money. Can you think of two reasons why this might be?

2 R.59 ▶ Listen to the radio programme and check your ideas.

Practice task

For questions **1–12**, read the text and think of the word which best fits each gap. Use only **one** word in each gap. There is an example at the beginning (**0**).

Write your answers IN CAPITAL LETTERS.

Example: | 0 | | F | E | W | | | | | | | |

Million dollar student

It took a twenty-one-year-old only a **(0)** *few* minutes to think of an idea which made him more **(1)** _____ one million dollars in four months. So what's his secret? It started when he had **(2)** _____ overdraft and a shortage of socks. Now it's a million dollar business.

One summer, as Alex Tew was about **(3)** _____ start a university course, he began to think about **(4)** _____ he could solve his financial problems. He already had a large overdraft, which was sure to multiply at university, and he felt his poverty was reflected by his lack **(5)** _____ decent socks. After a bit of creative thought, the 'Million Dollar Homepage' idea was born. The idea **(6)** _____ to sell pixels, the dots that make up a computer screen, as advertising space, costing a dollar **(7)** _____ dot. The minimum purchase was $100 for a 10x10 pixel square with the buyer's logo, **(8)** _____ has links to the buyer's website.

Alex designed the page himself. His friends and family paid the first $1,000, which he spent publicising the site. From then, the idea just took **(9)** _____. 'As I made money, more people talked **(10)** _____ it and the more people **(11)** _____ that, the more money I made,' he said. Alex believes his success is down to two things: **(12)** _____ power of word of mouth and the story of a student making a million, which enchanted the media.

3 R.59 ▶ Listen again and choose the best answer A, B or C.

1 These days, how much do people help their children financially?
   A more than our parents' generation
   B less than our parents' generation
   C about the same as our parents' generation

2 What does Jonathan Hynde say he wants to give his children?
   A almost nothing.
   B enough money to help them on their way.
   C some money, but only when they ask for it.

3 What does he say about kids who inherit a lot of money?
   A They spend it all too quickly.
   B They are ungrateful.
   C They lose their ambition.

4 How did Jonathan start making money?
   A He got a job.
   B He worked for his father.
   C His father gave him a small amount of money to start a business.

5 Sarah Hewitt talks about 'SKI-ing'. What does SKI stand for?
   A Saving your Kids' Income
   B Spending your Kids' Income
   C Spending your Kids' Inheritance

6 How does Sarah feel about spending the money on herself?
   A a little guilty but happy
   B excited and not guilty at all
   C mostly guilty and worried

7 How does her son feel?
   A happy for her and not worried at all
   B worried and annoyed
   C worried but happy for her

4 Read the quotes below from Jonathan and Sarah in the radio programme. What's your opinion about each one?

'I don't think it's right that our children should be handed money on a plate through an inheritance.'

'We think it's fair that now the children are off our hands, we should be able to live life to the full and enjoy ourselves as much as possible.'

premium plus 46 ▶

Grammar | *if* structures

1 Complete the sentences with the correct form of *have, ask* or *give*.

1 If you _____ your children a lot of money, you ruin their chances of success.
2 If I _____ my parents for some money, I'm sure they'll give it to me.
3 If I _____ more money, I'd go on a skiing holiday this year.

•• see grammar reference: page 183 ••

Grammar note | punctuation in *if* structures

We can use *if* structures to talk about the present and future (e.g. possibilities, hypothetical situations and general truths). We can also use *if* structures to talk hypothetically about the past.

Punctuation

Is the punctuation correct in these sentences?

1 *If I had more money, I'd travel more.*
2 *I'd travel more if I had more money.*

2 Look at these pairs of sentences. In what situations would you choose to say each one?

1 A If someone gives you €500, what will you spend it on?
  B If someone gave you €500, what would you spend it on?
2 A What will you do if you have some free time this weekend?
  B What would you do if you had some free time this weekend?
3 A If you have a holiday this year, where will you go?
  B If you had a holiday this year, where would you go?

3 For each set of prompts, decide which type of *if* structure is best and then write the question.

1 What / you do / if you / forget / pay / something in a shop?
2 you lend / a large amount of money / a friend / if they / ask / you?
3 If you / can choose / to be / famous person / for a day / who / you choose to be?
4 If you / hear / fire alarm / during this lesson / what / you do?
5 What / you change / if you / be elected / leader of your country?

4 Choose five questions from Exercises 2 and 3 to ask your partner.

5 Answer the questions about each of these examples.

1 *I **would have paid** by credit card if I **had** one.*
  Did I pay by credit card? Why/Why not?

2 *If I**'d** taken my credit card, I **would have paid** with that.*
  Did I pay by credit card? Why/Why not?

3 *If I**'d brought** my credit card with me, I**'d pay** with that now.*
  Am I going to pay by credit card now? Why/Why not?

6 Identify the verb forms in **bold** in Exercise 5.

•• see grammar reference: page 183 ••

7 There are mistakes in eight of these sentences. Find the mistakes and correct them.

1 She wouldn't have been able to buy her house if she didn't inherit so much money.
2 If I am better at maths, I would have trained to be an accountant.
3 You would have no problem exchanging the goods if you would kept the receipt.
4 If I hadn't left my old job, I'd be a lot wealthier now.
5 If I lived by the sea, I would buy a yacht a long time ago.
6 If I had had children, I would have gave them as much financial support as they wanted.
7 If I known you could donate money online, I would have done it like that.
8 You would passed many more exams if you hadn't messed around with your friends at school so much when you were younger.
9 I would have enough money to buy a new car if I hadn't been on that expensive holiday last year.
10 If I wouldn't have a family to support, I'd have taken last year off and travelled round the world.

8 Choose the correct linking word or phrase in each of these sentences.

1 I'll lend you £20 *unless/provided that* you pay me back by Friday.

2 You can borrow some money *as long as/even if* you don't ask me every week.

3 *As long as/Unless* you pay me back by Friday, this is the last time I'll lend you any money.

4 *Even if/Provided that* you promise to pay me back by Friday, I'm afraid I'm not lending you any money.

9 Look at the phrases in *italics* in Exercise 8 and answer these questions.

1 Which two have a similar meaning?

2 Which one means '*if not*'?

3 Which one is used to emphasise the idea in the *if* clause?

10 Complete these sentences.

If I won the jackpot on the lottery, I'd give up work immediately.

1 I'd carry on working even if …

2 It doesn't matter how much money someone has as long as …

3 If I had had the chance, …

4 Unless people plan their finances properly, …

5 Provided that you give your children the right advice, …

6 Generally, people's salaries tend to increase over time as long as …

7 I don't think I'd give money to people begging in the street even if …

8 If I could do the last five years again, …

9 I don't mind how much I earn provided that …

10 Unless people stop throwing away so much, …

11 Do you agree with the sentences you've written? Tell another student.

premium plus **47** ▶

Speaking

1 **R.60** ▶ Listen to two people discussing one of these statements. Which one are they talking about?

1 Teenagers shouldn't get pocket money unless they do jobs around the house.

2 It's fine to borrow money from people as long as you know they can afford it.

3 Everyone has a moral duty to give money to charity on a regular basis.

4 Credit card companies should drastically reduce the amount of credit available to customers.

'I have enough money to last me the rest of my life, unless I buy something.' *Jackie Mason (American comedian)*

2 **R.60** ▶ Look at the Exam Reviser. Listen again and tick the phrases you hear.

exam reviser **p19 | 1** ▶

3 What ways of responding to opinions and agreeing/disagreeing can you remember?

exam reviser **p19 | 2** ▶

4 Work in pairs and choose one of the statements in Exercise 1. Write down two arguments for and two against the statement.

5 Discuss the statement with your partner using the language in the Exam Reviser. Do you agree with each other?

exam reviser **p19 | 2** ▶

6 Choose another statement and repeat Exercises 4 and 5 with a different partner.

Grammar

1 Complete the text with *who, whose, which, that* or *where*.

A Picasso portrait of his lover, Dora Maar, has been sold for $95.2m, _____¹ is the second highest amount ever paid for a painting at auction. The picture, _____² is entitled *Dora Maar with Cat*, was sold at Sotheby's in New York in May 2006. Sotheby's said Dora's beauty and the gorgeous colours made it worth so much. 'It's the fact that the model is Dora, _____³ was one of Picasso's most famous subjects, and the perfection of the actual painting _____⁴ makes it so valuable,' said David Norman from Sotheby's. The most expensive picture ever sold is another Picasso, *Boy with a Pipe*, _____⁵ fetched a record $104m in 2004.

But who are the art lovers _____⁶ can afford to bid such astronomical sums? And what do they do with their multimillion-dollar purchases? Sotheby's keeps the identity of the buyers secret. But Godfrey Barker, of *Art and Auction* magazine, guesses at a likely buyer – Guido Barilla, _____⁷ pasta business Barilla has made him a billionaire. And he suspects that the Picassos will be kept in a bank vault in Switzerland, 'the one country in the world _____⁸ these things can be hidden very well'.

2 Combine these pairs of sentences to make one sentence, using a relative clause.

1 My sister's got a new boyfriend. He works in a garage.
2 You told me about a shop. I went to the shop, but I couldn't find anything I liked.
3 I met that man at the sales conference last week. He's wearing a dark blue suit.
4 Every year we go on holiday to Cornwall. I think it is one of the most beautiful places in Britain.
5 I met Nelson Mandela. I'll never forget that time.
6 My next-door neighbour is the best neighbour I've ever had. Her house is up for sale.
7 Barcelona is a city. I've always wanted to visit it.

3 Complete each of these *if* structures with the correct form of the verbs in the box.

> catch   look after   be able to   (not) speak
> (not) like   know   want   go   rain   find

1 That car will last for years provided you _____ it properly.
2 If he _____ working with numbers, he shouldn't have trained to be an accountant.
3 If you _____ to improve your spoken English, you have to practise regularly.
4 If I hadn't had such a late night, I _____ concentrate better today.
5 I can usually understand what people say in English as long as they _____ too fast.
6 If I _____ you needed help, I'd have come round earlier.
7 If you spoke a bit more slowly, I _____ it a lot easier to understand you.
8 If I wasn't so busy all the time, I _____ to last week's conference.
9 We might have a picnic later unless it _____.
10 If I _____ the earlier train, I'd be there already.

Vocabulary

4 Complete the sentences with a word from the box. Three of the words cannot be used.

> deposit   debt   fine   fare   fees   freebies
> refund   receipt   tip   insurance   overtime
> balance   bargain

1 It's normal to pay a 10% _____ to make a booking for a holiday.
2 You should take out _____ on all your valuable possessions in case they get stolen.
3 I've never borrowed any money in my life. I'd hate to be in _____.
4 I decided not to leave a _____ because the service was so slow and the waiter was very rude.
5 You'll get a complete _____ as long as you bring it back within twenty-eight days.
6 I should have used a better lawyer but I couldn't afford the _____.
7 I got a really good DVD player online for a very low price. I think I got a real _____.
8 They're giving away ten CDs as _____ when you buy one of their latest CD players.
9 I'm so annoyed. I had to pay a £50 _____ for parking on a yellow line.
10 In my new job, you can work at the weekends if you want and get paid _____.

Does crime really pay?

investigation

clue

forensics

Unit 12

Introduction

1 What do you know about the people/stories in the pictures? Which is the 'odd one out'? Why? Discuss with other students.

2 R.61 ▶ Listen to two people. Compare your ideas with what they say. Do they have any extra information?

3 Complete these descriptions of unusual American laws with the words in the box.

> permit   illegal   arrested   jail   forbidden   law

1 In Glendale it is _____ to drive a car in reverse.
2 In California it is against the _____ to eat oranges in the bath.
3 In South Bend monkeys are _____ to smoke cigarettes.
4 In Fargo you can be _____ for wearing a hat while dancing.
5 In Wisconsin you can be put in _____ for using a lasso to catch a fish.
6 In Vermont the law does not _____ you to whistle underwater.

4 Are there any laws that you would like to create? Discuss with other students.

exam reviser   p15 | 12.1 ▶

premium plus   48 ▶

FCE close-up | Reading Gapped text (Paper 1, part 2)

Exam information

This part of the exam consists of a text in which there are seven gaps. You complete the gaps with the sentences which follow the text. There is one extra sentence which does not fit any of the gaps.

Approach

1 Read the whole text through, including the title, to get the general idea of what the text is about.

2 Read all of the extracted sentences to get a sense of the subject of each one.

3 Look at each gap in the text and what comes before and after it. If you are sure about what should go in any of the gaps, make a note of your ideas.

4 Look carefully at the remaining gaps. Look for clues to help you decide which sentences complete them. Are there words like *that*, *it* or *he* which refer to something or someone in the sentence before? Are there any synonyms of words which were used in the previous sentence or two? (Sometimes synonyms help connect sentences.)

5 Decide on one sentence for each gap. Read the text through with the completed gaps. Does it all make sense?

6 Make sure you have filled all the gaps and have not used any sentence more than once

Practice task

You are going to read a newspaper article about an unusual German criminal gang. Seven sentences have been removed from the article. Choose from the sentences A–H the one which fits each gap (1–7). There is one extra sentence which you do not need to use.

Modern-Day Robin Hoods Have Hamburg Cops Baffled

They steal from the rich and give to the poor. And just like Robin Hood and his men, a gang in Hamburg, Germany are proving difficult to catch, despite the fact they dress as superheroes when they raid high-class stores.

A bunch of egalitarian criminals who go by such names as 'Spider Mum', 'Santa Guevara' and 'Multiflex' are being referred to as modern-day Germany's version of Robin Hood and his Merry Men. And just like the Sheriff of Nottingham in the legend of Sherwood Forest's most famous outlaw, the Hamburg police are at a loss when it comes to stopping them.

The group, which calls itself 'Hamburg Umsonst' – loosely translated as Hamburg For Free – started by handing out flyers with tips on how to forge cinema tickets and travel illegally on public transport. **1**

Their most high-profile job to date came last week. Dressed in a variety of comic book hero costumes, the gang raided a well-known delicatessen last Friday during work hours and got away with a large amount of fine food and drink. **2**

Standing inside his delicatessen, Carsten Sievers gestures miserably to where a giant Spanish cheese used to sit. 'They took it,' he says, pointing to an empty shelf. 'They also took my Ruinart champagne. It costs €99 a bottle. **3**

Hamburg cops called to the crime scene failed to arrest anyone despite deploying fourteen patrol cars and a police helicopter. According to eye witnesses, the raiding party consisted of around thirty people who apparently knew what they were doing when it came to fancy food and wine.

In a note posted on the Internet, the gang said it had distributed the food among Germany's new poor – interns who work for months in big publishing houses for no pay, low-wage nursery assistants and mums forced to take part-time jobs as cleaning ladies.

'To survive under the present economic conditions you need to be a superhero,' says Multiflex, after agreeing to meet me at a secret location. In her first interview with a newspaper since the gang staged the raid, she tells me that surviving on a low budget in Hamburg is extremely hard. **4** Wasn't she afraid she might get caught, though? 'It was a risk. But it was a well-planned operation. We were very organised. We tried to do it all with a bit of humour.' How did the gang escape? 'We flew away,' she says, with a twinkle in her eyes.

But even the best-laid plans of criminal masterminds have the odd weak spot. **5** Just recently, in what could eventually be their undoing, they have been leaving notes at the scene of their crimes which carry statements such as: 'Without the abilities of a superhero, survival is impossible in the town of the millionaires.'

Hamburg's police, meanwhile, are not amused. 'Hamburg has always been a very tolerant city which allows many different opinions,' says a spokeswoman for the Hamburg police. But, she adds: 'We are talking here about theft. It is forbidden. This was criminal activity. **6** She admits, however, that they stand little chance of identifying the thirty people who carried out the raid, all of whom were masked.

Meanwhile, Carsten Sievers feels his shop was the wrong target. **7** 'If I had a message for the gang,' says Sievers, 'I would say, "Try to come up with an idea next time that doesn't involve crime."'

A While carrying out their raids in order to support exploited employees and those on benefits, the gang have been unable to resist the temptation to show off.

B Fortunately, my vintage wines were all locked up.

C The shop regularly donates surplus poultry and vegetables to Hamburg charities.

D We can't tolerate it, even if they say they were behaving like Robin Hood.

E And because of their website, interest in the group is growing around the world.

F Not, however, before posing for a publicity photograph with bemused staff.

G Of all the German cities, it has the highest number of millionaires and at the same time there is a growing number of people who don't share in this wealth.

H Now, however, it has moved on to raiding the most expensive stores and delicatessens and then distributing the stolen money to the city's poor.

Grammar | reported speech

1 What do you think of the Hamburg gang in the article on pages 122–123? Are they heroes or villains? Discuss with other students.

2 Read what some people have said about the gang. Who do you think made each comment?

1 a member of the public
2 a member of the Hamburg Umsonst gang
3 a member of the local police

A 'They're just ordinary criminals.'

B 'We're trying to help the poor and low-paid in our city.'

C 'We've been following their activities closely for the last year.'

D 'They should be locked up.'

E 'We can't tolerate this kind of behaviour.'

F 'We will continue with our activities until the government does more to help local people.'

3 Change each of the comments in Exercise 2 from direct speech into reported speech making any appropriate changes.

A member of the public said they were just ordinary criminals.

•• see grammar reference: page 184 ••

Grammar note	tense changes after a reporting verb

Which one of these sentences is grammatically incorrect? Why?

1 Did you hear about Teri? Jon told me she lives in Lima now.

2 Jo, what are you doing here? Sarah said you are on holiday in Spain.

premium plus **49**

4 R.62 Listen to a reporter interviewing someone about an incident with a stranger. Do you think a crime was committed?

5 R.62 Listen again and then prepare the story for an evening news broadcast.

And our final story involves a warning for our listeners. Earlier today, we interviewed Terry Mayfield of Suffolk Square, Chichester who told us about a well-dressed young woman who had recently come to his house. He said that she had rung his doorbell and told him that her car had broken down and that she needed to phone her husband. Our reporter asked him why the woman hadn't used her mobile and Terry explained that ...

6 Read out your news broadcast to other students.

The news

Try to read or listen to the news in English at least once a week. Get into the habit of

- buying an English newspaper;
- going to an English news website, e.g. www.timesonline.co.uk;
- listening to the news on the radio, e.g. the BBC World Service.

Follow the stories that you know about in your language, too. This will help you to understand them more easily.

Don't try to listen or read too much! Just choose a few stories or articles you are interested in and focus on those.

If possible, do this with a friend. Then you can discuss the news stories together.

Task: What are the big stories in the English-speaking news at the moment? Are any about serious crimes?

learning tip

Listening

1 R.63 Listen to an interview and say how these pictures are connected.

2 R.63 Listen again and answer these questions.

1 What is Andrew Savage's collection called?
2 How much money did the National Lottery give the Nikon Gallery?
3 Does Jonathan Witkins confirm that Andrew Savage shoplifted some items?
4 What did the police do?
5 What happens in Andrew Savage's new works?
6 What does Jonathan Witkins say his gallery aims to do?

3 Discuss with other students.

- Do you think Andrew Savage is a criminal?
- Do you think that what he does will encourage other people to steal?
- Do you think that art should provoke debate and discussion? Why/Why not?
- Do you know of any other controversial pieces of art? If so, what are they and why are they controversial?

FCE close-up | Writing Letter/email (Paper 2, part1)

Exam information

Part 1 of the Writing paper consists of one question that all candidates must answer – it is compulsory. You are required to read some input material (e.g. an advertisement with some handwritten notes next to it) and then write an email or letter based on the notes. The email/letter may be formal or informal and may involve requesting, giving information, suggesting, complaining, etc. You will be asked to write between 120 and 150 words.

Approach

1 Read the rubric for the task and all the input material carefully. Underline the key parts.

2 Make a plan of what you are going to write before you start. Organise your points into logical paragraphs.

3 Make sure you begin and end your email or letter appropriately, e.g. *All the best, Sarah.* (However, you will *not* need to put addresses at the beginning.)

4 Include everything the rubric and the task ask you to do. Also, be careful not to include irrelevant information which is not asked for.

5 Do not copy large phrases or sentences from the input material.

6 Think about the tone of your email/letter. It is very important that it has a good effect on your reader.

7 When you have finished writing your letter/email, take some time to check what you have written. Make sure you have:

- organised it into paragraphs;
- used linking words to connect your sentences/ paragraphs where appropriate;
- used an appropriate style, i.e. formal or informal;
- included everything you were asked to do;
- checked for any mistakes of grammar and vocabulary;
- checked for any mistakes of spelling and punctuation;
- written approximately the correct number of words.

Practice task

You have received an email from your English-speaking friend, Paula, who has recently been the victim of a crime. Read Paula's email and the notes you have made. Then write an email to Paula, using **all** your notes.

email	
From:	Paula Larsen-Freeman
Sent:	15th March 2008
Subject:	Some news

Hi there,

Just wanted to let you know about something that happened to me yesterday. It's not very nice really and I'm not sure what to do about it.

Give advice → I was looking at my credit card account online and I was surprised at how much I seemed to owe. When I checked through the statement I realised that I hadn't actually bought some of the things that were down there. You can imagine the shock! It looks like there's ← *Express sympathy* about £175 worth of things which I never ordered – mainly CDs and sports equipment. The trouble is that I'm not sure what to do now. Maybe I should forget about it because it's not likely to happen again, is it?

This whole thing has made me feel quite nervous about using my credit card over the Internet. Do you ever buy things online? Have you ever had any bad experiences? *Tell her* →

Anyway, enough of all that. I do hope you and Francis are well and I'm really looking forward to seeing you both next month.

Do write and let me know your news.

Paula x

Write your **email**. You must use grammatically correct sentences with accurate spelling and punctuation in a style appropriate for the situation.

Vocabulary | phrasal verbs (crime)

1 Look at the pictures and explain what you think is happening.

2 Read the story. Check your ideas.

A New York teacher and his wife weren't getting on very well. He decided to hire two of his students to *break into* his house so he could impress his wife by *fighting them off*. Trent Darcy, twenty-seven, paid the teenagers $100 each to *tie up* his wife with tape and attempt to *make off with* the TV and computer. Darcy then came home and *set on* the boys with a piece of wood that had been pre-cut so as to break in half on impact. But while the mock fight was going on, his wife, who had been completely *taken in*, managed to *get away* and call the police. When officers arrived at the scene, the schoolboys tried to *make up* a story to explain what had happened but finally *owned up* to everything. They were later *let off* with a warning. Mr Darcy has been charged with filing a false report. He and his wife have since split up.

3 Match the phrasal verbs in *italics* in the story to these definitions.

1 invent
2 released with little or no punishment
3 enter illegally or by force
4 escape
5 admit
6 deceive
7 steal and take something with you
8 fasten rope, etc. around someone so they cannot move or escape
9 stop someone doing something by fighting them
10 make a sudden and unexpected physical attack

exam reviser p15 | 12.2

4 Complete the sentences with the correct forms of the phrasal verbs in Exercise 2.

1 When I was out shopping this morning, a young man grabbed my bag and _____ _____ _____ it.
2 I'll _____ you _____ this time, but you mustn't be late again.
3 He _____ _____ the dog outside the shop while he went in to get some milk.
4 They were _____ _____ by two men who were pretending to be police officers.
5 The bank robbers _____ _____ in a sports car that was waiting for them at the front of the building.
6 It looks like they _____ _____ the flat through the downstairs bathroom window.
7 When she asked him why he was late, he _____ _____ an excuse about his train being delayed.
8 He _____ _____ that he was the one who had broken the window after his teacher threatened to punish the whole class.

5 Write a short story about a crime. Use five of the phrasal verbs from Exercise 2.

Listening

1 In your opinion, what is the purpose of prison? Do you know of any good alternatives? Discuss with other students.

2 R.64 You will hear five people talking about their attitudes to dealing with crime. Choose from A–F which view each speaker expresses. Use the letters only once. There is one extra letter which you do not need to use.

A He/she thinks we are forgetting one of the main reasons for prison.
B He/she gives an example of the good effect of this approach.
C He/she thinks other countries have better systems.
D He/she thinks this type of punishment can be very appropriate.
E He/she thinks it's important not to be soft on people who break the law.
F He/she has some doubts about how well this idea is working.

3 R.64 Listen to the extracts again. Who refers to each of these and what do they say about them?

1 a joyrider
2 old people
3 the rest of society
4 graffiti
5 judges
6 a mediator
7 not very serious offenders

4 Do you agree or disagree with the opinions of each speaker? Discuss with other students. (If necessary, refer to the audioscript on page 166.)

Grammar | reporting verbs

1 Complete these sentences with different reporting verbs.

1 He _____ (that) he had seen the thief.

2 He _____ us (that) he had seen the thief.

3 He _____ seeing the thief.

2 Check that you understand the meaning of the words in the box. Then use them to complete sentences 1–5.

> congratulated promised blamed insisted advised

1 He _____ on telling the police.

2 He _____ me to tell the police.

3 He _____ me on telling the police.

4 He _____ to tell the police.

5 He _____ me for not telling the police.

3 Match these verbs to the verbs in Exercise 2 which have similar grammatical patterns.

> remind refuse encourage offer promise threaten

remind – advise, i.e. remind/advise someone to do something

> ### Grammar note | *suggest*
> Which of these patterns following *suggest* is not possible?
>
> | She suggested | going to | to the Sherlock Holmes museum. |
> |---|---|---|
> | | that they go | |
> | | that they should go | |
> | | that they went | |
> | | them to go | |

4 Complete the second sentence so that it has a similar meaning to the first sentence, using the word given. Do not change the word given. You must use between two and five words, including the word given.

'Well done on finding out who stole the money!'

on

He **congratulated me on** finding out who stole the money.

1 'You shouldn't try to catch the thief by yourself.'

not

She _____ try to catch the thief by myself.

2 'I'm not going to pay the speeding fine.'

refused

He _____ the speeding fine.

3 'Don't forget to bring my Agatha Christie novel!'

him

She _____ bring her Agatha Christie novel.

4 'It's not true – I didn't cheat in the exam.'

denied

He _____ in the exam.

5 'Let's go to the police.'

suggested

She _____ go to the police.

6 'It was the weather that made me late for court.'

for

He _____ him late for court.

7 'It's true that I didn't ask permission to use the computer.'

not

She _____ asked permission to use the computer.

8 'I'll sit with you at the trial, if you like.'

to

He _____ her at the trial.'

5 Tell another student about four of these occasions.

- When you congratulated someone on something.
- When you warned someone not to do something.
- When you refused to do something.
- When you advised someone to do something.
- When you reminded someone to do something.
- When you explained to someone how to do something.
- When you offered to do something for someone.

Vocabulary | prefixes

1 Answer these questions. If necessary, check your ideas in audioscript 64 on page 166 (sections 1 and 5).

1 What prefixes make the opposite of these words?
   A fortunately
   B responsible

2 What prefix adds the meaning of 'again' to words like *offend* and *build*?

2 Look at the prefixes and the examples in the table. Complete the meaning column for each one, using the explanations in the box. (You can use the explanations more than once.)

> negative/opposite   wrongly/badly   again/back   too much
> too little/not enough   former   together   after   before

Prefix	Meaning	Example
un	1 *negative/opposite*	*unfortunately*
ir	2 *negative/opposite*	*irresponsible*
re	3 *again/back*	*re-offend*
ex	4	*ex-husband*
il	5	*illegal*
in	6	*invisible*
over	7	*overworked*
under	8	*undercook*
pre	9	*prejudge*
post	10	*postgraduate*
co	11	*co-worker*
mis	12	*misbehave*
im	13	*impolite*
dis	14	*disappear*

3 Read these guidelines.

• The prefixes *co-* and *ex-* are often separated from what follows by hyphens.

• Sometimes other prefixes may also use hyphens in order to avoid strange combinations of letters (e.g. *pre-arrange, re-examine*).

4 Which of the words in *italics* should have hyphens?

1 Our company employs a lot of *exoffenders*.
2 He handed over control of the plane to his *copilot*.
3 Celebrities often write *premarital* agreements.
4 He was *reelected* as president three times.

5 Complete each question with the word in brackets and the correct prefix.

1 Do you think using mobile phones while driving should be <u>*illegal*</u>? (legal)
2 Have you ever done anything slightly _____? (honest)

3 What would you do if you were _____ in a restaurant and your bill was £3 too much? (charged)
4 Have you got any _____ hobbies? (usual)
5 Would you say that you were an _____ person? (patient)
6 Are there any words you often _____? (spell)
7 Do you think professional footballers are _____? (paid)
8 Do you have any _____ that you keep in touch with? (colleagues)
9 Have you got any _____ fears or phobias? (rational)

6 Choose five of the questions in Exercise 4 to ask another student.

> premium plus   **50**

Speaking

1 Look at the phrases in *italics* in the speech bubbles. What other things can you do or say to make sure other people are involved in a discussion?

A: So, *what do you think?*

B: I'm not sure I completely agree.

C: *Do you agree with that?*

D: Yes, up to a point.

E: *How do you feel about this?*

F: I'm not really sure. I can see both sides of the argument.

> exam reviser   **p20 | 3**

2 Work in groups. Each of the people on page 129 has committed a crime of some kind. Discuss each case, then decide what you think should be done. Consider these things:

• possible reasons for the crime
• how likely it is that the person will re-offend
• possible punishments
• what you hope the punishment will achieve

1 Mark, fifteen years old, often misses school. Caught by police spraying artistic graffiti on the side of motorway bridges. First time in trouble with the police.

2 Sarah, twenty-six, single parent with two small children. Third time she has been arrested for shoplifting items of food from a local supermarket.

3 Nick, twenty-four, arrested for fighting and vandalism at a football match. Often gets aggressive after drinking too much. One previous conviction for drink driving.

4 Petra, fifty-three, guilty of murdering her husband with poison. Considered a kind and loving woman by friends and family. Her husband was known to have had a number of affairs.

5 Alan, forty-two, wealthy accountant. Found guilty of stealing hundreds of thousands of pounds over many years from various clients, including famous pop stars and footballers.

3 Listen to what the other groups decided for each case. Discuss with your group if you would like to change any of your decisions.

> premium plus 51 ▶

Writing | essay

1 Read this task. <u>Underline</u> the key words.

> ## Writing task
>
> You have had a class discussion about crime and punishment. Your teacher has now asked you to write an essay giving your opinion on the following statement.
>
> *Prison causes more problems than it solves.*
>
> Write your **essay** in 120–180 words.

2 Compare the words you have <u>underlined</u> with another student.

3 With a partner, brainstorm ideas for your essay on the subject in Exercise 1.

4 Now group your ideas into four paragraphs. What is the main purpose of each paragraph?

5 Put the linking expressions in the box into four groups. Tell other students how the expressions in each group are connected.

> although   in addition   because of this   in conclusion
> whereas   nevertheless   so   however   to sum up
> moreover   therefore   what's more   as a result

6 Look at the Exam Reviser. Add any new linkers from Exercise 5 in the correct columns.

> exam reviser   p24 | 15 ▶

7 Write your essay for the task in Exercise 1. Follow the paragraph plan you decided on. Use a good range of linking expressions.

8 Look at the marking criteria for Paper 2 in Writing Reference page 207 and decide which of these things the examiners will be looking for.

1 A clear and complete answer to the question
2 An awareness of who the essay is being written for
3 Quotations from reference books or journals
4 Correct spelling and punctuation
5 A good range of linking expressions
6 An appropriately formal or informal style
7 References to statistics
8 Accurate use of grammar and vocabulary
9 Helpful and logical organisation of ideas in paragraphs

9 Look at your last three or four essays. Which areas are they strongest in? What are they weakest in?

10 Read through your essay. Check the areas that you are usually weak in. Make any changes you think could improve it.

Vocabulary

1 There are mistakes in some of these sentences. Find the mistakes and correct them.

1 My sister hasn't been getting on very well with our father recently.
2 The thieves cut the main alarm before they broke it into the museum.
3 They fought off tough competition to get a place in the finals.
4 As a joke, they tied up him and locked him in a store cupboard.
5 Somehow they got into the company safe and made nearly €100,000 off with.
6 It took them a little while to work out what was going on it.
7 He was taken in by a young woman who said her car had broken down.
8 I was surprised that they owned up taking the money so quickly.
9 The judge let off them with a small fine because it was their first offence.
10 Jennifer and I split up a few months ago but we're still good friends.

2 Replace the underlined words with a single word + prefix.

1 She left her last job because she was made to work too hard.
2 If you don't cook this meat for long enough there is a risk of food poisoning.
3 In some countries it is considered bad manners not to take off your outdoor shoes when you go into someone's home.
4 You shouldn't leave a dog in a hot car for a long time. It's not sensible and means you are not thinking about the possible bad results.
5 We shouldn't form our opinion about the new prime minister before she has had a chance to put her ideas into practice.
6 It's a well-known fact that 70% of young men who go to prison will break the law again at some point.
7 I really hate going in lifts. It's not based on any clear thought or reason but it makes me feel panicky!
8 I know the waiter's been a long time but you shouldn't get so annoyed at having to wait. You can see how busy they are.

Grammar

3 Complete the text with the linkers in the box.

> Nevertheless Therefore Although In conclusion
> What's more

I am here to report to you today the latest situation regarding crime in the local area. _____[1] in some ways we have had a difficult year, there are many areas of progress to report. Firstly, in terms of car crime, I'm pleased to say that the number of car thefts has gone down by 15%. _____[2], the recent campaign against drink-driving seems to have paid off as the police report a 20% reduction in drivers who are over the permitted alcohol limit.

This is all good news. _____[3], we can't afford to be complacent. We are all well aware of the problems of graffiti and vandalism in some of our local estates. _____[4] we are proposing a youth project aimed at providing more activities and facilities for young people. This will be based at the local community centre.

_____[5] I would like to thank our local police force for the invaluable work they do and urge everybody here to support them in any way they can.

4 Read the dialogue. Then report it making all the necessary changes.

Avril asked Ben if he had read about the stupid shoplifter.

Avril: Did you read about the stupid shoplifter?
Ben: No, what happened?
Avril: Well, apparently, a woman called Joyce Lebron lost consciousness in a supermarket in Berne, in Switzerland. At first, the checkout assistants thought she'd had a heart attack.
Ben: So what had really happened?
Avril: As she was being treated by paramedics, they found a frozen chicken under her clothes.
Ben: Are you serious?
Avril: Yes. It was the chicken that had made her body temperature fall dramatically, causing her to faint.
Ben: That must be the craziest crime I've ever heard of.

5 Put these sentences into direct speech.

1 They advised us to call the police if it happened again.
2 He blamed his teachers for his poor results.
3 She congratulated Tim on coming first.
4 He refused to let the police come into his flat.
5 His parents warned him not to borrow so much money.
6 She reminded him to put the diamonds in a safe place.
7 Her father suggested that she had a burglar alarm put in.
8 His teacher encouraged him to enter the competition.

Weird and wonderful

haunted

illusion

mystery

Unit 13

Introduction

1 What different kinds of mysterious, weird or puzzling things can you see in the pictures?

2 Complete the phrases in these questions using the words in the box. Use a dictionary if necessary.

> haunted   suspense   cryptic   illusions   treasure   unanswered
> solving   working

1 Do you like films or books about ghosts and _____ houses?
2 Do you like _____ out the answers to 'Whodunnit' type films or books?
3 Can you think of any films or books which are *full of* _____?
4 What do you think of shows in which magicians perform tricks and *optical* _____?
5 There are many _____ *questions* about UFOs. Can you think of any other things which are mysterious?
6 Do you know anyone who is good at doing _____ *crosswords*?
7 Have you ever taken part in a _____ *hunt*?
8 Are you the sort of person who is good at _____ *problems*?

3 Ask each question in Exercise 2 to two other students.

exam reviser   p16 | 13.1

Reading

1 Look at the pictures from the popular TV drama series, *Lost*. Read the information about the characters Jack and Kate and discuss these questions with other students.

- Have you seen this series? If so, tell other students about it. Did you like it? Why/Why not?
- If you haven't seen it, where do you think the story is set? What do you think has happened? Do you think you would enjoy watching it? Why/Why not?

2 Read the article quickly and answer the question that is relevant to you.

- If you've seen the series, do you think the article gives a correct impression of it?
- If you haven't seen it, were your ideas in Exercise 1 correct or not?

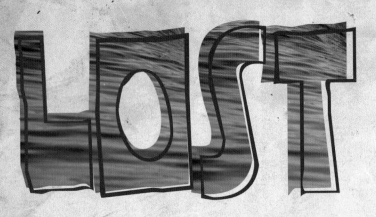

Forty-eight survivors of a mid-Pacific plane crash have been stranded on a mysterious island of harsh terrain, cruel weather and dark secrets,
5 including a terrifying creature that stalks the jungle. And some of the castaways have dark secrets of their own. Thousands of miles off-course and with no rescue in sight, they must
10 work together to survive. But the survivors' pasts keep coming back to haunt them and this threatens the group's ability to get through it all. Among the survivors, there's a doctor,
15 a convict, a rock star … they are all different. But in one way, they are all the same. They are all lost …

The first episode begins in a tropical jungle.
20 A man, Jack, is lying on the ground. He is bruised, bloody and disoriented. A terrible memory flickers across his face. Silently, he begins to run through the trees,
25 **wincing** with pain as he goes. As he gets near a beautiful beach, he hears the sounds of people screaming. He rounds a bend to find the wreckage of a plane crash, surrounded by
30 survivors in shock. His doctor's instincts kick in and he runs to help those he can. After treating the injured, the able-bodied survivors rescue what they can from the
35 body of the plane, but the cockpit, where the radio transceiver is kept, is missing. As darkness falls, a monstrous howl rings out from the forest. The tops of the trees shake, but eventually
40 whatever is making the sound goes away, leaving the survivors marooned and exhausted – and now terrified.

Jack, it turns out, is a neurosurgeon from the USA. With his inner strength
45 and sharp brain, he quickly emerges

as a leader to the survivors, who look to him for guidance. Jack's closest ally is Kate, whose positive qualities are clear from her first moments on the
50 island. She is intelligent and level-headed and in the initial crisis, she shows bravery and determination. Jack is impressed by her stitching of the wounds on his back despite
55 having no medical training.

The next day, Jack and Kate head into the jungle to look for the cockpit, accompanied by Charlie, a musician from Manchester, England.
60 Struggling through a torrential rainstorm, they find the wreckage, where the apparently dead pilot regains consciousness. The terrifying howls begin again – this time just
65 outside the cockpit. And when the pilot crawls out to see what is making the sound, he is snatched up by a mysterious force. Jack, Kate and Charlie run for their lives, but quickly
70 discover the body of the pilot hanging

Jack (Matthew Fox) With his inner strength and medical skills, Jack quickly emerges as the group's leader. But he is tormented by the search for his dad. Why is his father's coffin empty when it is later found?

3 Read the text again and choose the answer A, B, C or D which you think fits best.

1 Why does the group find it hard to cope with the situation?

  A They are haunted by ghosts.

  B They have a lot of their own individual problems to deal with.

  C They have no past experience of this kind of thing.

  D They all come from different backgrounds.

from the top of a tree. They stand there, wondering what on earth could do something like that …

The twists, turns and puzzles have turned the story of this group of plane crash survivors into one of the
75 most talked-about TV series on Earth. And that's just one of the mysteries. Is it set on Earth? Or perhaps in an alien land? Is time-travel involved? Or is it even all just in one of the survivor's heads?

One thing we do know is that, in reality, it's filmed
80 in Hawaii. There, we caught up with one of the main stars, Matthew Fox, who plays Jack Shephard. He was staggered to discover the show had turned into an international phenomenon. 'I've never experienced anything like it, but it's very exciting.' It's been an even
85 bigger adjustment for Evangeline Lilly, who was a complete unknown before she landed the part of bad-girl Kate. 'It's been overwhelming,' she admits. 'There are not many things in my life that are the same as two years ago. I was a student with five jobs to get
90 myself through college, and now I have photographers following me around to get one picture.'

What the cast won't give away, however, are the show's secrets, because they, like the massive audience, don't know the answers themselves. It makes it easier
95 to play the roles in a really authentic way and be genuine about it all when they are kept just as much in the dark as everyone else. 'We've just begun to scratch the surface of the mysteries,' says Fox, 'but *Lost* is like a good dessert; you want to take it slowly.'

Kate (Evangeline Lilly) Although her past is shrouded with mystery, Kate's positive qualities are clear from the start. But not everyone warms to her. Will we finally learn her secrets?

2 *wincing* in line 25 describes a way of

  A moving.

  B eating or drinking.

  C showing emotion.

  D communicating with someone.

3 What is it that particularly scares them at the end of the first day?

  A Some of the survivors can't stop screaming.

  B They see some monsters in the darkness.

  C The bodies in the plane are moving about.

  D They hear a terrifying sound from the jungle.

4 An important factor in Kate and Jack's relationship is

  A Kate manages to help Jack with his injury.

  B Jack decides to give Kate medical training.

  C Jack is uncertain about how brave Kate is.

  D they were close friends before the crash.

5 When Jack and Kate find the pilot,

  A he is already dead.

  B he is unconscious.

  C he is howling in pain.

  D he is crawling around silently.

6 Before taking part in *Lost,* Evangaline Lilly had been

  A a photographer.

  B a well-known actress.

  C studying and working part-time.

  D in trouble with the police.

7 What is the writer's main point in the last paragraph?

  A *Lost* is a hugely-popular, slow-moving drama series.

  B The characters in *Lost* are based on genuine people.

  C The cast are not told what happens at each stage of the series.

  D The cast are told they must keep the show's mysteries secret.

8 How would you describe the writer's tone in the article?

  A surprised but interested

  B impressed and intrigued

  C confused and slightly irritated

  D overwhelmed and slightly puzzled

4 Discuss these questions.

- What does the text say about: the setting of *Lost*? the different characters? the mysteries?

- What do you think about the way the article is written? Does it give an interesting impression of the TV series? Why/Why not?

- Why do you think TV dramas like *Lost*, which have mysterious elements and unanswered questions in them, are so popular?

- What other kinds of TV dramas do you like and why (e.g. historical dramas, science fiction dramas, comedy dramas, etc.)?

Grammar | possibility and certainty

1 R.65 ▶ Listen to two people discussing the TV drama series *Lost*. Which two mysteries in the programme are they talking about? What different theories do they have about them?

2 Look at these sentences and decide if one or both of the modal verbs in *italics* are grammatically possible.

1 I'm absolutely certain that the monster *must/might* be something really weird – not just an ordinary wild bear.

2 I'm sure that the monster *can't/couldn't* be a normal wild bear. It's just not possible.

3 I'm certain that the island is real. The survivors *can't/mustn't* be imagining the whole thing.

4 I'm not sure, but I think the whole thing *might have/may have* been set up as a huge scientific experiment.

5 I'm not certain, but possibly they *could/can* be in the middle of some sort of a scientific experiment.

6 It's possible that the scientists *could/might* be doing some research into how people behave in a crisis.

7 I feel certain that the survivors *can't have/couldn't have* known anything about the island before landing on it.

8 I'm certain the crash was an accident. The scientists *couldn't have/mustn't have* made it happen on purpose.

•• see grammar reference: page 186 ••

Grammar note | *may, might, could, can*
Which one of these sentences is grammatically incorrect? Why?

1 *I think it might rain today.*

2 *It's possible she may be late today.*

3 *It could be the best thing that's ever happened to me.*

4 *I'm not sure, but I suppose he can still be at work.*

3 Complete the second sentence so that it has a similar meaning to the first sentence, using the word given. Do not change the word given. You must use between two and five words, including the word given.

1 Jenny will possibly lend me the first series of *Lost* on DVD.
   might
   Jenny _____ me the first series of *Lost* on DVD.

2 I can't work out how people managed to build the Great Pyramid.
   have
   I can't work out how the Great Pyramid _____.

3 It's possible that there's a piece missing from this jigsaw puzzle.
   be
   There _____ a piece missing from this jigsaw puzzle.

4 It's impossible that they have finished the treasure hunt already.
   have
   They _____ the treasure hunt already.

5 She's really good at crosswords – I'm certain she does them a lot.
   do
   She's really good at crosswords – she _____ them a lot.

6 I don't know what's going on in this episode of *Lost* – I'm pretty sure I missed the last one.
   must
   I don't know what's going on in this episode of *Lost* – I _____ the last one.

7 It's not possible for a watch to disappear like that – it's just an illusion.
   could
   A watch _____ like that – it's just an illusion.

8 It was obvious who the murderer was from the start – you certainly weren't concentrating properly.
   been
   It was obvious who the murderer was from the start – you _____ properly.

4 Read this story. After each sentence answer the question by speculating about a reason for what happened at each stage.

On Monday last week, a smartly-dressed man was walking along the beach. *[1 Why? He might have been going to a party.]* He was completely soaked to the skin. *[2 Why?]* When a member of the public spoke to him, he didn't answer. *[3 Why?]* Later that day, he was taken to hospital by the police. *[4 Why?]* Despite the staff talking to him, he stayed silent for weeks. *[5 Why?]* One day, someone gave him a piece of paper and pencil. *[6 Why?]* He drew a detailed sketch of a grand piano. *[7 Why?]* The hospital staff took him to a room with a piano. *[8 Why?]* He played the piano for hours at a time, day after day. *[9 Why?]* Police have put his picture in the newspaper. *[10 Why?]*

5 Find out more about the mysterious pianist on page 169.

premium plus 52 ▶

6 Work with other students and follow these instructions.

1 Choose *one* of the following mysteries to talk about:

A the TV series *Lost*

B a mystery from a different TV series or film of your choice

C the mystery of the man in Exercise 4

D a different mystery from real life of your choice

2 Discuss these questions about the mystery you chose.

- What are the main mysteries involved?
- What different theories are there about the mysteries?
- What do you think are the most likely explanations? Do you all agree?

Vocabulary | speculating

1 Work in pairs. Look at phrases A–J. Find them in context in audioscript 65 on page 166 and discuss these questions with your partner.

1 In which four of the phrases is the speaker fairly sure of his/her ideas?

2 In which three of the phrases is the speaker not sure of his/her ideas or has no ideas?

3 In which three of the phrases is the speaker responding directly to someone else's ideas.

A I knew right from the start …

B I've got a feeling …

C I think it's probably some sort of …

D At first I thought … but now I'm not so sure.

E I just can't work out how …

F I think it's more likely …

G I don't see how it could be …

H I suppose you're right.

I It doesn't make sense.

J I hadn't thought of that.

exam reviser p21 | 6

2 Cover the phrases in Exercise 1. Then, complete the phrases in *italics* in the dialogue.

A: Where do you think it is?

B: *I think it's some* _____[1] *of* lake that's frozen over.

A: Do you? *I hadn't* _____[2] *of that. I think it's more* _____[3] *that* it's a street because of the houses and other buildings, here and here.

B: *At first I thought that, but now I'm not so* _____[4] because the people look like they're skating on water … you know, frozen water.

A: *I* _____[5] *you're right.* Hmm, *it doesn't make* _____[6], though. I mean, *I don't see* _____[7] *it could be* a lake because the houses would be right next to the water, you know, *in the water.*

B: Yes, but look there are boats here. It must be a lake. *I knew right from the* _____[8] *that* it was a lake. It's obvious now.

A: Mmm, what about this bit? *I just can't* _____[9] *out what* these people in the middle are doing – the ones holding hands …

B: *I've got a* _____[10] *that* they're dancing. Look, they're all in a line …

3 R.66 ▶ Listen and check your answers.

4 Look at the pictures on page 169. For each one, discuss and speculate with another student about the situation, the different people and their stories. Use these questions to help you.

- Where is the scene taking place? What clues are there?
- How long ago is the scene taking place? What clues are there?
- Who are the people in the picture? What do you think the connection is between them? What makes you think that?
- What are the people doing? Why? What have they done/been doing before this scene took place? What makes you think that?

premium plus 53 ▶

Speaking

1 Read the advert and answer these questions.
1 Where will the competition take place?
2 What are the two kinds of 'challenges' that the contestants will have to do?
3 What will the winner get?

SURVIVOR! HAVE YOU GOT WHAT IT TAKES?
Contestants wanted for new TV show

ChallengeTV is currently looking for twelve contestants to take part in the new series of *Survivor!* – the most challenging and exciting survival competition on television.

There will be twelve contestants divided into two teams of six each. You will live on a desert island off the coast of Panama for a month. Water will be available, but you will have to make your own camp and hunt, fish or find and cook your own food. Plus you will have to deal with the heat, the insects and each other!

The format of the game is simple, following a three-day cycle. On the first day, you will do a 'Reward Challenge'. The team that wins will get something to make their lives easier (e.g. extra food, bedding, etc.). On the second day, you will take part in an 'Immunity Challenge'. The team that loses will have to vote one of its members off the island on the third day – whereas the winning team will be immune from this. Then the cycle will start again.

Towards the end of the competition, the two groups will become one, with individuals then competing against each other for rewards and immunity. At the end of the month, there will be one winner, who will receive £1,000,000.

2 Discuss these questions with other students.
• Would you like to take part in *Survivor!*? Why/Why not?
• Do you think you would be successful? Why/Why not?

3 R.67 ▶ Listen to two people discussing the question 'Which essential items would you want to take to the island?' What do they agree on?

4 R.67 ▶ Listen again and tick the phrases you hear.

Starting the discussion:	
1 *Why don't we start by ...?*	☐
2 *Shall we ... first?*	☐
3 *Let's begin with ...*	☐
Moving the discussion on:	
4 *And what about ...?*	☐
5 *What else do you think is important?*	☐
6 *Let's see. What's left?*	☐
Finishing the discussion:	
7 *Shall we check that we agree on ...?*	☐
8 *So, have we decided which ones ...?*	☐
9 *Anyway, we have to decide which ...*	☐

5 You and your partner have been selected to take part in the television competition *Survivor!* You can only take six items. Talk about which items you would take and why. Use at least three of the phrases in Exercise 4.

Listening

1 R.68 ▶ Listen to five people talking about strange or puzzling things. Which five of these things do they talk about?

1 a number puzzle
2 a crossword puzzle
3 a TV game show
4 a detective story
5 a science fiction film
6 a children's treasure hunt
7 a dream/nightmare
8 an Internet game

2 R.68 ▶ Listen again and choose from the list A–F how each speaker feels about what he or she is talking about. Use the letters only once. There is one extra letter which you do not need to use.

A He/she felt differently from how he/she had anticipated.
B He/she felt unsure about where he/she was.
C He/she found it hard to stop what he/she was doing.
D He/she feels worried about having to do it again.
E He/she is inspired to do something he/she has seen.
F He/she feels very differently from someone he/she is describing.

Speaker 1 _____
Speaker 2 _____
Speaker 3 _____
Speaker 4 _____
Speaker 5 _____

3 Look again at the list of things in Exercise 1 and choose three that you are interested in. Tell another student how you feel about each one, including any experience you have of them or future plans.

exam reviser p21 | 7 ▶

Grammar | -ing forms/infinitives

1 Look at the verb forms in *italics* in the sentences. Match them with the correct rules A–H.

1 It must *get* so boring doing puzzles all the time.
2 I went to my friend's house *to play* on his computer.
3 *Reading* detective stories is one of my favourite hobbies.
4 I'd rather *read* a book than do crosswords.
5 I find those TV game shows really exciting *to watch*.
6 I'm too impatient *to bother* with those Sudoku things.
7 My brother makes me *play* computer games with him.
8 She trained for the competition by *doing* five puzzles a day.

> Use the infinitive without *to* (e.g. *do*)
> A after modal verbs
> B after *make* and *let*
> C after *I'd better* and *I'd rather*
>
> Use the infinitive with *to* (e.g. *to do*)
> D after certain adjectives
> E after the construction '*too … to …*'
> F to express purpose
>
> Use the -*ing* form (e.g. *doing*)
> G after prepositions
> H when an action (not a noun) is the subject or object of a sentence

2 Choose the correct alternatives in this text.

A man has praised the honest people in Utah, USA for *to return/returning*[1] his wallet forty years after he lost it. Fifty-seven-year-old Doug Schmitt left his wallet on the counter of a petrol station in Logan, Utah in the spring of 1967. 'I've wondered about it occasionally,' he said. 'But I knew that it was too long ago *having/to have*[2] any hope of getting it back. I couldn't *remember/to remember*[3] where I'd lost it anyway, and I thought I'd better just *to give up/give up*[4] the idea of ever *find/finding*[5] it again.

The owner of the petrol station, however, put the wallet in a drawer *keep/to keep*[6] it safe until Mr Schmitt came back to *collect/collecting*[7] it. Decades later, the owner's son found it in the drawer. '*Having/Have*[8] a student identity card in the wallet was great,' he said 'because I could track Mr Schmitt down on the Internet and *sending/send*[9] the wallet back.' The wallet also contained $5 in cash, some stamps and a dry-cleaning ticket. 'It makes me *to wonder/wonder*[10] if I've still got some dry-cleaning out there!' said Mr Schmitt.

3 Complete these sentences with the correct form of the verb in brackets.

1 I managed _____ (work out) who the murderer was in the end.
2 She offered _____ (help) me with my next task.
3 Do you fancy _____ (watch) that murder mystery film tonight?
4 I meant _____ (phone) Marco earlier, but I totally forgot.
5 In my dream, the stairs kept _____ (disappear).
6 I was expecting _____ (see) him at the meeting, but he wasn't there.
7 I really don't enjoy _____ (waste) my time playing computer games.
8 When I went camping, I really missed _____ (have) a proper bed.

•• see grammar reference: page 186 ••

4 Look at the two definitions for each verb pattern and then complete the pairs of sentences with the correct form of the verb in brackets.

1 A I love trying _____ (work out) all the answers in 'Whodunnit' books.
  B I tried _____ (write) down all the possibilities for each gap in a Sudoku puzzle, but I still couldn't do it.
  • try to do = attempt to do/make an effort to do
  • try doing = do something as an experiment or test
2 A Did you remember _____ (programme) the DVD player to record the match?
  B I only remember _____ (go) inside a dark building, but then I woke up.
  • remember to do = remember about something and then do it
  • remember doing = do something and then remember about it
3 A He only stopped _____ (play) that computer game when the computer crashed!
  B I stopped _____ (have) a coffee on my way to work this morning.
  • stop to do = stop doing an action in order to do something else
  • stop doing = stop doing an action while in the middle of that action

•• see grammar reference: page 186 ••

5 Tell other students about five of these things.

Something you …

• intend to do
• regret doing
• have given up doing
• usually avoid doing
• don't often remember to do
• miss doing
• sometimes pretend to do
• expect to do soon

premium plus 54 ▶

Vocabulary | feelings

1 Look at the words/phrases in the box. If there are any you don't know, check the meaning and pronunciation, using a dictionary if necessary.

> elated   enthusiastic   exhilarated   inspired
> relieved   thrilled to bits   distraught   downhearted
> overwhelmed   scared stiff   staggered   traumatised

2 Choose the correct alternatives in these sentences.

1 She's a positive person and is always *enthusiastic/relieved* about her studies.

2 Don't be *relieved/downhearted* about your driving test. I'm sure you'll pass next time.

3 I was *staggered/exhilarated* when he told me he was going bungee jumping. It's so out of character.

4 There are several people away at work and I'm feeling *inspired/overwhelmed* by the amount I have to do.

5 My cat was like my best friend and I was *downhearted/distraught* when she died.

6 After watching the Olympics on TV, I was *elated/inspired* to become a member of a running club.

7 She was *traumatised/thrilled to bits* for a while after the car accident.

8 I usually feel *exhilarated/scared stiff* in job interviews, but I felt quite relaxed for this one.

3 Complete these sentences. Make three of them true and three of them false.

1 Something I always feel enthusiastic about is …

2 Above all, I felt relieved when I …

3 I usually feel scared stiff when …

4 I felt completely elated as soon as I'd finished …

5 I can say that I was absolutely thrilled to bits when …

6 I've never felt as exhilarated as when I …

4 Read your partner's sentences and try to guess which ones are true and which are not. Tell each other more details about the ones that are true.

> exam reviser   p16 | 13.2
>
> premium plus   55

Writing | story

1 Look at these tips. Which should you do *before* you write and which should you do *after*?

1 Think about the story/situation.

2 Think about the character(s).

3 Check your writing for any mistakes.

4 Think about who will read your story.

5 Make sure there is a range of interesting vocabulary.

6 Plan the paragraphs.

2 Look at this task and answer the questions. Refer to the Writing Reference on page 196.

1 Who will read your story?

2 What three things will make it a good story?

Writing task

Your teacher has asked you to write a story for the school magazine. Your story must **end** with the following words:

It had been a strange and frightening day and John was relieved to be home at last.

Write your **story** (**120–180** words).

3 Work in pairs. Prepare for writing by discussing these questions and making notes.

1 In the sentence you must use to finish the story, what are the key words? What ideas do they give you about the story/situation?

2 What different kinds of feelings do you think your story could include? Try to think of interesting words (e.g. *thrilled to bits* instead of *happy*, etc.).

3 What different kinds of events do you think could happen in the story (e.g. an accident, a crime, etc.)?

4 Write down some details about one of the events that you want to include.

5 What is/are the main character(s) like? Build up a picture in your mind by thinking about his/her age, personality, appearance, etc.

> Key words: strange / frightening / relieved to be home at last
>
> Went on a journey? / Got lost? / met someone strange?
>
> Feelings: scared stiff / distraught / relieved
> Events:

4 Think about how many paragraphs you will include in your story. What is the purpose of each paragraph? Write the first draft of your story using your notes to help you.

5 Read your story and check that you have used:

- logical paragraphs
- interesting vocabulary
- correct narrative verb forms
- correct spelling, grammar and punctuation
- the correct number of words

6 Write a final draft, incorporating any changes you think will improve your story. In the exam, there won't be time to write a second draft of your story, but you still need to plan and check it carefully.

FCE close-up | Use of English Key word transformations (Paper 3, part 4)

Exam information

This part of the exam consists of eight key word transformations (plus an example). Each question contains three parts: a lead-in sentence, a key word, and a second sentence with a gap in the middle. You have to fill the gap in the second sentence so that it is as close as possible in meaning to the lead-in sentence. The answer must be between two and five words, including the key word. The key word must not be changed in any way.

The focus of this part is grammar and vocabulary. A wide range of structures is tested, e.g. modals, -ing forms and infinitives, verb tenses, *if* structures, passive voice and reported speech. Phrasal verbs and lexical phrases, e.g. *looking forward to -ing*, may also be tested.

Approach

1 Read both sentences carefully.

2 Look at the key word and try to identify what kind of word it is (e.g. verb, noun).

3 Look at the words before and after the gap and try to work out what kind of grammar or vocabulary the question is testing (e.g. modals, phrasal verbs, reported speech).

4 Write between two and five words in the gap including the key word. Don't change the key word. Remember that contractions count as two words (e.g. *don't* = two words).

5 Check that your sentence makes sense. Also check for spelling and verb form mistakes.

6 In the exam, remember not to write the complete sentence. You should write only the missing words in the space on your answer sheet. Always write something in each gap: you do not lose marks for a wrong answer.

Practice task

For questions **1–8**, complete the second sentence so that it has a similar meaning to the first sentence, using the word given. **Do not change the word given**. You must use between **two** and **five** words, including the word given. Here is an example (**0**).

Write your answers IN CAPITAL LETTERS.

Example:

0 It's not possible that you failed the exam – you studied so hard.
   CAN'T

   You _____ the exam – you studied so hard.

The gap can be filled by the words '*can't have failed*', so you write

Example: | 0 | | C | A | N | ' | T | | H | A | V | E | | F | A | I | L | E | D |

Write the missing words in **CAPITAL LETTERS**.

1 I finished the exam in the time available but it was difficult.
   MANAGED

   I _____ the exam in the time available, but it was difficult.

2 I couldn't understand the instructions for my new mobile phone.
   SENSE

   The instructions for my new mobile phone didn't _____ me.

3 My grandmother continued as a tennis player until she was seventy-two.
   STOP

   My grandmother _____ tennis until she was seventy-two.

4 I'm sure they were terrified when they thought nobody would rescue them.
   BEEN

   They _____ terrified when they thought nobody would rescue them.

5 'Perhaps we could go to the cinema,' said Jerry.
   SUGGESTED

   Jerry _____ to the cinema.

6 I think the more probable reason is that his train has been delayed.
   LIKELY

   I think _____ his train has been delayed.

7 I'm having difficulty understanding how to do my maths homework.
   OUT

   I can't _____ how to do my maths homework.

8 'I'll give you a lift to the airport,' said Delia.
   OFFERED

   Delia _____ a lift to the airport.

Go to www.iTests.com or your CD-ROM for interactive exam practice

Grammar

1 There are mistakes in the verb forms in *italics* in these sentences. Find the mistakes and correct them.

A: I can't find my keys anywhere. I *must left*[1] them at Sally's house.

B: They *mustn't be*[2] at her house because you drove home using them.

A: Oh, yes, so I did. Oh dear, they *can't have be stolen*[3], can they?

B: I don't think so. Where did you go after Sally's?

A: Well, I went to the supermarket – so I suppose I *can have dropped*[4] them somewhere there …

B: No, you *can't do*[5] because you drove home from there as well, didn't you?

A: Of course I did! Well, they *must to be*[6] somewhere in the house, then.

B: Have another look in your bag – you *could have miss*[7] them.

A: They're really not in there. Perhaps I *must have left*[8] them in the front door …

B: No, they're not there. They're probably somewhere really obvious – like in your pocket. Have a look, they *might have be*[9] in your pocket.

A: Oh, yes! Here they are – after all that! They're right here!

2 Match the sentence halves 1–10 with A–J to make complete sentences.

1 I'd rather …
2 I usually avoid …
3 I think you're too young …
4 I've always dreamt of …
5 You can …
6 I want …
7 I really regretted …
8 My parents don't let me …
9 I borrowed his puzzle book …
10 He said he regrets …

A … going to a desert island.
B … play computer games much.
C … to watch such scary horror films.
D … watch a detective film than a horror film.
E … borrowing things if I can.
F … borrow my puzzle book if you like.
G … to borrow Steve's puzzle book for the journey.
H … to have something to do on the journey.
I … to say that he won't be lending you any more money.
J … borrowing all that money from my parents last time.

Vocabulary

3 Six of these sentences have a word missing. Write the missing words in the correct place.

1 I suppose you right.
2 It doesn't make sense me.
3 I hadn't thought of that.
4 I've got feeling that someone's watching me.
5 I think it's some sort charity fund-raising event.
6 I don't how it could be brand new – it looks dirty.
7 At first I thought she was a bit unfriendly, but now I'm not so sure.
8 I knew right the start that he wasn't going to fit in with the team.

4 Choose the correct alternatives.

Hi Tim,

I just wanted to tell you about this fantastic holiday I'm on. It's a sort of adventure type holiday and we've been doing really exciting but sometimes scary things! At the end of every day, I'm exhausted but completely *distraught/ exhilarated*[1] by my achievements. The staff are lovely – very friendly and *enthusiastic/elated*[2] about all the sports.

On the first day, we went abseiling. At first, I really didn't want to do it – I stood at the top of the enormous cliff and was *staggered/scared stiff*[3]. Then I watched James – he was the first person to go over the edge and down the side of the rock. In the morning, he had been really *distraught/relieved*[4] at the whole idea of it. You have ropes and everything, but it's still scary! He did it though and I was really *inspired/ downhearted*[5] when I saw him – and suddenly I really wanted to do it myself.

When it was my turn, I was *staggered/ overwhelmed*[6] that I didn't feel more scared actually … I went over the edge at the top quite easily. It was a bit scary on the way down and I was very *exhilarated/relieved*[7] when I reached the bottom in one piece – but I would definitely recommend it.

I'll write more tomorrow. By the way, well done about your exam results. You must be *enthusiastic/thrilled to bits*[8]!

Michael

Work to live

special skills

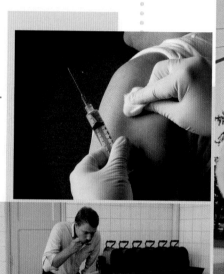

opportunity

dangerous

Unit 14

Grammar: passives; ability | Vocabulary: jobs and work; phrasal verbs | Writing: a letter of application; set book

Introduction

1 Look at the pictures, which show people earning money in different ways. Say what you think each job is and what skills or personality characteristics you would need to do these jobs well.

2 Explain the difference in meaning between the phrases in *italics* in these pairs of sentences.
1 A I *got the sack* on Friday.
   B I was *made redundant* on Friday.
2 A I'm on *maternity leave*.
   B I'm on *sick leave*.
3 A He's in a *dead-end* job.
   B He's got a *promising career* ahead.
4 A She has a *demanding job*.
   B She has a *high-powered job*.
5 A I was *promoted* to this job.
   B I was *headhunted* for this job.

3 What job would you *not* want to do however high the salary was? Tell other students and give your reasons.

premium plus 56

exam reviser p17 | 14.1

Unit 14

FCE close-up | Listening Sentence completion (Paper 4, part 2)

Exam information

In this part of the exam, you hear a monologue or conversation between interacting speakers, e.g. an interview. It will last about three minutes. You complete sentences with information you hear on the recording. The missing information will be one to three words or numbers and will come from the recording. You listen to the recording twice.

Approach

1 Read the rubric to the task and the sentences that follow. Try to predict what kind of information is missing from each sentence.

2 As you listen the first time, complete as many of the gaps as you can. Remember that you will hear the words you need in the recording. Use the exact words or numbers you hear, don't change them.

3 If you miss the words for one gap, don't worry, just move on to the next one.

4 When you listen the second time, check the answers you put the first time and try to complete any gaps that remain.

5 Read through all the completed sentences. Check they make sense and are grammatical and that the gaps are completed with one to three words or numbers. Remember you cannot lose marks for an incorrect answer.

6 Pay attention to spelling. Remember that small spelling mistakes may be accepted by the examiners if the meaning is clear. However, if a word has been spelt out letter by letter in the recording (e.g. someone's name), it must be spelt correctly in your answer.

Practice task

R.69 ▶ You will hear part of a radio programme about an unusual job. For questions **1–10**, complete the sentences.

AN UNUSUAL JOB

Diego's parents worked as [_____ **1**] in the circus.

Diego was only [_____ **2**] when he began to train in the circus.

The speed of flight of a 'human cannonball' can be as much as [_____ **3**]

He says the feeling of flying is similar to [_____ **4**]

It is very important to [_____ **5**] to make sure that things don't go wrong.

Marnie Dock says you have to finish the flight on your [_____ **6**]

They test the cannon a number of times with a [_____ **7**] of Diego.

One of the main disadvantages of having a career as a human cannonball is the [_____ **8**] .

As a result of his job in the circus, Diego has been offered [_____ **9**] such as working in a film.

His daily routine involves him spending at least [_____ **10**] hours in the gym.

Go to www.iTests.com or your CD-ROM for interactive exam practice

Grammar | passives

1 Discuss these questions with other students.
- How would you feel about being fired out of a cannon?
- What talents/skills are needed to be a 'human cannonball'?

2 Look at these sentences. What do the parts in *italics* have in common?
1 Diego, 'the human cannonball', *is fired* from a four-metre gun and travels through the air at speeds of up to 60 mph.
2 He says that he *has* always *been* well *looked after* by the circus.
3 Last year he *was offered* a part in a Hollywood movie.

3 Work with other students and discuss which of these do you think are common reasons why we use the passive.

1 We are not interested in who or what did the action.
2 We are writing a formal letter.
3 We want to keep a piece of new information until the end of a sentence.
4 We are describing a process.

• • see grammar reference: page 188 • •

Grammar note | the passive with *make, let, allow*

Which of these sentences are grammatically possible?

1 A His boss made him finish the report before he went home.
   B He was made finish the report before he went home.
   C He was made to finish the report before he went home.
2 A She let him have the day off work.
   B He was let to have the day off work.
   C He was allowed to have the day off work.

---

4 Complete the text with the verbs in brackets in the correct tense. Use the active or passive as appropriate.

| OME | Articles | Story of the Week | Weather |

tices

Visit

nu

tures

HIGH FLYER!

She (make) _____*makes*_____[1] swinging on a trapeze look far too easy, but acrobat Corinne Pierre is well aware of the dangers. 'I (have) _____[2] no serious injuries during my career so far, but I know it could happen at any time.' This is very obvious when you see her dangling from a ten metre rope swing, waiting to (catch) _____[3] by another acrobat. As she says, 'Safety standards need to (establish) _____[4], but without taking away the excitement.'

Corinne (join) _____[5] the circus in 1985 at the tender age of ten. While other children (read) _____[6] Harry Potter stories, she (teach) _____[7] how to do the Chinese balancing chair act. A couple of years later she (see) _____[8] by a scout for the world famous 'Cirque du Soleil' and invited to join them for a two-year tour. Since then she (never look back) _____[9].

Luckily for us she (recently settle) _____[10] in London and set up her own performing company. She now directs as well as performs what she calls 'physical theatre'. Money is an important issue for the company. As she points out, 'We (fund) _____[11] by government grants and these seem to be harder and harder to get.' Nevertheless, her company's ambitious productions (amazingly well receive) _____[12] by audiences and I, for one, have no doubts that we (see) _____[13] a lot more of this remarkable new talent in the future.

premium plus   57 ▶

Speaking

1 What jobs have you done in the past? How did you feel about them? Tell other students.

2 Look at the list of job features. Choose the four which are most important for you.

- short hours
- long holidays
- good salary
- mentally challenging
- pleasant physical surroundings
- opportunity to work with people
- good prospects for promotion
- security (pension, etc.)
- opportunity to travel
- responsibility/autonomy
- flexible hours
- opportunity to learn new things

3 Look at these comments. What is the purpose of each of the parts in *italics*?

> Flexible hours are crucial for me *as* I have young children and want to be able to see them as much as possible.

> I think 'mentally challenging' is important for me *because* otherwise I get bored and I hate that.

> I want a job where I have the opportunity to work with lots of people. *The main reason for this is* that I live on my own and I would like to get to know more people.

> Pleasant physical surroundings matter to me. *If* I feel comfortable where I'm working, *then* I can really give my best to the job.

4 Compare your four most important job features from Exercise 2 with another student. Explain why you chose them. Use the words/phrases from Exercise 3 where appropriate.

exam reviser   p22 | 8 ▶

5 Tell your partner about your present job or a future job you would like to do. Explain how well the job meets your priorities.

Grammar | ability

1 Look at these examples and answer the questions.

- *I hope **I'll be able to** do more work in films in the future.*
- *You must **be able to** fly straight and keep your body rigid if you want to be a human cannonball!*
- *I **can** use this new design program quite easily. I did a training course on it last month.*
- *I **could** speak Portuguese quite well when I was working in Brazil.*
- *I **managed to** communicate quite well on my business trip to Italy although I have never studied Italian properly.*
- *I **haven't been able to** attend many meetings recently.*

1 What is the past of *can* (when it refers to ability)?
2 When do we use *able to* rather than *can* or *could*?

2 Which of the alternatives in sentences **A** and **B** are correct? Why?

A He *managed to/could* get to the meeting on time in spite of the traffic.
B When Beatrice was younger, she *managed to/could* sing like an angel.

••• see grammar reference: page 188 •••

3 There are mistakes in some of these sentences. Find the mistakes and correct them.

1 How did he manage to finish writing the report so quickly?
2 I can't to speak any louder. I've got a sore throat.
3 I've been able to touch type since I was at college.
4 Apparently, a secretary got stuck in a lift this morning, but they were able to get her out quite quickly.
5 He could juggle quite well when he worked as a clown.
6 We've looked everywhere for the caretaker, but we don't be able to find him.
7 I was used to be able to work through the night if necessary.
8 We didn't managed to persuade Mikey to take the day off work.
9 The window in the conference room was stuck but we're able to open it in the end.
10 They must can lend us some money. They're very rich.

4 Complete the text with one word in each space.

ames was always something of an unusual child. To start with, he _____¹ walk by the time he was nine months old and then he was _____² to speak in proper sentences before he was a year and a half. There are other examples, but I particularly remember when he took us all by surprise shortly before his tenth birthday when he _____³ to memorise every capital city for fun one weekend. He does have an incredible memory. For example, if you ask him what he was doing on a particular day a year ago, he _____⁴ tell you exactly where he was, who he was with and what they were doing. James left university last year and unfortunately he hasn't _____⁵ able to find a job that really suits him yet. We really hope he'll _____⁶ able to put his talents to good use. He's a very special person.

5 Tell another student about something you:

- could do well as a child that you can't do now.
- have managed to do recently which you are really pleased about.
- can do quite well but not as well as you would like.
- hope you'll be able to do in the future.

Reading

1 Work with other students. Discuss these questions about writing a job application letter in English.

1 What style should the letter be written in?
2 How long should it be?
3 About how many paragraphs should there be?
4 What should go in each paragraph?
5 What should you do once you have written your letter?

2 Read this text and check your ideas from Exercise 1.

School leavers' handbook

✔ *Get it Write*

Never underestimate the __C__ [0] of the covering letter that you send for a job application. It is your ____[1] to sell yourself to the employer and to get the opportunity of an interview for the ____[2]. There is no strict formula for an application letter as different jobs may require different approaches. Employers can ____[3] standardised letters, so you must tailor every letter to be uniquely relevant to each job you apply for. You will need to make sure that the letter is essentially formal in style but also friendly and that you pay ____[4] to your spelling, punctuation and grammar. Many application letters are far too long. Try to keep to one side of A4 paper and no more than three to four paragraphs, otherwise you will lose the interest ____[5] the person reading it!

The first paragraph of the application letter is the most important. It ____[6] the tone and focus. It is a good idea to begin by addressing the letter to a ____[7] person if you can get hold of this information. This paragraph should be brief and to the point, indicating which job you are applying for as well as the ____[8] of your information and an explanation as to why you have applied for this job.

In the ____[9] parts of the letter, present your work experience, education, training – whatever makes the connection between you and the job you are seeking. Highlight why you are right ____[10] the job and list any relevant achievements. Be positive and confident and focus more on the future than the past.

In the final paragraph you should indicate how the prospective employer can get in ____[11] with you and when are the best times for an interview. It is important to end the letter strongly and on a positive note. Once you have written your letter, check it several times for any mistakes you may have made and check all the information you have provided them with is ____[12].

12

3 Read the text again and decide which answer A, B, C or D best fits each gap.

0 *A status* *B influence* *C importance* *D grandeur*

1	A luck	B chance	C fortune	D gamble
2	A position	B place	C spot	D site
3	A watch	B notice	C observe	D spot
4	A regard	B thought	C attention	D concentration
5	A by	B from	C with	D of
6	A sets	B starts	C presents	D shows
7	A unique	B special	C particular	D peculiar
8	A cause	B source	C root	D base
9	A majority	B chief	C main	D prime
10	A for	B with	C to	D on
11	A meet	B connect	C touch	D hold
12	A accurate	B legitimate	C authentic	D faithful

4 Is there any advice in the text which is new for you? Discuss with other students.

Writing | letter of application

1 Read the advert and this letter of application. Do you think it is a good letter? Does it have any problems? If so, what are they? (Refer to the Writing Reference page 200 if necessary.)

English-speaking Tour Guide Wanted

Our client is an English family with two young children who would like to spend two weeks travelling around the country, visiting all the most important tourist sites.

The successful applicant for this position will spend two weeks accompanying the family, ensuring they have a comfortable and informative trip.

You will have a good level of English and a good knowledge of the major tourist sites.

There is very generous remuneration for this position and all (first-class) travel and living expenses will be paid.

Please apply in writing to: Marsha Thorpe, LuxHolidays, 15 Cavendish Square, London W1 3PN.

Dear Ms thorpe i am writing to apply for the position you advertised in 'english Language Weekly' on 14th June

I am twenty-one years old and in the third year of a degree in tourism Im also studying English as a subsidiary subject. I have a good knowledge of all the major Tourist sites and can communicate well in English Last summer I worked as a tour guide for Thomas Holidays in addition I have two younger brothers and have always enjoyed being with and looking after children I am available during the months of july and august and would very much value the opportunity to work with this English family

I can be contacted at the above address or by phone on 07941 127123 if you have any further questions please don't hesitate to call me. I look forward to hearing from you.

yours sincerely,

(Silvia Nero)

2 Work in pairs. Read the section on punctuation in the Writing Reference page 205. Discuss how you could improve the letter in Exercise 1.

premium plus 58

3 You are going to reply to this advert with a partner. Decide how many paragraphs you will have. Make notes of what you will put in each paragraph.

Get Away From It All!

We have a few limited places for volunteers to join our round-the-world sailing expedition, which will carry out scientific research in various remote islands and other parts of the world. You can be part of this unforgettable experience for three months. No experience of working on boats is necessary, but it is important that you are flexible, hard-working and can be an enthusiastic member of a team. Food and accommodation provided.

Apply to Voyage International, PO Box 294, Croydon, Surrey.

4 Write your letter in 120–180 words. Pay careful attention to your punctuation.

premium plus 59

Listening

1 Have you ever had a formal interview, e.g. for a job, course, etc.? If so, what was it like? How did you feel? Discuss with other students.

2 R.70 ▶ Listen to an extract from a radio programme. Which of these do they talk about?
1 The increasing number of candidates for jobs
2 Typical modern-day salaries
3 How to respond to strange interview tasks
4 The increasing importance of qualifications
5 Strange experiences of interviewers

3 R.70 ▶ Listen again and answer these questions.
1 What two factors mean that applying for and getting jobs is harder now than previously?
2 What are companies doing these days to try to identify the best people for jobs?
3 What kind of job was Peter being interviewed for?
4 Why might interviewers ask strange questions?
5 How does Matt think candidates should react to this kind of questioning?
6 How were these things significant in four unusual job interviews that are mentioned?

- a Polaroid camera
- a therapist
- an iPod
- a shoe

4 Discuss these questions with other students.

- How do you think you would react if you were asked in an interview to stand in the corner of the room for one minute and describe the most embarrassing moment of your life, then tell a joke, then sing a song and finally, cluck around the room like a chicken.?
- How useful do you think an interview activity like this is?
- Can you remember a very embarrassing moment from the past? What happened?

Vocabulary | phrasal verbs (work)

1 R.71 ▶ Listen to a conversation between two work colleagues. What are they both worried about?

2 Look at the audioscript on page 167. Match the phrasal verbs in *italics* to these meanings.

1	depend on	6	take control
2	reduce (x 2)	7	employ
3	arrive	8	expand
4	postpone	9	arrange
5	fire (for economic reasons)		

3 Complete these sentences with the correct forms of the phrasal verbs in Exercise 2.

1 The government needs to _____ _____ the level of inflation urgently.

2 We have three candidates for the new job _____ _____ to see you this afternoon.

3 We've decided to _____ _____ our usual Tuesday staff meeting until Friday because so many people are off sick.

4 Steve finally _____ _____ nearly twenty minutes after the presentation had started.

5 We really must _____ _____ on travel expenses. From now on, all junior managers must fly economy class.

6 Our local big supermarket has _____ _____ into selling designer jeans and t-shirts.

7 Why does she want to leave? We only _____ her _____ in March.

8 Who do you think will _____ _____ as manager when Sue goes on maternity leave?

9 You know you can always _____ _____ Jamie in a crisis.

10 Apparently, due to falling demand EngCom have _____ _____ another 300 workers.

exam reviser p17 | 14.2

4 Work in pairs. Make a note of the ten phrasal verbs from the conversation in Exercise 1. Practise the same conversation with your partner by referring to the list of phrasal verbs to help you remember.

Speaking

1 R.72 ▶ Listen to a student comparing these two pictures. Which of these does she *not* do?

1 talk about similarities between the two pictures
2 talk about differences between the two pictures
3 give a personal reaction to the pictures
4 use a good range of vocabulary including linking expressions
5 use a variety of grammatical structures
6 keep talking

2 You are going to compare two pictures. Work in pairs, pair A and pair B. Pair A look at the pictures on page 169. Pair B look at the pictures on page 170. First make a note of any key vocabulary/ expressions from Exercise 1 you would like to use.

exam reviser p20 | 5

3 Work in A/B pairs. Take turns to compare your pictures. Then tell your partner how you felt when you did the task. Refer to the five points in Exercise 1.

FCE close-up | Reading Multiple choice (Paper 1, part 1)

Exam information

In this part of the exam, you read a text and then answer eight multiple-choice (**A, B, C** or **D**) questions. These questions may test your understanding of specific parts of the text, words and phrases in the text, the text as a whole, e.g. the attitude of the writer, the purpose of the text.

Approach

1 Read the rubric to the task. It will tell you where the text comes from.

2 Look through the whole text quite quickly to get a general idea of what it is about.

3 Look at each question but *not* the options (**A, B, C, D**). <u>Underline</u> the important words. Then, mark the part of the text each question refers to.

4 Now read the text carefully. When you come to a part you have marked, read through the relevant question and the options (**A, B, C, D**). Choose the option that best matches what the text says. Make sure you read *all* the options before you make a decision.

5 The last question may test your understanding of the text as a whole, so it may be appropriate to read the complete text from beginning to end, one more time.

Practice task

You are going to read an extract from a novel. For questions **1–8**, choose the answer (**A, B, C** or **D**) which you think fits best according to the text.

Animal Farm

Mr Jones, of the Manor Farm, had locked the hen-houses for the night and made his way up to bed, where Mrs Jones was already snoring.

As soon as the light in the bedroom went out there was a stirring and a fluttering all through the farm buildings. Word had gone round during the day that old Major, the prize boar, had had a strange dream on the previous night and wished
line 5 to communicate it to the other animals. It had been agreed that they should all meet in the big barn as soon as Mr Jones was safely out of the way.

At one end of the big barn, on a sort of raised platform, Major was already settled on his bed of straw, under a lantern which hung from a beam. He was twelve years old and had lately grown rather stout but he was still a majestic-looking pig, with a wise and benevolent appearance.

line 10 Before long the other animals began to arrive and make themselves comfortable after their different fashions. When Major saw that they had all made themselves comfortable and were waiting attentively, he cleared his throat and began:

'Friends, you have heard already about the strange dream that I had last night. But I will come to the dream later. I have something else to say first. I do not think that I shall be with you for many months longer, and so I feel I must pass on to you such wisdom as I have acquired. **This** is my duty.

line 15 Now, what is the nature of this life of ours? Let us face it: our lives are miserable, laborious and short. We are born, we are given just so much food as will keep the breath in our bodies, and those of us who are capable of it are forced to work to the last atom of our strength; and the very instant that our usefulness has come to an end we are slaughtered with hideous cruelty. No animal in England knows the meaning of happiness or leisure after he is a year old. No animal in England is free. The life of an animal is misery and slavery: that is the plain truth.

line 20 But is this simply part of the order of nature? Is it because this land of ours is so poor that it cannot afford a decent life to those who dwell upon it? No, a thousand times no! The soil of England is fertile, its climate is good, it is capable of affording food in abundance to an enormously greater number of animals than now inhabit it. This single farm of ours would support a dozen horses, twenty cows, hundreds of sheep – and all of them living in a comfort and dignity that are now almost beyond our imagining. Why then do we continue in this miserable condition? Because nearly the whole of the produce of our labour is
line 25 stolen from us by human beings. And there is the answer to all our problems. It is summed up in a single word – Man. Man is the only real enemy we have. Remove Man from the scene, and the root cause of hunger and overwork is abolished for ever.

Man is the only creature that consumes without producing. He does not give milk, he does not lay eggs, he is too weak to pull the plough, he cannot run fast enough to catch rabbits. Yet he is lord of all the animals. He sets them to work, he gives back to them the bare minimum that will prevent them from starving, and the rest he keeps for himself.

line 30 Only get rid of Man and the produce of our labour would be our own. Almost overnight we could become rich and free. What then must we do? Why, work night and day, body and soul for the overthrow of the human race! That is my message to you: Rebellion! I do not know when that Rebellion will come, it might be in a week or in a hundred years, but I know, as surely as I see this straw beneath my feet, that sooner or later justice will be done.

Go to www.iTests.com or your CD-ROM for interactive exam practice

1 The animals had planned to have a meeting when

   A   Mrs Jones was asleep.

   B   Mr Jones had gone to bed.

   C   Major switched a light off.

   D   someone gave a signal.

2 What does the writer say about Major's physical state?

   A   He had recently lost a lot of weight.

   B   He had become too old to stand up.

   C   He needed to lean against a piece of wood.

   D   He basically looked as good as in the past.

3 When did Major start speaking?

   A   as the animals were arriving

   B   when all the animals had arrived and were listening carefully

   C   while some animals were still talking

   D   even before some animals had managed to get comfortable

4 Major wanted to speak to the animals because

   A   he had an important message.

   B   he felt ill.

   C   they asked him to.

   D   he was told to in a dream.

5 *This* (line 14) refers to Major

   A   dying soon.

   B   becoming wise.

   C   informing the animals.

   D   looking after the animals.

6 Major says there are better conditions for animals who

   A   are less than one year old.

   B   are particularly strong.

   C   don't eat much.

   D   don't live in England.

7 According to the text, what is the reason for the terrible situation of animals?

   A   bad environmental conditions

   B   the laziness of animals

   C   the people who control them

   D   overcrowding on farms

8 What is the general tone of Major's speech?

   A   relaxed

   B   resigned

   C   despairing

   D   passionate

Speaking

1 You have just read an extract from *Animal Farm* by George Orwell. Discuss these questions.

- What do you think happens next in the book?
- Do you feel sympathy towards the animals or not?
- Read this comment. Then say what you think the 'significant underlying meaning' of the novel is.

> 'The most important thing about *Animal Farm* is that it is an *allegory*. An allegory, like a *fable*, is a story with two levels of meaning. An allegory is usually longer than a fable and it is read and enjoyed for its surface meaning as well as for its more significant underlying meaning.'

Writing | set book

In Paper 2, part 2 of the Cambridge FCE exam there is a question which asks you to write about one of two set books (there is one question about each book). You can be asked to write the answer in the form of an article, a letter, a report or an essay.

1 Look at these examples. What do you think are the advantages and disadvantages of answering this question in the exam? Discuss with other students.

1 *Animal Farm* by George Orwell

You have just read *Animal Farm* and it made a big impression on you. Write a **letter** to a friend describing why you think it is an important book for people to read.

2 *Great Expectations* by Charles Dickens

There are many interesting and colourful characters in *Great Expectations*. Write an **essay** saying which character you found most interesting and why.

3 *The Phantom of the Opera* by Gaston Leroux

Jealousy and envy are central themes of *The Phantom of the Opera*. Write an **essay** explaining the consequences of such feelings in the story.

2 You are going to write an essay about a book you have read. First, prepare your writing by following these instructions.

1 Choose a book you have read that you want to write about.

2 Choose a question to answer about it. This could be:

- one of the three questions in Exercise 1 above;
- a question your teacher gives you;
- a question you have found on an old exam paper;

3 Decide how many paragraphs your answer will have.

4 Make notes of what you will write in each paragraph.

3 Write your essay in 120–180 words. Remember to use your paragraph plan and to answer the question directly and completely.

Grammar

1 Rewrite this text with correct punctuation.

the leaning tower of pisa in italy was begun in 1174 as a bell tower for the nearby cathedral the foundations were laid in sand and only three of the eight storeys were finished before it began to lean the plans were altered to compensate for the problem and the building was eventually completed in 1350 the 54.5 m tower continued to lean a little more each century until 1990 when engineers did work to help correct the problem the work cost $25m but the tower should now survive for another 200 years at least

2 There are mistakes in six of these sentences. Find the mistakes and correct them.

1 I think my bike has been stole.
2 Your new computer will been sent as soon as possible.
3 Have you any idea when this picture was taken?
4 The gym can be used by any of our members.
5 I'm afraid this flat has already being sold.
6 Eddie, our dog, needs be taken for a good walk at least once a day.
7 All personnel are requested to make their way towards the nearest fire exit.
8 The hole in the road was being repair when I left home this morning.
9 My boss has said that I'm going to be given a company car from the start of next year.
10 When I finally got to the meeting, everyone had already told about the disastrous sales figures.

3 Complete these sentences with one word connected with ability.

1 I'd like to _____ able to swim.
2 Did you manage _____ change Derek's mind?
3 They haven't _____ able to decide where they want to get married.
4 Surely you _____ ask your boss for a few hours off on Friday?
5 You must be _____ to work evening shifts in this job.
6 My brother and I _____ both play tennis quite well in our teens.
7 I hope you _____ be able to come to the party on Saturday.
8 I'm afraid they didn't _____ to finish painting the kitchen.

Vocabulary

4 Match the sentence halves 1–10 with A–J to make complete sentences.

1 When you didn't turn up on Friday,
2 You can't put off
3 His daughter will probably take over
4 We want to avoid laying off
5 Better farming methods have brought down
6 We're thinking of branching out
7 It might be a good idea to take on
8 The government is going to cut back
9 We've lined up some
10 You can always count on

A any of our permanent members of staff.
B into new markets in Asia.
C making your decision again.
D the price of food.
E fantastic bands for Saturday night.
F its funding for adult education colleges.
G we tried to call you.
H the business when he retires.
I Marta to have an interesting idea.
J another marketing assistant.

5 Match the definitions 1–8 to the words/phrases in the box.

> headhunt   demanding (job)   maternity leave
> promising (career)   promote   be made redundant
> high-powered   get the sack

1 time that a mother is allowed to spend away from work when she has a baby
2 when someone is dismissed from their job
3 find someone with special skills and experience needed for a particular job and persuade them to leave their present job
4 give someone a more responsible, higher paid job in a company
5 important or influential
6 showing signs of being successful or good in the future
7 needing a lot of ability, effort or skill
8 when someone has to leave their job because there is not enough work

State of mind

strange dream

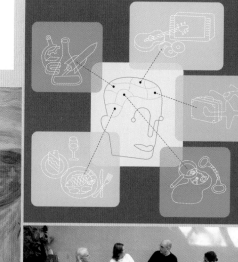

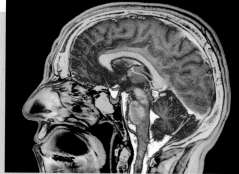

mental health

on my mind

Unit 15

Introduction

1 Look at the pictures. What does each one make you think about?

2 Check that you understand the words in the box. Which syllable has the main stress in each word? (Refer to a dictionary if necessary.)

> memory subconscious health depression feeling mind
> psychologist interpretation mood experiment analysis

3 Complete these sentences using words from the box in Exercise 2.
1 Blood samples were sent to the laboratory for _____.
2 He managed to recite the entire poem from _____.
3 I thought the director's _____ of *Hamlet* was very interesting.
4 Billy seems to have a lot on his _____ at the moment.
5 Why are you in such a bad _____? Has something happened?
6 I've decided to re-train and become a child _____.

4 Discuss with other students.
- Do you remember your dreams? What do you usually dream about?
- What kinds of things put you in a bad/good mood?
- Do you think you have a good memory or not? Why do you think this?

exam reviser p18 | 15.1

Grammar: hypothetical meaning; verb–subject agreement | Vocabulary: idioms with *mind* | Writing: an article

Unit 15

Reading

1 Discuss with other students.
- What kinds of things make people happy?
- Do you think people are happier now than in the past? Why/Why not?

2 You are going to read an article about happiness. Seven sentences have been removed from the article. Choose from the sentences A–H the one which fits each gap 1–7. There is one extra sentence which you do not need to use.

How to be happy

Happiness is hard to define. For some people it's about being in love or the birth of a child, for others, winning the lottery or being in touch with nature. **1** Positive psychology expert, Sheila Panchal, explains:

5 'Psychologists have identified three elements to happiness – having pleasures in life, being engaged and using your strengths on a regular basis, and experiencing a sense of meaning by feeling part of something greater than yourself.'

10 Happy people have stronger immune systems – when exposed to the flu virus, they are more able to resist it – and they recover from surgery faster. **2** That's the conclusion from an analysis of the attitudes of new nuns entering an American convent in 1932. Psychologists rated

15 each of them for the level of positive feeling expressed and found a correlation with how long each nun lived.

The relationship between money and happiness is complex. 'If you're below the breadline, then extra money makes a difference to your happiness,' says Panchal.

20 But after a certain level of income, extra money does not make you that much happier. **3** In one study, Harvard students were asked what they would prefer – a world where they got $50,000 a year and everyone else got $25,000, or one where their income was doubled to

25 $100,000, but others got more – $250,000. The majority preferred the first world, where they got less in absolute terms, but at least it was more than everyone else.

Studies on twins show a strong genetic component in happiness and depression. This is not just because twins

30 share the same environment – research on identical twins brought up apart shows the same. However, the genes involved in happiness are unknown and, as with all psychological attributes, it is likely that many different genes are responsible. **4** Low levels of serotonin are

35 linked to depression. Drugs like Prozac boost serotonin levels and so lift depression and improve mood. But even if you are born miserable, you can still learn to be happier by changing your outlook and attitude.

Relationships are one of the most important sources of our

40 happiness. Socioeconomic surveys in Germany suggest that both men and women become happier when they marry. Happiness increases as the marriage approaches, peaks in the first year and then decreases a little as people get used to their new status. **5** Children, as

45 you might expect, are a source of joy when they are born, but within two years, their parents' happiness tends to revert to its former level.

Happiness around the world is tracked by projects such as the World Database of Happiness. **6** This appears to

50 be true despite massive increases in the standard of living and quality of life. Dr Stevens identifies two major barriers to achieving happiness in the 21st century – the car and the media. Cars isolate you from the local community so that your neighbourhood and town centre more often feel

55 like threatening places rather than a positive resource. Television (and to a lesser extent print media) exposes people to violence, bad news and consumer pressures which create fear and discontent. TV watching is also passive and takes away time that could be used for much

60 more satisfying activities.

According to the US General Social Survey, the main sources of happiness are, in order of importance: family relationships, finances, work, social networks and health. Added to that are personal values and freedom. Based on

65 his long-standing research, Dr Stevens claims happiness comes from the body, relationships and learning to direct your thoughts in a positive way. **7** It means taking definite steps to improve your life. 'Take exercise and watch your diet, work at caring, loving relationships and

70 give them the time they need,' he says. 'Smile at strangers, make small gestures and, above all, list the good things you have to be grateful for. If you think like this, wellbeing and good feelings will follow.'

3 Read the article again. In your own words, explain the significance of each of these phrases 1–7.

1 three elements (line 5)
2 immune systems (line 10)
3 below the breadline (line 18)
4 serotonin levels (line 34)
5 source of joy (line 45)
6 standard of living (line 50)
7 be grateful for (line 72)

4 Work in groups and discuss these questions.

1 Which part of the article did you find most interesting? Why?
2 Read the 'Happy Hints'. Which do you think are the three best pieces of advice? Why? Is there *one* which you would consider trying to follow? Could you add one more 'happy hint'?

A One key factor seems to be that we start to compare ourselves with others and this creates discontent.

B That doesn't just mean vaguely wishing that things in your life were different.

C However, it still remains at a higher level than in the single state.

D In scientific terms, happiness has different dimensions.

E This is something governments don't appear to be very concerned about.

F One group of genes that may be involved in positive mood are those dealing with the brain chemical serotonin.

G Happy people also tend to live longer.

H It seems that populations in Western countries, such as Britain, have not got any happier since 1950.

HAPPY HINTS – TIPS TO IMPROVE YOUR MOOD

1 Go nuts > Instead of eating sweets and crisps, snack on nuts, seeds, bananas and avocados – they all help to boost levels of serotonin, the brain's 'feel good' chemical.

2 Be optimistic > Learn to be an optimist. Look for temporary and specific explanations when things go wrong – 'I wasn't on top form', rather than 'I'm useless'. Take time to identify what you are really good at.

3 Get a pet > Consider getting a pet to look after. Choose an animal that suits your personality or lifestyle.

4 Socialise > Do something to connect you to the community – join an evening class, volunteer for a campaign or invite a neighbour in for coffee.

5 Keep dancing > See what happens if you cut your TV watching and newspaper reading in half. Replace with something more active, e.g. try a dance class, learn a new language, etc.

6 Smile > Be really daring – smile and say 'hello' to someone you don't know; even consider stopping for a chat.

7 Keep a diary > Keep a journal of the good things that happen – aim to list three to five items, however small, every day.

8 Go running > Twenty to thirty minutes exercise, outside if possible, three times a week will boost your mood.

9 Say thank you > Develop the habit of gratitude and learn the art of forgiveness – let go of the bad things that happened in the past. Live as much in the present as you can.

10 Happy talking > Take time to talk. Schedule an hour-long conversation with your partner or closest friend every week and guard the time jealously.

Vocabulary | mispronounced words

1 Look at the dictionary entry and discuss these questions with other students.

1 What is the correct pronunciation of *scientific*?
2 Which letter is not pronounced?
3 How many syllables does it have?
4 Which syllable has the main stress?

---

scientific /ˌsaɪənˈtɪfɪk◂/ *adj*
1 relating to science: *scientific discoveries* | *a **scientific experiment** | advances in **scientific research*
2 using an organised system: *we keep records, but we're not very scientfic about it*
—**scientifically** /-kli/ *adv*

LONGMAN
Exams
Dictionary
YOUR KEY TO EXAM SUCCESS

---

2 Look at these word families 1–5. What is:
A the correct part of speech of each word in the family?
B the position of main stress in each word?
C the correct pronunciation of each word?

1 science, scientist, scientific
2 psychology, psychologist, psychological
3 analyse, analysis, analytical, analytically
4 photograph, photographer, photographic, photography
5 economics, economist, economy, economical, economise

3 Look at the words in the box. Tick the ones you feel confident about pronouncing and put a cross next to the ones you don't feel confident about.

> secretary recipe comfortable cupboard cough
> receipt muscle interesting apostrophe scissors
> law chocolate comb dessert

4 Go through the list with another student. Compare how you think you pronounce each word.

5 R.73 ▶ Listen and check the correct pronunciation of each word in Exercise 3.

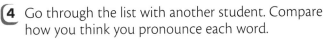
premium plus 60 ▶

---

6 Work with another student and take turns to read these sentences out loud. Pay special attention to the pronunciation of the words in *italics*.

1 Is it against the *law* to take a *comb* on a plane?
2 He wanted to know the *recipe* for the *chocolate* cake which they had for *dessert*.
3 It's *interesting* the way an *apostrophe* can change the meaning of a sentence.
4 Do you have a *receipt* for the *scissors* that you want to return?
5 The *secretary's* chair isn't very *comfortable*.
6 You can see his *muscles* in that *photograph*.
7 William can't decide whether to study *law*, *economics* or *psychology*.
8 My grandmother keeps the *cough* medicine in the top *cupboard*.

premium plus 61 ▶

Grammar | hypothetical meaning

1 Look at these statements. Who do you think is speaking? Why do you think they each say this? What is the context of the statement?

1 I wish I *lived* by the sea.
2 I wish I *could spend* more time with my family.
3 I wish I *had travelled* more when I was younger.
4 I wish you *wouldn't worry* so much.

2 R.74 ▶ Listen and check your ideas.

3 Discuss these questions with other students.

1 Look at the tenses of the verbs in *italics* in Exercise 1 sentences 1–3. What is surprising about them?
2 How is a person usually feeling when they say *I wish you wouldn't …*!

•• see grammar reference: page 188 ••

Grammar note | *wish + would(n't)*

Which of the following sentences is not possible? Why?

1 I wish they wouldn't play their music so loudly.
2 I wish I would lose weight.
3 I wish it would stop raining.

---

4 Read this extract from an email and complete each space with the correct form of the verb in brackets.

In your last message you asked me how everything was going. Well, to be honest, I really wish I (have) _____¹ a bit more money coming in every month. I'd really like to pay off some of my credit card debts and start renting a flat on my own. I also wish I (live) _____² a bit closer to my parents. It takes me nearly three hours to go and see them, which is quite hard especially if it's just for a day.

In terms of work, as you know, I've had a few problems getting a decent job recently. I suppose now I really wish I (do) _____³ a more practical degree at university. I mean I did enjoy psychology, but it's not very relevant to the jobs I've been applying for. The other thing I regret a little in terms of getting a good job is not making more effort with Spanish. You know my mum's Spanish and she tried to speak to me in Spanish at home when I was younger, but I never wanted to. In fact I really wish I (can speak) _____⁴ Spanish fluently now because it would be a big help in my job interviews!

Oh, yes, and while I'm doing all this wishing ... the only other thing I wish is about my boyfriend! I really wish he (not whistle) _____⁵. It's never in tune and it's very annoying!

5 Complete these sentences so that they are true for you. Tell another student about your wishes and explain why they are your wishes. Also, say if there is anything you can do to make your wishes come true.

- *I wish I ...* (+ past simple)
- *I wish I ...* (+ past perfect)
- *I wish I could ...*
- *I wish (name of someone you know) would/wouldn't ...*

6 The expressions in *italics* are also followed by past tense forms to show hypothetical meaning. Complete the second sentence so that it has a similar meaning to the first sentence. Decide if you need to add to or change the form of the words in the first sentence.

1 *If only* she hadn't left the meeting early.
  I wish …
2 *It's time* I joined a gym. I need to get fit.
  I should …
3 *I'd rather* you painted the bathroom first.
  I would prefer it …
4 *Suppose* you were offered the job. Would you accept it?
  Imagine …

• • **see grammar reference: page 188** • •

7 There are mistakes in some of these sentences. Find the mistakes and correct them.

1 I wish I can afford to buy a new car.
2 If only I'd listen to my dad!
3 She'd rather we helped her in the garden.
4 It's time you to found somewhere to live.
5 Suppose he asked you to marry him, what would you say?
6 She wishes she had never borrowed his car.
7 If only she knows how sorry we were.
8 I wish she wouldn't spend so much time with Terry.
9 It time we had a chat about your exam results.
10 Suppose someone asked you where you did get the money from.

premium plus 62 ▷

8 Discuss these questions with other students.

- If you were to give yourself one piece of advice for this week beginning: *It's time I …*, what would the advice be?
- Suppose you had the chance to meet one famous living person. Who would you choose and why?

Writing | article

1 Work in pairs. Make a list of the characteristics of a good article. How many different points can you think of?

An interesting title

2 Check your ideas on page 76 or Writing Reference page 202.

3 Read this task. <u>Underline</u> the important words/phrases.

Writing task

You see the following notice in an airline magazine.

> *Are young people in your country happier today than 50 years ago?*
>
> Write us an article giving your opinions. The best article will be published and the writer will receive £200.

Write your **article** for the magazine.

4 Read this answer to the task in Exercise 3. Look at the band descriptions (0–5) for writing in Writing Reference page 207 and decide which band you think the article should go in.

Happy young people

This is a very interesting question. It is something I have thought about a lot. I have also talked to many of my friends about this. They have many different opinions. I am going to present my points in order.

Young people have many more opportunities than in the past. They have more money, more chances to get a good education and more freedom to do what they want. There is also a lot of new technology for young people to enjoy. There are mobile phones and the Internet. These make lots of possibilities for communicating with friends, getting to know new people and learning about the world.

On the other hand, there are many pressures on young people now to get a good degree, to have a career, to earn lots of money, to look good and to be in a happy relationship. When things don't go well, you can think you are a failure.

5 What are the main strengths and weaknesses of the article in Exercise 4? Discuss with other students.

6 Complete these expressions for comparing and contrasting with the words in the box.

> comparison   contrast   opposed   unlike   compared

1 Young people today have much more freedom _____ with young people in the past.

2 There's quite a bit more pressure on young people now in _____ with a few years ago.

3 Children seem to spend much more time indoors using or playing with technology _____ when I was growing up. We were always outside, running around or playing with a ball.

4 In _____ to most of her friends, my daughter hates mobile phones.

5 Our teachers encourage us to have our own ideas as _____ to just learning other people's opinions off by heart.

exam reviser   p24 | 13

7 Write your answer to the task in Exercise 3. Try to improve on the areas of weakness you identified in the sample answer in Exercise 4. Use appropriate expressions for comparing and contrasting from Exercise 4.

Listening

1 Do you know any of the films in the posters? Do you know any of the actors? If so, tell other students what you know about them.

2 R.75 ▶ You are going to hear a radio interview with Sam Jones, a film critic, about recent films involving memory. For questions 1–7, choose the best answer A, B or C.

1 What does the main character (Joel) in *Eternal Sunshine of the Spotless Mind* find out one day?

A His girlfriend has been killed.

B His girlfriend has no memories of him.

C He can't remember anything about his girlfriend.

2 What does Joel do as a result?

A He persuades his girlfriend that she has made a mistake.

B He gets into a fight with someone.

C He has his memories of his girlfriend removed.

3 What does Sam Jones think of Jim Carrey's performance?

A He doesn't say.

B That it's very good.

C That it's not as good as Kate Winslet's.

4 What is Leonard Shelby's problem in *Memento*?

A He can't remember new things.

B He can't remember anything about his wife.

C He can't remember what happened when his wife was killed.

5 What does Sam Jones find most interesting about *Memento*?

A Guy Pearce's performance

B the way the story is told

C the action sequences

6 What was Samantha Caine in *The Long Kiss Goodnight* before she became a schoolteacher?

A a private detective

B a prison convict

C a government agent

7 Who is prepared to help Samantha Caine?

A Charly Baltimore

B Mitch Henessey

C Samuel L Jackson

3 Discuss your answers with other students. Give reasons for your choices.

4 Discuss with other students.

• Which of the three films do you think you would be most interested in seeing? Why?

• If you have seen any of the films, tell other students what you think of it/them.

• If you know any of the actors referred to, tell other students what you know about them and what you think of them.

Grammar | verb–subject agreement

1 Choose the correct alternative in these sentences. Both alternatives are possible in two sentences.

1 All of my choices *is/are* connected to the subject of 'memory'.

2 Hardly anyone *is/are* prepared to help her.

3 My family *is/are* very good at making plans.

4 None of these films *has/have* been a major success.

5 The police *has/have* asked for help from the public in finding a missing teenager.

6 Two years *is/are* a long time to be unemployed.

7 The news *is/are* much the same as it was last night.

8 Politics *was/were* my main subject at university.

9 These jeans *is/are* similar to my old ones.

10 Our local football team *need/needs* to practise more.

11 Scissors *is/are* not allowed on the plane.

12 The United States *is/are* the home of baseball.

•• see grammar reference: page 189 ••

2 Read this extract from an email message. Complete each gap with one word.

◉◉◉

I'm afraid my news _____¹ not very exciting at the moment – everything _____² much the same as usual. I'm working hard on all my courses – especially economics. _____³ is a really difficult subject but the staff _____⁴ been very helpful. One professor has been giving extra tutorials for anyone who _____⁵ questions. Even so, almost nobody I know _____⁶ they're going to pass the end-of-term exams!

   Did I tell you that our house was broken into? The police _____⁷ great and came round straight away but _____⁸ is not a lot they can do. Can you believe it my Gucci sunglasses _____⁹ taken? I was so upset. They cost me nearly £100! And £100 _____¹⁰ a lot of money to me at the moment!

---

3 Write five sentences which are meaningful for you, with words/phrases from the box.

> the news   politics   hardly anyone   jeans   my family
> the majority of   £5   one of my   everybody   the police

One of my sisters has just got married.

4 Listen to another student's sentences. Do any of them surprise you?

premium plus   **63** ▶

Vocabulary | idioms with *mind*

1 What do the phrases in *italics* mean? Discuss with other students.

1 Do you have something *on your mind*? You look worried.

2 It never *crossed my mind* that Arthur might be lying.

3 When I looked at the first exam question, my *mind* just *went blank*.

4 He found it difficult to *keep his mind* on what she was saying.

5 I meant to get my dad a present, but it completely *slipped my mind*.

6 She couldn't *make up her mind* whether to accept the job or not.

7 If it'll *put your mind at rest*, why don't you go and see a doctor?

8 I'd definitely be interested in buying your car, if you want to sell. Will you *keep it in mind*?

9 I was worried my dad would *change his mind* and say he wouldn't give me a lift to the airport.

10 'Patient' is not the word that *springs to mind* when you think of Bill.

2 Match the phrases in Exercise 1 to these meanings.

A to forget about something

B to continue paying attention to something

C to be unable to think of anything

D to decide

E to help someone to stop worrying

F to remember information when deciding to do something

G to think about something for a short time

H to change your decision, plan or opinion about something

I to think of something immediately

J to be worrying you

exam reviser p18 | 15.2

3 Choose the correct alternative in each sentence.

1 I'm afraid we don't have any jobs at the moment but we will certainly *keep you in mind/put your mind at rest* if anything comes up.

2 Have you *crossed your mind/made up your mind* where you're going to go on holiday?

3 I'm afraid the meeting completely *crossed my mind/slipped my mind*. Was anything important decided?

4 The interviewer asked me quite an easy question, but *my mind just went blank/it slipped my mind*.

5 I'll phone you as soon as we land in Costa Rica if that will *cross your mind/put your mind at rest*.

6 After the phone call with his girlfriend, he couldn't *keep his mind/change his mind* on his revision.

7 What's *on your mind/put your mind at rest*? You're very quiet!

8 I have no ideas for a present for Amy. Nothing *keeps it mind/springs to mind*.

4 Complete these sentences so that they are true for you.

1 Something I do to keep my mind on my work when I am studying is to …

2 I sometimes find it difficult to make up my mind when I …

3 The last time my mind just went blank was when …

4 Something which can occasionally slip my mind is …

5 Compare your sentences with another student.

FCE close-up | Speaking (Paper 5, part 2)

Exam information

In this part of the exam, you speak for one minute without interruption. You compare two colour photographs on the same topic and give a personal reaction to them. It is not necessary to describe the photographs in detail. You must pay attention while the other candidate is speaking as you will be asked to comment briefly when they have finished speaking.

Approach

1 Make sure you have revised the language of comparing photos (see Exam Reviser page 20).

2 Listen carefully to what the examiner asks you to do. If necessary, ask the examiner to repeat anything you don't understand, e.g. 'Would you mind saying that again, please?'

3 Don't just describe what you see in the photos. Do what the examiner has asked you to do.

4 Keep talking until the examiner tells you to stop. Don't worry if the examiner interrupts you while you are still talking – it does not mean you have done something wrong!

5 While the other candidate is speaking, look at their photos and listen carefully to what they say. Be ready to answer the examiner's question to you when they have finished speaking.

Go to www.iTests.com or your CD-ROM for interactive exam practice

Exam FAQs

1 Read the information about the exam on pages 29–30 to check that you have a good idea of the form of each part of the exam.

2 Now answer these questions.

First Certificate in English Quiz

1 How many papers are there in the FCE exam? What is each one called?

2 How many marks is each paper worth?

3 If you fail one of the papers, do you fail the whole exam?

4 How long does each paper last?

5 Are you allowed to use dictionaries in the exam?

6 Do you lose marks if you put down an incorrect answer?

7 In Paper 1 (Reading), how many parts are there?

8 In Paper 2 (Writing):

   A What different types of text might you be asked to write?

   B What happens if you write too many words?

   C What happens if you write too few words?

9 In Paper 3 (Use of English):

   A What are the four different parts?

   B In which part do you get two marks for each question rather than just one?

   C Is correct spelling essential?

   D If you give more than one answer but only one of your answers is correct, do you get a mark?

10 In Paper 4 (Listening):

   A How many times do you hear each text?

   B Will you hear any regional accents?

11 In Paper 5 (Speaking):

   A How many examiners will you have?

   B Is it OK to ask an examiner to repeat a question or instruction?

12 How long after the exam must you wait before you will hear your results?

13 When will you receive your certificate?

Practice task

R.76 ▶ Work in pairs (Candidate A and Candidate B). Decide who will take the long turn first. Listen to the recording and follow the instructions.

Which person seems most interested in what they are doing?

What are the different people trying to remember and why?

3 Find out exactly when you will take each of the five papers. Plan how much time you have between now and each paper and what you need to revise before each one. Plan a sensible revision schedule between now and then.

   exam reviser ▶ **p30**

4 Think about these questions:

  1 How are you going to use/refer to:

    • the Grammar Reference?

    • the Writing Reference?

    • the Exam Reviser?

    • the Workbook?

    • your vocabulary notebook?

    • old essays you have written?

  2 When are the best times of day for you to revise?

  3 What is best to study alone and when it could help to revise with other people?

  4 What motivates you to revise? For example, does it help to plan a 'reward' for yourself at the end of a study period, e.g. going out with friends, watching a new DVD, etc.?

Grammar

1 There are mistakes in five of these sentences. Find the mistakes and correct them.

1 The majority of our class was at the end-of-term party.
2 Two weeks wasn't a long enough holiday.
3 A number of local people has asked for better lighting in this street.
4 A rugby team are made up of fifteen players.
5 My company has given €100,000 to charity this year.
6 The police is sure that the thief must have been in the house before.
7 These jeans aren't very comfortable.
8 The statistics shows that people who live in the south live longer than those who live in the north.

2 Complete these sentences with the words in the box.

> had   rather   suppose   time   only   could
> would   wish

1 I wish I _____ shut all the windows before it started to rain.
2 I'd _____ you tidied up your room before you went out.
3 I wish I _____ develop my own photographs.
4 It's _____ you got a proper job.
5 They _____ they had never bought their house in the country.
6 _____ someone asked where you got the money, what would you say?
7 If _____ I hadn't invited so many people to my birthday party!
8 I wish Simon _____ be a bit more friendly to my sister.

3 Complete these sentences using the prompts.

1 This car / making / strange noises. / Time / we buy / new one.
2 I wish / go / university / instead / get / a job / straight after I left school.
3 Suppose you / have / chance / be part / a scientific expedition / the Amazonian rainforest, / you go?
4 Julian / rather / we get / something to eat / before / go / the cinema.
5 I wish / he / not do / his trumpet practice / so early / Sunday morning.
6 It's time / you get / new jacket. / This one / have holes / the elbows!

Vocabulary

4 Unscramble the letters in *italics* to make words.

1 Everyone was in a confident *odom* and they were sure that they would win.
2 I think that being in good *lhhaet* is much more important than being rich.
3 I've been *gneilef* quite anxious about my job recently.
4 Our conclusion is that further *sasaiyln* of the data is needed.
5 They carried out an *teeemnpxri* on a group of university students to test their theory.
6 He's been suffering from a kind of *nersdeoips* ever since he lost his job.
7 I don't know where it comes from but my therapist says I have a *ccssoobiuuns* fear of failure.
8 Do you know what qualifications you need in order to become a *ohcysigoltps*?

5 Put the words in the box into the correct columns according to the underlined sounds.

> ec<u>o</u>nomy   ph<u>o</u>tograph   s<u>e</u>cretary   c<u>o</u>mfortable
> c<u>ou</u>gh   m<u>u</u>scle   ap<u>o</u>strophe   c<u>u</u>pboard   l<u>aw</u>
> ch<u>o</u>colate   c<u>o</u>mb,   r<u>e</u>cipe

s<u>u</u>n	d<u>oo</u>r	<u>e</u>gg	h<u>o</u>t	n<u>o</u>

6 Rewrite the sentences using an idiom with the word *mind* to replace the words in *italics*.

1 I meant to go to the bank today but I *forgot about it*.
2 I wish Michael would *decide* – does he want to go out tonight or not?
3 I promise I'll be home by 11.00 p.m. if that *makes you feel less worried*.
4 Please try to *concentrate on* your homework. Your exams are coming soon.
5 If you need anyone to do overtime, I'd be grateful if you could *remember that I'm interested*.
6 What's *worrying you*? You can always talk to me about your problems.
7 It was awful. I recognised him but then I *couldn't remember anything* about him.
8 What's *the first thing you think of* when I say 'childhood'?

Progress Check 3 Units 11–15

1 Complete the sentences with the correct form of the verbs in brackets.

1 If you _____ (mix) yellow and blue, you _____ (get) green.

2 If I _____ (bring) more cash with me, I _____ (have) enough to lend you some now.

3 As long as you _____ (not mind) sleeping on the floor, you _____ (be) welcome to stay.

4 If only you _____ (tell) her how much you loved her. It's too late now.

5 Unless you _____ (start) being more punctual, we _____ (have) to reconsider your position.

6 I'd rather you _____ (not interrupt) me while I'm on the phone.

7 Suppose you _____ (be) the manager. What would you do?

8 I _____ (tell) you what she said provided you _____ (promise) not to tell anyone.

2 There is a mistake in *italics* in each of these sentences. Correct the mistakes.

1 Go and talk to her and put your mind at *peace*.

2 I tried to remember his name but my mind went completely *blind*.

3 It's important to keep your *recipe* if you want to bring something back to the shop.

4 I'm working long hours and getting paid a lot of *overwork* as well as my regular salary.

5 They want someone who's good with figures and Diana *screams* to mind.

6 I don't like borrowing money and I've never been *with* debt in my life.

7 It is against the *legal* to use a mobile phone while driving.

8 The company didn't need him anyone more and he was made *refund* after twenty-five years.

9 You must take *over* insurance before you travel in case something happens.

10 I'd like to be a psychologist and work with people with *mind* health problems.

3 Complete the gaps using the correct form of the verbs in brackets.

Have you read these Agatha Christie novels?

Dead Man's Folly

Sir George and Lady Stubbs fancy _____[1] (do) something different for the village fête and eventually decide _____[2] (stage) a 'mock murder mystery'. The well-known crime writer, Ariadne Oliver, agrees _____[3] (organise) the murder hunt with the help of Hercule Poirot. But it seems that something weird is about to happen …

Dumb Witness

Emily's fall on the stairs seems _____[4] (be) an accident. She remembers _____[5] (trip) on a ball belonging to her dog. But the more she thinks about it, the more she feels that one of her relatives is trying _____[6] (kill) her. She writes to Hercule Poirot about her suspicions but mysteriously, by the time he receives the letter, Emily is already dead …

Black Coffee

A famous physicist, Sir Claud Amory, tells Poirot that he fears someone in his household is attempting _____[7] (steal) his latest discovery, a formula critical to England's defence. Poirot rushes to Amory's house and tries _____[8] (stop) the thief. He fails _____[9] (achieve) his mission, however, as Amory has died, his formula is missing and anyone could have been responsible …

4 Complete the second sentence so that it has a similar meaning to the first sentence, using the word given. Do not change the word given. You must use between two and five words, including the word given.

'Why don't we buy her a CD?' Jules said.

suggested

Jules *suggested buying her* a CD.

1 It's a pity I didn't know you were going to be here.
   wish
   I _____ you were going to be here.

2 Alex got the sack because he was always late.
   not
   If Alex _____, he wouldn't have got the sack.

3 She said she would never tell anyone else our secret.
   promised
   She _____ anyone else our secret.

4 'Do you like horror films?' she asked me.
   if
   She _____ horror films.

5 I didn't ask David because I wasn't able to contact him.
   managed
   If _____ David, I would have asked him.

6 He deceived us by all the lies he told us.
   taken
   We _____ by all the lies he told us.

7 'You stole my bicycle,' he said to me.
   accused
   He _____ his bicycle.

8 She works such long hours and I really don't like it.
   not
   I wish _____ such long hours.

5 Read the text and decide which answer A, B, C or D best fits each gap.

A survey carried out last year by a recruitment agency investigated the influence of the small screen on our big decisions. These days, it seems, more and more students say that their choice of job was _____¹ by a TV show. 62% of eighteen to twenty-four-year-olds said that *CSI* and other crime programmes made forensics look so _____² that they would consider it as a _____³.

An obsession with the CSI series led Emma Wade, twenty-two, to study forensic science at university. She explains, 'It was something that had never _____⁴ my mind before seeing that show. But I found I could identify with the characters – I wanted to be one of them. I wanted to _____⁵ in investigations and help _____⁶ the right people for crimes they have _____⁷. At first, I wanted to go for a _____⁸-powered job in the FBI, but my teachers _____⁹ me to think about forensic science.'

Engineering organisations, worried about low numbers of young people _____¹⁰ to train as engineers, are _____¹¹ about using the TV to address this shortfall. They are going so far as to _____¹² scriptwriters a £35,000 prize if they create a positive engineering character for TV.

	A	B	C	D
1	excited	inspired	elated	interested
2	enthusiastic	thrilled	puzzling	exciting
3	career	promotion	living	work
4	changed	crossed	slipped	made
5	turn out	work out	make sense	take part
6	punish	permit	forbid	let
7	done	made	punished	committed
8	high	fast	quick	strong
9	insisted	encouraged	promised	warned
10	studying	advising	applying	graduating
11	enthusiastic	staggered	exhilarated	overwhelmed
12	encourage	offer	blame	congratulate

6 Complete the text with one word in each gap.

Oxfam is a charity whose main aims are to achieve change and save lives. _____¹ provides help in emergencies as well as setting up longer-term development projects. Cecil Jackson-Cole, _____² was a London businessman in the 1940s, was one of the first pioneers of Oxfam and led the charity for many years. After World War II, Oxfam _____³ involved in helping people to rebuild their lives, and food parcels and clothing _____⁴ sent to many parts of Europe.

In 1951, Howard Leslie Kirkley _____⁵ appointed. By insisting _____⁶ a rapid response to emergencies and by his own presence in disaster situations, he _____⁷ to bring Oxfam to the attention of a wider audience than before. The 1960s brought even bigger changes and Oxfam's income trebled _____⁸ the decade. The charity's success depends _____⁹ public donations and it now raises millions of pounds every year.

7 Use the word given in capitals at the end of some of the lines in this text to form a word that fits in the gap *in the same line*.

How to make small talk	
It's time to stop pretending to be (0) *invisible* at parties and start mastering	VISIBLE
the art of small talk. Small talk can be a big challenge, but a little (1) _____ is all	PREPARE
you need. You may know how to nod and smile, but you need to talk, too – it's	
(2) _____ to stay completely silent. So,	POLITE
make the (3) _____ not to be shy any	DECIDE
more and just follow the tips below.	

Tips:
1 Practice. Talk to all kinds of people; those similar to you, but also people (4) _____ yourself, from older people to teenagers to tourists. — LIKE

2 Keep a diary. Write down (5) _____ or funny stories you hear, beautiful things you see, quotes you like and interesting (6) _____ you have with people. — USUAL / CONVERSE

3 Give yourself some (7) _____. Talk to yourself in the mirror and retell stories you've heard. Make a random list of topics and see what you have to say on the subjects. Baseball, Russia, butter, hip-hop, shoes … the more (8) _____ the better. — ENCOURAGE / VARY

4 Read everything, however (9) _____ it might seem at the time: cookbooks, newspapers, magazines, reviews, signs and catalogues. Everything is a source of (10) _____ that can be discussed. — RELEVANT / INFORM

Remember, the more you know, the more you know you can talk about!

8 Complete the sentences with the correct particle.

1 He was very lucky to be let _____ with just a fine for speeding.

2 I've had my house broken _____ three times in the last five years.

3 The director is ill so the meeting has been put _____ until next week.

4 She turned _____ five minutes after the film had started.

5 The restaurant is taking _____ extra staff for the busy summer period.

6 At first he denied taking the money but in the end he owned _____.

7 The company is cutting _____ on how much they spend on marketing.

8 Our local supermarket is being taken _____ by a huge multinational company.

Selected audioscripts

UNIT 01

R.03
a <u>block</u>buster
the dress <u>circle</u>
a <u>gig</u>
ce<u>ra</u>mics
<u>arch</u>itecture
<u>wat</u>ercolours
a <u>dance</u> floor
a <u>DJ</u>
<u>house</u> music

R.05
1 A: Do you go to concerts much?
   B: Well, not much … I mean, I'd like to but <u>I've always thought that</u> the tickets cost far too much. Don't you think so?
   A: Well, I know what you mean, but <u>from my point of view</u>, it's sometimes worth it. I have such a good time when I go that it's worth saving up and having an experience you won't forget.
2 C: I quite like going to concerts but <u>I think that</u> they're often disappointing …
   D: Really? <u>I don't think that</u> that's always the case. I've been to some great concerts …
   C: Well, in my experience, you often end up in a seat so far away you can't see anything. And also, they often don't play the songs you really want them to …
   D: That can be true, I suppose.
3 E: <u>I strongly believe that</u> people should pay to download music … instead of getting it free from the Internet… You know, singers must miss out on record sales … I just think it must be very difficult for musicians to make enough money these days.
   F: Well, I agree in a way, but <u>I have my doubts about</u> how it would work … It's almost impossible to stop people from finding a way to download things for free …
4 G: What did you think of the *Bjorn Again* concert last night?
   H: Well, I was really disappointed. I mean, they were quite good, but <u>as far as I'm concerned</u>, tribute bands like that just aren't the same as the real thing.
   G: True, they're not the same. But <u>in my opinion</u>, they're still worth seeing … I mean they give a very good performance, even though they don't look or sound exactly the same as the real Abba.

R.06
1 I've <u>always</u> thought that the tickets cost <u>far</u> too much.
2 I know what you <u>mean</u>, but from my point of view, it's worth it.
3 I <u>quite</u> like going to concerts but I think that they're often <u>disappointing</u>.
4 I <u>don't</u> think that that's <u>always</u> the case.
5 I <u>strongly</u> believe that people should <u>pay</u> to download music.
6 I agree in a <u>way</u>, but I have my doubts about <u>how</u> it would work.
7 As far as <u>I</u>'m concerned, tribute bands just aren't the <u>same</u> as the real thing.
8 In <u>my</u> opinion, they're <u>still</u> worth seeing.

R.07
Sandi Thom song
Oh, I wish I was a punk rocker with flowers in my hair
In '77 and '69 revolution was in the air

I was born too late and to a world that doesn't care
Oh I wish I was a punk rocker with flowers in my hair

When the head of state didn't play guitar,
Not everybody drove a car,
When music really mattered and when radio was king,
When accountants didn't have control
And the media couldn't buy your soul
And computers were still scary and we didn't know everything

Chorus

When record shops were on top
and vinyl was all that they stocked
and the super info highway was still drifting out in space
kids were wearing hand-me-downs,
and playing games meant kick arounds
and footballers still had long hair and dirt across their face

Chorus

I was born too late to a world that doesn't care
Oh I wish I was a punk rocker with flowers in my hair

R.08
1 A: I'm so tired … I just feel like chilling out in front of the TV tonight …
   B: Yes, I know what you mean … I'm exhausted too …
   A: I don't know what's on. Do you? I really fancy watching one of those animal <u>documentaries</u> … You know the ones … lions in Africa or undersea creatures … I love that kind of thing …
   B: Umm … well, there's something called *The Wild World* on at 8.30 … Shall we see what that's about?
   A: Yes, good idea … Sounds perfect.
2 A: I'm just off to the library … Do you want to come with me?
   B: Oh yes, … good idea. Actually I need to get a couple of books out to take on holiday with me.
   A: Yes, that's why I'm going … It's a really good chance to catch up with some reading, isn't it? What kind of books do you like?
   B: Umm … well, the last one I got out was a <u>biography</u> of David Beckham – it was really good. I'm not that keen on fiction but I really like reading about the lives of famous people …
3 A: I'm thinking of buying a new computer …
   B: Oh really? I thought you had one …
   A: Yes, I have got one … well, I've got two … I've got the laptop which I use for work and the one at home. But the thing is, the laptop is fine but the one at home is quite old and a bit slow now …
   B: What do you use the one at home for?
   A: Almost the only thing I use it for is <u>playing games</u> … and it's really annoying because there are loads of games I can't get to work on it at the moment …
4 A: Oh dear … I'm completely rushed off my feet today … I've got so much to do and now I've invited some friends round for dinner and I haven't even been shopping …
   B: What are you going to make for them?
   A: Well, that's it … I'm not sure yet … and I think at least one of them is a vegetarian so I've got to be careful to get something she can eat …
   B: When was the last time you had friends round for dinner?
   A: Oh, not for ages and ages … it's not something I do much at all … We <u>usually go out to restaurants</u> or get a take away or something …

Selected audioscripts

UNIT 02

R.12

A: So … what do you think about this one about who your best friends are?

B: Hmmm … I'm not quite sure what I think about that …

C: Yeah … it depends really … doesn't it?

B: I mean I have one or two friends who I've known since primary school …

A: Wow!

B: … we don't see each other all that often but we do know each other incredibly well. But on the other hand I've made one or two friends in the last year who I talk to a lot and we're very close. So … which are my 'best friends' … it's hard to say.

C: And what about this one about not liking to spend time by yourself?

B: Oh, that's never been the case for me. I've always enjoyed having time just for me … What about you?

A: Well, funnily enough, that used to be true for me but it isn't any more.

B: How come?

A: I don't know really … but I used to get really anxious if I wasn't going out with friends in the evening … or doing something with people … but now I can quite happily mess around at home at the weekend or whenever … just reading or doing stuff on the computer … not seeing anyone … and it's not a problem …

UNIT 03

R.18

Both pictures are connected to the theme of houses or where people live. In both pictures, you can see people in their living rooms. I think they're in their living rooms. But they are very different – the styles are completely different. In this picture, the style they have chosen is very ornate, whereas in this one, it is a modern, minimal look. The room in the first picture is quite dark and crowded with a lot of furniture and decorations. In contrast, the room in the second picture is very airy and light.

As far as I can tell, the people in the first picture live there and have chosen that style themselves. I'm not sure if the people in the second picture live there or not. It could be a hotel, I suppose. Personally, I much prefer the more modern kind of style to this one. I'd rather live in a place that was quite empty than somewhere like that. I'm not very keen on that kind of style. I think it would feel too crowded and you would get tired of it very quickly.

R.19

1 syllable: quaint
2 syllables: sprawling; bustling; leafy
3 syllables: supportive; upmarket; historic; comfortable; fashionable
4 syllables: isolated; overcrowded; inner-city

UNIT 04

R.25

1 I never used to do much sport.
2 I used to love finding a good book.
3 We would all get to school really early.
4 I didn't have time for any sport. It took ages to get used to that.
5 I used to be pretty good in my teens.

6 I'm not as fit as I was … I can't really get used to that.
7 When I was younger we would always be outside.
8 I'm used to getting up an hour or so before I go to work.

R.26

1 What sports did you use to play?
2 What other things did you use to do in your free time?
3 How would you typically spend your weekends?
4 When was the last time you had a big change in your life?
5 Which new things are you used to?
6 Which new things are you getting used to?

UNIT 06

R.31

1 They've been planning the party for weeks.
2 I've been writing the invitations and I posted them today.
3 She's been looking for a hat to wear, but she hasn't found one yet.

UNIT 07

R.36

As you know, at the moment,
I'm working in the marketing department
of a small advertising firm.
I have some exams in June
and then I'll probably take a few months off
and go travelling.
I'm not sure what I'll do after that.
If I enjoy it, I might do a course
to learn to be an English teacher.
The one thing I'm sure about
is that I won't still be working in an office
this time next year!

UNIT 08

R.38

A 1 crunchy, tough, well-done, succulent
  2 cooker, cook
  3 chop
  4 roast
B 1 bake, tasty, grate
  2 stir
  3 raw
  4 rare
C 1 fry, slice, spicy
  2 grill, whisk, bitter, mix
  3 juicy
  4 boil

R.42

1 The habit of chewing gum was first popular with the Ancient Greeks. They chewed mastic gum, a resin obtained from the mastic tree. Modern chewing gum, however, originated around the 1860s in America. A substance called chicle was found in the sapodilla trees of Mexico and made a smoother, more elastic gum than previously. William Wrigley, a flour factory owner, found a way to flavour it with mint and started making the first mass-

produced gum. Nowadays 90% of chewing gum is manufactured by Wrigley, and the basic process has changed little since manufacture began in 1892.

2   Sales of chewing gum are at record levels; last year in the UK, £317 million was spent on gum. This figure has risen nearly 40% in the last five years, with the sugar-free brands now making up three-quarters of the total market. Consumer analysts say it's no longer considered just a sweet. It's become more relevant to today's consumer with people regarding it as a kind of two-in-one: a sweet fix and a breath-freshener at the same time. Stress relief is another factor, although not so many gum users admit to that one.

3   I've just heard the most incredible story about Britney Spears' chewing gum! Apparently, she's always spitting her chewing gum out onto the pavement and one day, someone saw her spit some out, picked up the piece of gum and decided to sell it online … you know, on eBay. Basically they sold her piece of chewed chewing gum by online auction! Nobody could guarantee it was real, of course, but lots of people bid for it – and in the end, it was sold for about $100. I can't believe anyone would want chewing gum that's been in someone else's mouth – whoever that person is!

4   An incredible three and half billion pieces of gum are disposed of in the UK every year. In London, there are 300,000 pieces of discarded chewing gum on the pavement in Oxford Street alone. Better enforcement of fines has helped to reduce the problem slightly, but it is almost impossible to catch people spitting out their gum. Some areas have installed special boards which people are invited to stick their used gum to. Meanwhile, biodegradable gum is being developed which in the end may well be the ultimate answer to the seemingly never-ending problem of chewing gum litter.

5   A man from north London has come up with a new idea for dealing with chewing gum on our pavements – not by removing it or cleaning it, but by painting on it. Forty-one-year-old Ben Wilson says he intends to paint gum all the way across London, from north to south. Using acrylic paint and varnish, and a little burner to dry it, he paints different things including animals, flowers and tiny landscapes. Many people stop and look at his work and most have praised him for trying to make beautiful what is, ultimately, just rubbish on our pavements.

UNIT 10

R.48

1   The first text message was sent in 1992.
2   Over 85% of teenagers in Europe own a mobile phone.
3   95% of all text messages are delivered within ten seconds.
4   The peak hours for texting are between 10.30 – 11 p.m.
5   On New Year's Day 2006, the highest daily total ever recorded was reached in the UK, when 165 million messages were sent.
6   The current speed record for typing a 160-character text message is held by Kimberly Yeo Sue Fern from Singapore. She typed: 'The razor-toothed piranhas of the genera Serrasalmus and Pygocentrus are the most ferocious freshwater fish in the world. In reality they seldom attack a human' in just in 43.2 seconds.

R.49

Oh brother I can't, I can't get through
I've been trying hard to reach you, cause I don't know what to do
Oh brother I can't believe it's true
I'm so scared about the future and I want to talk to you
Oh I want to talk to you

You can take a picture of something you see
In the future where will I be?
You can climb a ladder up to the sun
Or write a song nobody has sung
Or do something that's never been done

Are you lost or incomplete?
Do you feel like a puzzle, you can't find your missing piece?
Tell me how do you feel?
Well I feel like they're talking in a language I don't speak
And they're talking it to me

So you take a picture of something you see
In the future where will I be?
You can climb a ladder up to the sun
Or a write a song nobody has sung
Or do something that's never been done
Do something that's never been done

So you don't know where you're going, and you want to talk
And you feel like you're going where you've been before
You tell anyone who'll listen but you feel ignored
Nothing's really making any sense at all
Let's talk, let's talk
Let's talk, let's talk

R.50

1   A: I'm really nervous about my presentation later …
    B: Oh, don't worry – you'll be fine. Just remember, it's a big room so you'll need to speak loudly so that everyone can hear.

2   A: How's your new job going?
    B: Well, to be honest – I'm not really enjoying it. My boss spends his whole time talking to me like I'm a bit stupid … or like he's better than me.

3   A: What's the matter? You're looking really stressed out … what's been going on?
    B: Ohh! I've spent the whole morning on the phone trying to contact someone about fixing my TV. They just give you a machine … but never a real person to speak to … it's so frustrating!

4   A: Have you heard? Sylvia and Mark have just got engaged. They're getting married in June, I think.
    B: Oh really? Say congratulations to them from me when you see them, won't you?

5   A: He's such a good speaker, isn't he?
    B: Yes, what I like about him is that he communicates his point clearly but he's not boring … Actually, often he's quite funny …

6   A: How did the council meeting go today?
    B: Well, it was good to see so many people standing up and complaining about the new parking restrictions round here … I'm just not sure how much difference it will really make …

7   A: Have you ever had Spanish lessons?
    B: No, I just learnt it while I was living in Spain – obviously everyone around me was speaking Spanish, so I had to learn pretty quickly.

8   A: You know all that unpaid rent you told me about? Have you talked to your flatmate about it yet?
    B: No, I really must … I find it so hard to start talking about a subject like money …

Selected audioscripts

R.51

1 It's a big room so you'll need to speak up.
2 My boss spends his whole time talking down to me.
3 I've spent the whole morning on the phone trying to get through to someone.
4 Pass on my congratulations to them.
5 He gets his point across clearly.
6 It was good to see so many people speaking out about the new parking restrictions round here.
7 I just picked it up while I was living in Spain.
8 I find it so hard to bring up a subject like money.

R.53

1 A: Well, I'm not sure but I think the one about that woman is interesting because it would be interesting to hear about her life. I want to know about her and why she was living in a car. What do you think? Which one are you interested in?
   B: Well, I'd like to look at the news one actually, because I think that sounds interesting. Sometimes I hear something on the news and I want to give my opinion.
2 C: I can't understand why people write blogs. I think it's very strange for people to write about normal things and put it on the Internet for other people to read. And why do people read these blogs? It's strange. Do you agree?
   D: I suppose you're right. And also it's strange that people write things like this and they don't know who will read it. I certainly wouldn't write one.

UNIT 11

R.57

1 thousands
2 fifty per cent
3 sixteen megabytes
4 the thirty-first of May
5 a hundred pounds
6 seven
7 oh eight four five seven, four six four, five double three
8 eight a.m. to six thirty p.m.

R.58

1 A: What's your date of birth?
   B: It's 20.05.83.
2 A: What time did you get up today?
   B: At 7.15 a.m.
3 A: How much did your bag cost?
   B: It was £5.50.
4 A: What's your phone number?
   B: It's 07739 456997.
5 A: What's the speed limit in this country?
   B: It's 120 kph.
6 A: How much do you weigh?
   B: About 65 kg.
7 A: What's another way of writing 0.5?
   B: 1/2.
8 A: What's another way of writing 1/4?
   B: 0.25.
9 A: How far is your home from here?
   B: It's about 17 km.
10 A: What's the interest rate at the moment?
    B: It's just over 3.2%.
11 A: How much water do you drink a day?
    B: 2 litres.
12 A: What's the temperature today?
    B: It's at least 27°C.

UNIT 12

R.64

1 Well, everybody knows that, unfortunately, crime is going up, year in, year out. It's getting so bad that some old people are afraid to leave their homes. As far as I'm concerned, there's only one thing for it – judges have to give out tougher sentences ... and we need more prisons. Letting people off with a fine or a bit of community service is both irresponsible and a waste of time. Criminals need to be taught a proper lesson and the only place for that is prison.
2 I do actually think that community service is a good idea. I mean, where it's a case of making the punishment fit the crime, it can make perfect sense. If you get some kid who thinks it's clever to spray graffiti all over the wall of a building, let him spend a weekend cleaning it all off. I mean, as well as that, there are so many jobs that need doing around the area – like picking up litter for example. Why not use the people who otherwise would be locked up in a cell all day?
3 I'm not exactly sure about this electronic tagging business, you know. I suppose it's a good idea, you know, to let people out of prison a bit earlier – I mean there's such a problem with too many people in prison. As I understand it, it means that the police can keep a track of them ... and they have to be at home at a certain time. Probably a good idea for not very serious offenders, but I do think they've had some problems with people cutting off their tags so I'm not sure ...
4 I was just reading about this new thing where they get victims and offenders of certain crimes together with a kind of mediator. There was this one woman whose car had been stolen by a teenage joyrider. The woman needed to take her daughter to hospital urgently but she didn't have her car. Apparently, the effect of hearing this story had a big effect on the teenager. I think it sounds like a really good new idea – they should do more like this with certain types of crime ... not all of them, though.
5 Sometimes I think we need to keep a hold of what the point of prison is. I mean, yeah, of course, we need to lock some people up and keep the rest of society safe ... and yes, it's right people should be punished for hurting other people, but surely one of the big things is that we should help people to get to a point where they can get work and settle into normal society when they leave prison. I read somewhere that over 70% of criminals re-offend! Too often prison just seems to be a training ground in how to be a better criminal!

UNIT 13

R.65

Man: Have you been watching the new series of *Lost*?
Woman: Have I? Yes, I'm completely obsessed!
Man: Me, too! It's great. I love mysteries, don't you? Talking of which, where do you think they are? Do you think it's just a normal desert island ... or something a bit weirder?

Woman: Well, I don't know. I mean, <u>I knew right from the start</u> that something really bizarre was happening. <u>I've got a feeling</u> it might be a complete set up. In fact, <u>I think it's probably some sort of</u> scientific experiment. Maybe some scientists designed the island to watch how people cope under extreme conditions?

Man: Do you think so? That would be sick though … you know, making them crash just so they could observe them. <u>At first I thought</u> it was something like that, <u>but now I'm not so sure</u>. <u>I just can't work out how</u> they would make them crash. The plane went off-course by a thousand miles and then split into three bits, didn't it? Scientists couldn't make that happen.

Woman: Well, I'm not sure …

Man: <u>I think it's more likely</u> to be a normal island with some strange wild animals on it. I mean, you know, the survivors think there are monsters … when they see the trees swaying around madly and when they hear strange noises and everything …

Woman: Yes?

Man: Well, my guess is that they're just imagining things. You know, after the trauma of the plane crash. And really it's all just some wild bear or something …

Woman: No, really? But <u>I don't see how it could be</u> … I mean, it really can't be … That monster savaged one of them to death and the body ended up at the top of a tree, don't you remember? That wasn't in their imagination and a normal bear certainly couldn't have done that. It must be something really savage and weird … it's just not normal …

Man: <u>I suppose you're right</u> …

Woman: And anyway, there was that bit when they actually shot a bear … and it turned out to be a polar bear. <u>It doesn't make sense</u> – a polar bear on a tropical island!

Man: Hmm … yes … <u>I hadn't thought of that</u>.

R.66

A: Where do you think it is?

B: I think it's some <u>sort</u> of lake that's frozen over.

A: Do you? I hadn't <u>thought</u> of that. I think it's more <u>likely</u> that it's a street because of the houses and other buildings, here and here.

B: At first I thought that, but now I'm not so <u>sure</u> because the people look like they're skating on water … you know, frozen water.

A: I <u>suppose</u> you're right. Hmm, it doesn't make <u>sense</u>, though. I mean, I don't see <u>how</u> it could be a lake because the houses would be right next to the water, you know, *in* the water.

B: Yes, but look there are boats here. It must be a lake. I knew right from the <u>start</u> that it was a lake. It's obvious now.

A: Mmm, what about this bit? I just can't <u>work</u> out what these people in the middle are doing – the ones holding hands …

B: I've got a <u>feeling</u> that they're dancing. Look, they're all in a line …

UNIT 14

R.71

A: Did you hear that Steve <u>turned up</u> half an hour late for his meeting with Michael Tate, the Marketing Director!

B: Really?

A: And he'd already <u>put</u> the meeting <u>off</u> once from last week.

B: Was Michael annoyed?

A: What do you think? And it's really not very clever of Steve. You know that Michael will probably be <u>taking over</u> as Regional Director in October.

B: I heard that, too.

A: And if he does, they say that he intends to <u>lay off</u> quite a big part of the workforce.

B: That's ridiculous!

A: Apparently he's determined to <u>bring down</u> labour costs.

B: But we should be <u>branching out</u> into new areas, opening new stores. We should be <u>taking on</u> new people, not <u>cutting back</u>! I think they should fire Michael!

A: I couldn't agree more.

B: So, are *you* worried about being laid off?

A: Well, put it this way, I've made a few calls and I've got one or two interviews <u>lined up</u>.

B: Really? Listen, if you get anything … will you mention my name?

A: Of course I will. You know you can <u>count on</u> me.

UNIT 15

R.73

<u>se</u>cretary
<u>re</u>cipe
<u>com</u>fortable
<u>cu</u>pboard
<u>cou</u>gh
re<u>cei</u>pt
<u>mus</u>cle
<u>in</u>teresting
a<u>pos</u>trophe
<u>sci</u>ssors
<u>law</u>
<u>cho</u>colate
<u>comb</u>
des<u>ser</u>t

Communication Activities

Unit 3 page 31, Exercise 6

Student A

Take turns to compare your pictures. Use the headings in Exercise 4 and at least four of the highlighted phrases in Exercise 3.

Picture 1

Picture 2

Unit 8 page 80, Exercise 2

Group B

Read your text quickly and check your ideas from Exercise 1.

Encounter, Los Angeles, USA

It's the most recognisable landmark at Los Angeles International Airport and one of the most famous buildings in Los Angeles as a whole. I am, of course, talking about the amazing landmark Theme Building situated at the USA's third busiest airport; this twenty-one-metre-high monster looks like a giant futuristic insect. With its unique arches and multiple lighting changes, the building has been a fixture since 1961 and is now home to *Encounter* – restaurant with a difference.

For many years, the structure housed a coffee shop providing snacks for travellers waiting to board the next flight. Just a few years ago, Walt Disney Imagineering completely redesigned the interior.* It was converted into a kind of *Star Trek* restaurant, complete with multi-coloured patterns on the carpeting, blue and red lights and moon-cratered walls. You might hear sci-fi or James Bond music in the space-age elevator that takes you up to the top of the building.

There seems to be a separate life at the crater-shaped, metallic bar, too. There are guns that emit laser lights and sound effects when bartenders pour a drink. The barstools seem to hang in mid-air. The overall scene looks like some kind of a vision of an alternate universe in the distant future. Visually, there's nothing like this place anywhere.

But then there's the food. *Encounter*'s management has a daunting challenge on its hands. The building itself is a major attraction with its unusual location and famous architecture. It's easy in such a scenario for the food to become an afterthought. However, you will be in for a surprise if you stop in for dinner at the *Encounter*, as the cuisine is fabulous.

The *Encounter*'s Executive Chef, Michel Audeon, continues the tradition at the restaurant of a menu featuring 'art-food'; a Los Angeles speciality that focuses not only on taste but also on creating incredible sculptural arrangements on the plate. Whatever your taste, you're sure to find something you will enjoy looking at as well as eating: my favourites are roast chicken, grilled salmon and best of all, the delicious California Summer Spinach Vegetable Wrap. And if you're coming with kids, don't worry; there's a menu for them and *Encounter*'s party atmosphere ensures they'll enjoy themselves without **disrupting** the ambience a bit.

The sceptics may think *Encounter* is just a 'theme park' with second-rate food. Don't make that mistake. The chef has a good thing going here. At *Encounter*, Audeon incorporates his flair for genuinely good food, eclectic menus and innovative presentation. You wouldn't want to miss his mouth-watering menu, regardless of the location and décor. In fact, I'd take a bet you wouldn't want to miss the location and décor either.

*Walt Disney Imagineering were contracted by CA One Services, Inc. now trading as Delaware North Companies Travel Hospitality Services, Inc.

Unit 9 page 93, Exercise 5

The original moral of the story was *'When force fails, gentleness often succeeds'*. Do you agree with it?

Unit 13 page 135, Exercise 4

Look at these pictures. For each one, discuss and speculate with another student about the situation, the different people and their stories. Use the question in Exercise 4 to help you.

Unit 14 page 147, Exercise 2

Pair A

Look at the pictures. First, make a note of any key vocabulary/ expressions from Exercise 1 you would like to use.

Unit 7 page 73, Exercise 5

With another student, take turns to compare pictures 3 and 4.

Picture 3

Picture 4

Unit 13 page 135, Exercise 5

The mysterious pianist

Andreas Grassl (born October 25, 1984) is a German man who was found in England in April 2005. He remained unidentified for a long time due to his refusal to speak; he communicated instead through drawing and playing the piano. When he was first brought to a piano, he reportedly played music from various genres (ranging from classical music by Tchaikovsky to pop by The Beatles) non-stop for four hours.

During the more than four months that passed until he revealed his identity, the mysterious story created interest and speculation across the world, and he became known as the 'Piano Man'.

Many of the questions in the story remain unsolved, however. It is still unclear why he was so smartly-dressed or why he was soaking wet. In fact, nobody knows quite how and why he came to be on a beach in Kent, but it is assumed he either suffered some kind of mental breakdown or that he was pretending all along and it was a complete hoax.

Communication Activities

Communication Activities

Unit 3 page 31, Exercise 6

Student B

Take turns to compare your pictures. Use the headings in Exercise 4 and at least four of the highlighted phrases in Exercise 3.

Picture 3

Picture 4

Unit 14 page 147, Exercise 2

Pair B

Look at the pictures. First make a note of any key vocabulary/ expressions from Exercise 1 you would like to use.

Unit 2 page 23, Exercise 4

November 4:

This weekend was fantastic. I went with some friends from my English class down to Brighton (a town on the south coast). I'd never been before but everyone says it's really nice – and they were right!

Then on Sunday I had a long phone call with my sister in Spain. It was her birthday and we hadn't chatted for ages, so it was good to catch up with all her news (she's got a new boyfriend!) and find out how our parents are. I told her I was keeping a diary in English. She was very impressed.

I think keeping a diary in English is good for me. It makes me write a little English every day. (I don't worry about making mistakes). And sometimes I give it to my English teacher to look at.

Communication Activities

Index

Unit 01

Question forms

Direct questions

There are three main types of direct questions:

A *Yes/No* questions (which expect the answer 'yes' or 'no')

1 Most verbs need to use the auxiliary *do/does/did* to make questions.

Do you like nature documentaries?

2 Verbs with *be*, *can* and *have* (*got*) don't need the auxiliary *do/does/did*.

Is he playing computer games?
Can you play the guitar?
Have you got the tickets?

3 Negative *Yes/No* questions expect a particular answer.

Didn't she go to Barcelona last weekend? (expected answer 'yes')
Aren't you going to the party? (expected answer 'yes')
Hasn't he paid you back yet? (expected answer 'no')

B *Wh-* questions

1 Question words (*who, what, where, when, whose, why, which* and *how*) come at the beginning of the question.

Where did you go last night?
What do you think about horror films?

2 If *who, what* or *which* is the subject of the sentence, we don't use the auxiliary *do/does/did*, and we use normal sentence word order (not the inversion of subject and verb as for other questions).

Who gave you that CD?
What happened yesterday?

Compare:

Who gave you that CD? (asking about the subject)
Who did you give that CD to? (asking about the object)

3 If there is a preposition, it comes at the end of the question (unless it is very formal speaking or writing).

Who did you buy that for?
(Very formal: *For whom did you buy that?*)
What were you talking about?
(Very formal: *About what were you talking?*)

C Alternative questions (which expect the answer to be one of two options)

There are two types of alternative questions; (a) a *Yes/No* type and (b) a *Wh-* type.

Do you want to go to the cinema or watch a DVD?
Which would you rather do, book tickets now or buy them on the night?

Other types of questions

Indirect questions

Indirect questions use statement word order (you don't invert the subject and verb). They are often used to be more polite or tentative when you're asking a question (e.g. if you don't know someone very well/at all, if you're asking for something quite big or difficult). We use *if/whether* for *Yes/No* type indirect questions.

Common ways of starting indirect questions are in **bold**:
I'd like to know if you're coming to the cinema with us.
Could you tell me where the theatre is, please?
Would you mind telling me how long the performance lasts?
Do you know if the single has been released yet?

Question tags

Question tags are short questions at the end of a statement. The speaker often expects a particular answer and is using a question tag to confirm what he/she already knows.
The most common question tags are formed as follows:

1 positive statement + negative question tag
She loves singing, doesn't she?
You've seen that film before, haven't you?
2 negative statement + positive question tag
You didn't get me a ticket, did you?
He isn't learning the piano, is he?

Prepositions of place, time and movement

In 'time' phrases: *at/in/on*

at
Used for clock times, points of time in the day, weekends and holidays, points in time, e.g. *at 9.30 a.m., at midnight, at lunchtime, at the weekend, at New Year, at the moment, at the beginning, at the end*

in
Used for the main parts of the day, months, years, seasons, centuries, a point of time during a period or at the end of a period, e.g. *in the morning, in August, in 2006, in the summer, in the 21st century, in the night, in an hour, in a couple of minutes*

on
Used for specific dates and days, e.g. *on 20th May, on Friday, on New Year's Day, on Sunday morning*

In 'place' phrases: *at/in/on*

These prepositions can be used to indicate actual position, and they can also be used in expressions.

at
Shows a point in space where something is happening, e.g. *at the bus stop, at the bottom, at the top, at the corner (of a street), at home, (sitting) at the table, at the party, at the end*

in
Shows that something taking place is inside (not outside), e.g. *in a chair, in bed, in a book, in the centre, in the corner (of a room), in the country, in the world, in the park, in Italy, in an area*

on
Shows that something taking place is on something (not inside); e.g. *on the sofa, (put something) on the table, on page 1, on the beach, on a trip, on the coast, on an island, on the pavement, on TV, on the radio*

In 'movement' phrases: *at/to/into/towards*

at
We use *at* with 'arrive', e.g. *We <u>arrived at</u> the party*.
We use *at* to show the person or thing the action is aimed at, e.g. *She <u>shouted at</u> me*.

Compare:
He threw the ball <u>at</u> her. (implies it's aimed at her and he wants to hit her)
He threw the ball <u>to</u> her. (implies he wants her to catch it)

to
We generally use *to* with verbs of movement e.g. *come, go, travel, run, send, take, return, get, walk*; e.g. *I <u>walked to</u> work yesterday.*
We usually use *to* with nouns that suggest movement e.g. *journey, trip, welcome*; e.g. *I'm going on a <u>trip to</u> Italy.*

Compare:
I've been <u>to</u> Spain three times. (implies travelling/movement)
I've been <u>in</u> Spain for three weeks. (implies staying/place)

into
We use *into* with verbs that mean 'to move from outside to an inside area'; e.g. *Everybody looked at her when she walked <u>into</u> the room. I got <u>into bed</u> to read my book.*

towards
Towards means moving or pointing in a particular direction; e.g. *I saw someone coming <u>towards me</u>.*
We also use towards with nouns to suggest aiming to achieve; e.g. *I'm working <u>towards my gold medal</u> in swimming.*

at the end/in the end

At the end is a prepositional phrase which is usually followed by a noun. It refers to the final point or part, e.g. *<u>At the end</u> of the film, they all live happily ever after.*
At the end is also an adverb which refers to the point at which something occurs, e.g. *We'll read it through <u>at the end</u>.*
In the end is a linking phrase which means 'finally, after a long time', e.g. *<u>In the end</u>, we found a bank and got some money out.*

Unit 02

Present simple

FORM

1 Positive statements
   I/you/we/they play tennis.
   He/she/it plays tennis.
2 Negative statements
   I/you/we/they don't play tennis.
   He/she/it doesn't play tennis.
3 Questions
   Do I/you/we/they play tennis?
   Does he/she/it play tennis?
4 Short answers
   Yes, I/you/we/they do.
   No, I/you/we/they don't.
   Yes, he/she/it does.
   No, he/she/it doesn't.

USE

We use the present simple:

1 With routine or regular repeated actions (often with adverbs of frequency like *always, often, sometimes, never, every Saturday morning, once a week*).
   My father goes to the gym twice a week.
   We visit my grandmother in Scotland every summer.
   I always have a coffee before I leave for work.

2 In time clauses with a future meaning after *when, as soon as, if, until*.
   Please tell Mike to call me if you see him.
   I'll start making dinner when/as soon as I get home.
   I can't afford to buy a new car until I get a pay rise.

3 When we are talking about permanent situations.
   I come from Innsbruck.
   Does he still live with his family?

4 When we are talking about the future as expressed in timetables, regulations and programmes.
   The tour of the castle starts at 11.00 a.m.

5 With scientific facts.
   Water boils at 100 degrees Celcius.
   The sun rises in the east.

6 With 'state' verbs which are not normally used in continuous forms: *be, have, depend, know, think, understand, disagree, like, want, hear, love, see, smell, taste.*
   I don't have any brothers or sisters.
   Do you know why your father is upset?
   This soup tastes delicious.

7 In spoken instructions, sports commentaries, jokes and formal letters.
   First you make sure there are batteries in the camera.
   Murray serves and runs towards the net.
   Two men decide they want to make a lot of money, so the first man says to the second man …
   I enclose a copy of my last bank statement as requested.

Present continuous

FORM

The present form of *be* + the *-ing* form of the verb.
Contracted forms: *I'm (I am), you're (you are), s/he's (s/he is), it's (it is), we're (we are), they're (they are)* + *-ing* form.

USE

We use the present continuous when we are talking about:

1 Actions happening now.
   I think she's revising for tomorrow's exam.
2 Changing/developing situations.
   The hole in the ozone layer is getting bigger.
3 Temporary situations.
   I am staying with my sister for the next few weeks.
4 Plans and arrangements in the future.
   Are you doing anything special over New Year?
5 Annoying or surprising habits with *always*.
   She's always borrowing money from me.

Modifiers

1 *Fairly* usually modifies adjectives and adverbs. It does not suggest a high degree.
   It's a fairly large flat but I don't think there's enough space for all our furniture.
   Pete is fairly good at science but he wants to study languages at university.

2 *Quite* suggests a higher degree than *fairly*. It can be used with *a/an* + *noun*. It normally comes before *a/an* if there is a gradable adjective (e.g. *large, hot*, etc.) or no adjective. It can modify verbs and nouns as well as adjectives and adverbs.
   It's quite a large flat so there should be space for all our furniture.
   She's quite tall for her age.

3 *Pretty* is stronger than *quite*. It can suggest 'more than was expected' and similar ideas. It is more informal than *fairly* and *quite* and is more often used in speaking than in writing.
   It's a pretty large flat. I didn't realise that it would have four good-sized bedrooms.

4 *A bit* is often used with the same meaning as *a little*.
   He's a bit more interested in sports than his brother.
   When *a bit* or *a little* are used with non-comparative adjectives, the meaning is usually negative or critical.
   She's a bit young to go to school on her own.
   (It is not possible to say ~~a bit nice, a little happy~~, etc.)

5 *Really* is used to show emphasis. It can be used with adjectives, adverbs and verbs. It can be used with both gradable and non-gradable adjectives.

I really like Janice.

That film was really awful.

She played really well in the match on Saturday.

6 *Extremely*, *incredibly* and *terribly* are also used to show emphasis. They are used in a similar way to *very* (i.e. with gradable adjectives) but they are stronger than *very*.

My boss was extremely pleased that we finished the report on time.

I was terribly embarrassed when he proposed to me in the middle of a large restaurant.

Unit 03

Comparison

Types of comparison

There are three types of comparison of adjectives and adverbs:

A to a higher degree (comparative form + *than*)

*The town centre is **busier than** it used to be.*

*My mother drives **more carefully than** my father.*

B to the same degree (*as ... as*)

*Walking is **as fast as** taking the bus.*

*I'm **not as tired as** I was last week.*

C to a lower degree (with *less* + *than* and *the least*)

*He's **less keen** on going to the gym **than** he was.*

*I usually buy **the least expensive** t-shirts I can find.*

1 The comparative and superlative forms of **one-syllable adjectives and adverbs** are generally made by adding *-er/-est*.

*Petrol prices are **higher** than they were this time last year.*

Exceptions:

Adjectives which end in a vowel plus a consonant. These comparatives and superlatives are made by doubling the consonant and adding *-er/-est*.

*They've just moved to a **bigger** house.*

Adjectives which end in *-e*. These comparatives and superlatives are made by adding *-r/-st*.

*That's **the nicest** thing you've ever said to me.*

2 The comparative and superlative forms of **two- and three-syllable adjectives and adverbs** are generally made by using *more* and *most*.

*The second week of the holiday passed **more quickly than** the first.*

Exception:

Two-syllable adjectives ending in *-y*. These comparatives and superlatives are made by changing the *y* to *i* and adding *-er*.

*She is usually here **earlier than** this.*

3 (*not*) *as ... as*

A We use *not as ... as* to compare things which are different.

*I'm **not as good** at the guitar **as** I used to be.*

B We use *as ... as* to compare things which are the same.

*The film is **as boring as** the book.*

so ... as can be used in negative sentences to mean the same as *as ... as* (but not in positive sentences and questions)

*Computers are not **so expensive as** they were.*

*She worked **as hard as** she could.*

*Could you get here **as quickly as** you can please?*

Some adjectives and adverbs have irregular forms. The most common irregular forms are:

1 Adjectives

good better best

bad worse worst

little less least

much more most

far further/farther furthest/farthest

old elder eldest (used for people only; the regular forms, *old older oldest*, are used for buildings, towns, animals, trees, etc.)

*Carol is a **better** player than I am, but Tess is **the best**.*

*That was **the worst** book I've ever read.*

*I live **further** from school **than** I used to.*

*David is **the eldest** of seven children.*

2 Adverbs

well better best

badly worse worst

late later last/latest

much more most

little less least

*I can speak English **better than** I could six months ago.*

*I don't see Mike **much** but I see him **more than** I used to.*

Modifying comparison

You cannot use *very* with comparatives, but you can use the following:

much faster

a lot cheaper

far less expensive

a bit bigger

very much better

a little happier

*I don't think it will be **any** quicker to go by car.*

Reflexives

There are three main ways we use reflexive pronouns:

1 When the object is the same person/thing as the subject. In this case, the reflexive pronoun is essential to the grammar of the sentence.
*I **forced myself** not to watch television for two whole weeks.*
*The computer **turns itself off** after fifteen minutes of no use.*
Common verbs which take reflexive pronouns include: *enjoy yourself, behave yourself, help yourself, make yourself at home.*
Common verbs which don't take reflexive pronouns include: *relax, concentrate, hurry, feel.*

2 When you want to emphasise the subject or object (to say 'that person/thing and nobody/nothing else'). In this case, the reflexive pronoun is not essential to the grammar of the sentence, but is added for emphasis.
*I'd like to speak to the director **himself**.*
*The film **itself** is very good, but some of the acting is a bit weak.*

3 With *by* to mean *alone*.
*More and more people in their twenties live **by themselves** these days.*

own

There are three main ways we use *own*:

1 *on my own/on his own*, etc. to mean 'without the help of others'
*I organised the whole thing **on my own**, which was tiring but satisfying in the end.*

2 *on my own/on his own*, etc. to mean 'alone'
*She doesn't seem to mind going to the cinema **on her own**.*

3 *my own/her own*, etc. to mean 'belonging to no other person'
*I've just bought **my own** flat.*

Unit 04

Past simple

FORM
verb + *-ed* (remember there are many irregular verb forms)

USE
We use the past simple:

1 To talk about events in the past that are now finished.
We had a great skiing holiday in Austria in January
She opened her suitcase, took out her swimming costume and went straight down to the hotel pool.

2 To talk about habits in the past.
My family went to the south of Spain for a two-week holiday every summer.

3 To talk about situations in the past.
When I was younger, I was very interested in motorbikes.

4 In reported speech.
She said she didn't want to go out for the evening.

Past continuous

FORM
was/were + *-ing*

USE
We use the past continuous:

1 To talk about actions in progress in the past.
She was lying on the grass, looking at the stars.

2 To talk about temporary situations in the past.
Last June I was doing part-time work in my father's insurance company.

3 To talk about anticipated events that did not happen.
They were sailing around the Greek islands that summer, but his dad got ill and so they decided to postpone the trip.

4 To talk about an event that was in progress when another event happened.
He was reading a holiday brochure when Pete called him on his mobile.

5 To talk about actions in progress at the same time in the past.
While Tara was preparing dinner, Cassie was making a list of everyone they wanted to invite to the party.

Past perfect simple

FORM
had + past participle

USE
We use the past perfect simple:

1 To refer to a time earlier than another past time.
The next time I spoke to Josie, she had had the baby.

2 In reported speech.
She said she had already sent us an invitation.

Past perfect continuous

FORM
had been + *-ing*

USE
We use the past perfect continuous:

1 To talk about actions or situations which had continued up to the past moment that we are thinking about.
I decided to take my bike to a garage as the engine had been making some strange noises.

Time conjunctions

As, *when* and *while* can introduce a background action/situation which is going on while something else happens.
I heard the phone ring while I was having a shower.

As-, *when-* and *while-* clauses can go at the beginning or end of sentences, but *as-* clauses usually introduce less important information and often go at the beginning of sentences.
As I was sitting in my car, I saw two masked men run out of the bank.

We usually use *while* to describe two longer actions or situations going on at the same time.
While I was making dinner, Tina was finishing her essay.

As is used (with simple tenses) to talk about two situations which develop or change together.
As I get older, I don't worry about things so much.

We often use *when* to refer to periods of life.
When I lived in London, I had a lot more money than I do now.

Eventually and *finally* mean 'in the end'. We use them to say that something happens after a long time or a lot of effort.
It was a very close match which lasted for hours but eventually Tim won.

At first and *to begin with* refer to the beginning of a situation, to make a contrast with something different that happens later.
At first she enjoyed her new job, but after a while she wanted more of a challenge.

As soon as and *then* can be used to talk about two actions or events that happen very quickly one after the other.
As soon as I saw him, I gave him the letter.

After is not usually used alone. Instead we use other expressions like *afterwards* or *after that*.
We're going to see an early film and afterwards we're all going out for a drink.

By the time is used before a verb and means 'not later than'.
I will have finished painting the bedroom by the time you get home.

Unit 05

Asking for and giving permission

1 *can*

We use *can* to ask for and give permission.
Can I borrow your tennis racket for the weekend?
You can come with me to watch the football match if you help me in the garden on Sunday.

2 *could*

We use *could* to ask for permission when you are not sure what the answer will be.
Note: *could* is not used for giving permission
A: **Could** *I see you for a minute?*
B: *Not now, but after lunch will be possible.*

3 *may*

We use *may* to ask for or give permission in formal situations.
May *I take these files home with me tonight?*
*You **may** have the rest of the day off.*

Obligation: *should* and *ought to*

We use *should* and *ought to* to talk about obligations and duties in the future, present and past.
*You **ought to/should** do more exercise.*
Oughtn't *we to/**Shouldn't** we do some revision for tomorrow's exam?*
Shouldn't *we have/**Oughtn't** we to have bought Sara a birthday present?*

Should + *have* + past participle is often used to criticise your own or other people's behaviour.
*We **should have won** yesterday's match.*
*She **shouldn't have taken** my car without asking.*

Strong obligation and necessity

A *must*

We use *must* to:

1 Talk about present and future strong obligations and necessities that come from the speaker.
   *You **must** drink lots of water after having a sauna.*
   *I **must** remember to ask the tennis coach for another lesson this week.*

2 Ask about what the listener wants you to do.
   ***Must** I wear any special clothing?*

3 Tell people not to do things.
   *You **mustn't** use your mobile phone in here.*

B *have to/have got to*

We use *have to/have got to* to:

1 Talk about present and future strong obligations that do not come from the speaker. *Have got to* is used more in British English than it is in American English.
   *We **have to** pay our rent on the first of every month.*
   *When do we **have to** register for the exam?* (more common in American English)
   *I **haven't got** to go to team practice tomorrow.* (more common in British English).

2 Talk about past and reported obligations of all kinds.
   *She told me I **had to** change my diet.*
   *We **had to** do a cross-country run every term when I was at school.*

Lack of obligation

1 *needn't, don't need to* and *don't have to*

  We use *needn't, don't need to, don't have to* to talk about a lack of obligation in the present or future.

  You **don't need to/needn't** come and watch me on Saturday. It's not an important match.

  We **don't have to** get up early tomorrow. It's a holiday.

2 *needn't + have + past participle*

  We use *needn't + have + past participle* to say that somebody did something, but that it was unnecessary.

  You **needn't have done** all the washing-up. I was going to do it.

3 *didn't need to + infinitive*

  We use *didn't need to + infinitive* to say that something wasn't necessary without saying whether the person did it or not.

  We **didn't need to** bring our sweaters.

used to

FORM
Positive statements
used to + infinitive

Negative statements
did/didn't + use to + infinitive

Questions
did you/she/they, etc. *use to + infinitive*

USE
We use *used to* to talk about past habits and states that do not occur now or no longer exist.

I **used to** play a lot of sport, but now I hardly ever do.

How did they **use to** keep in touch without email?

He **used to** be great at volleyball, but he's put on a lot of weight recently.

Notes:

1 *Used to* is not used to say how often things happened or how long they took.

2 *Used to* can be used for things you still do now but the place or time has finished.

  I **used to** ride a motorbike when I lived in Egypt. I still do, but now I live in Portugal.

3 Be careful not to confuse *used to* with *be/get used to + noun/gerund* which means 'be/become accustomed to something' because you have been doing it for a while.

  I'm **used to** getting up early.

  I can't **get used** to living in the middle of the city.

  Do you think we'll ever **get used to** the heat?

would

Would is also used to talk about past habits and repeated actions but not about past states.

When I was a child, I **would** go to the park after school and kick a ball around with my friend Peter for hours.

Present perfect simple

FORM
have/has + past participle

USE
We use the present perfect simple:

1 To talk about an experience or an action in the past when the time is not important or not known. (Often used with *ever* and *never*.)

  I've **never** been to Greece.

  Have you **ever** been on a skiing holiday?

2 To talk about an action that started in the past and continues to the present. (It is often used with *for* and *since*.)

  When you're focusing on the finished action.

  I've revised everything I can for the test tomorrow.

  When you're focusing on the number of times the action has been completed up to the time of speaking.

  I've seen that film three times since it came out.

  With 'state' verbs, e.g. *be, have, like, believe, know*.

  He's known about the letter since last week.

3 To talk about an action that happened in the past but has the result in the present. (It is often used with *just, yet* and *already*.)

  She's **just** had her hair cut.

  Have you booked that holiday **yet**?

  I've read that magazine **already**.

4 To talk about our first/second experience of something with the phrase *This is the first/second time …*

  This is the first time I've driven a car on my own.

5 When used with the superlative. (Often used with *ever*.)

  My first job interview was the most difficult thing I've ever done.

Present perfect continuous

FORM
have/has + been + -ing

USE
We use the present perfect continuous:

1 To suggest that an action is not complete.

  I've been reading this book all morning and I'm halfway through.

2 To emphasise how long the action has been going on for.

  He's been having driving lessons for over a year.

3 To describe a recent activity when you can still see the results of that activity.

  A: What's all that mess?

  B: I've been painting the bathroom.

ever

Ever indicates that the speaker is talking about 'at any time in your life'. It generally comes before the past participle in questions.
Have you ever tried Thai food?

for/since

For is used to talk about a period of time.
I've lived here for three years.

Since is used to talk about the starting point.
We've been friends since 1999.

just/yet/already

Just means a short time ago. It usually comes between *has/have* and the past participle.
I've just seen David.

Yet shows that the speaker expected something to happen before now. It is used at the end of negative sentences and questions.
I haven't bought the tickets yet.
Have you heard from Paula yet?

Already shows that something happened sooner than expected. It usually comes between *has/have* and the past participle or at the end of the sentence.
He's already passed his driving test.
She's invited me to the dinner party already.

so/such

MEANING

So and *such* are used to emphasise the great extent or high degree of what you're talking about.
*I wish he wouldn't drive **so fast**.*
*I'm lucky to work with **such interesting people**.*
*We had **such a lovely time** at your party.*

Note: *so/such* vs. *very*:
very is usually used for new information.
so/such are usually used when the information is already known.
*I've got a **very bad headache**.*
*I'm sorry you've got **such a bad headache**.*

FORM

so + adjectives and adverbs
so + quantifiers (*much, many, few, little*)
*He's **so kind**.*
*She speaks **so quickly**.*

*I've got **so many** books.*
*There's **so little** time left.*

(Don't use *so* with adjective + noun.)
such/such a + nouns and noun phrases
such good weather

such lovely trousers
such a beautiful day

Use *so* (not *very*) in *that* clauses.
*We were **so late that** we took a taxi there.*
*He wanted to make her feel **so ashamed** of her bedroom **that** she would tidy it up.*

too/enough

MEANING
Too is different from *very*:
too = more than is necessary or wanted

Compare:
*It's **very hot** today.*
*It's **too hot** to sit in the sun today.*
enough = as much as is necessary or wanted

FORM
too + adjectives and adverbs
*These trousers are **too small** for me.*
*Don't eat **too quickly** – you'll be sick.*

too much/too many + noun phrases
*There's **too much salt** in this soup.*
***Too many people** wanted tickets.*

Adjectives and adverbs + *enough*
*I'm not **old enough** to vote.*
*You're not speaking **slowly enough**.*

enough + noun
*Have you got **enough milk**?*

Also:
Adjective + *enough* + noun OR *Enough* + adjective + noun

Compare:
*These aren't **fresh enough vegetables**.*
*I haven't got **enough fresh vegetables**.*

too/enough + infinitive
*It's **too cold for me to go out** today.*
*She's **old enough to make** her own decision.*
*This food is **too spicy for her to eat**.*
NOT: *This food is too spicy for her to eat it.*

Unit 07

like and as

1 *like* as a verb

FORM
like + object
I like my new flat, but I would prefer to be closer to the centre of town.

like + *-ing* (= enjoy doing)

Do you like working for a small family firm?

like + *to* + infinitive (= choose to do)

I like to go to the gym for an hour before work.

Note: short answers to *Yes/No* questions with *like* are always formed with *do, does* or *did*.

A: *Did you like the film?*

B: *Yes, I did.*

Would like + (object) + infinitive with *to* is used as a polite way of saying 'want'. It refers to one occasion in the future.

I'd like you to help me paint the spare room this evening.

2 *like* as a preposition, which means 'similar to' or 'in the same way as'. We use *like*, not *as*, before a noun or pronoun to talk about similarity.

This perfume smells like the one my grandmother used to wear.

My brother looks very like me.

3 *As* is a conjunction. We use it before a clause and before an expression beginning with a preposition.

I think the stock market will crash soon, as it did in 1989.

4 We can use *as* to talk about function – the jobs that people or things do.

He worked as a waiter over the summer.

5 *like* which means 'such as/for example'

I want to do something active this afternoon, like going swimmin g or playing tennis.

6 *feel like* + object/*-ing*, used to talk about something that we want or want to do

I feel like going for a long walk by the sea.

7 *As* can be used to talk about actions or situations that take place at the same time.

As I was having my breakfast, I heard a loud crash upstairs.

8 *As if* and *as though* are both used to say what a situation seems like. They can refer to something that we think may be true.

It looks as if the rain will stop soon.

9 Some expressions beginning with *as* are used to introduce facts which are known to both speaker and listener e.g. *as you know, as we agreed, as you suggested.*

So, we'll all meet back here in an hour, as we agreed.

Overview of future forms

FORMS

will (*shall*) + infinitive

going to + infinitive

Present continuous

Present simple

Future continuous (*will* + *be* + *-ing* form)

Future perfect (*will* + *have* + past participle)

USES

1 We use *will* +infinitive for predicting something based on what you know or believe.

I think it will rain later this afternoon.

I'm sure you'll pass your exam because you've worked really hard.

Note: *going to* + infinitive is also possible in this case.

2 We use *going to* + infinitive for predicting something based on what you can see or hear.

Look at those clouds. It's going to rain.

He's going to fall if he tips his chair back like that.

Note: we cannot use *will* + infinitive or the present continuous in this case.

3 We use *will* + infinitive for promises, threats, offers and requests.

If you shout at me one more time, I'll leave.

I promise I won't tell anyone.

I'll give you a lift to work if you like.

Will you make the dinner tonight?

Note: we cannot use *going to* in this case.

4 We use *going to* + infinitive and the present continuous to talk about things that have already been decided. We usually use present continuous if the plans are more certain and more details have been decided.

I'm going to see that new film at the weekend.

Jim and Sarah are getting married on Saturday.

Note: We cannot use *will* + infinitive in this case.

5 We use *will* + infinitive to talk about future actions decided at the time of speaking.

I think I'll lie down for a moment.

I'll make a cup of tea.

Note: We cannot use the present continuous in this case.

6 We use the future continuous (*will* + *be* + *-ing*) to say that an action will be in progress at a definite time in the future.

I'll be lying on a beach this time tomorrow.

7 We use the future perfect (*will* + *have* + past participle) to describe something that will be completed before a definite time in the future.

I'll have finished this book by the end of the day.

Unit 08

Countable and uncountable nouns

Uncountable nouns

These have no plural. The following are common nouns that are usually uncountable:

accommodation, advice, behaviour, bread, copper (and all other metals), *English* (and all other languages), *furniture, health, information, knowledge, luggage, news, progress, research, rice* (and all other grains and cereals), *rubbish, salt* (and all other condiments, e.g. pepper), *scenery, spaghetti, traffic, travel, trouble, water* (and all other liquids), *weather, work.*

Nouns which can be countable or uncountable

The following nouns can be both countable and uncountable:

1 Nouns we think of as single things or substances.

   Egg: *I'll have a fried egg and two sausages. You've spilt egg on your shirt.*

   Chicken: *I bought a chicken to have for Sunday lunch. Would you like some more chicken?*

   Iron: *I'm going to buy a new iron – this one's broken. They found some old tools made of iron.*

   Glass: *Could I have a clean glass, please? Did you know that glass is made from sand?*

   Hair: *I found a hair in my soup. He's got short red hair.*

2 Normally uncountable nouns which are used to refer to particular varieties.

   Would you like red or white wine?

   They produce a very good white wine on that island.

3 Words for drinks, e.g. *coffee, tea, beer.* The countable noun means a glass of, a cup of, a bottle of, etc.

   Coffee is very expensive at the moment.

   Do you fancy going for a coffee?

   He usually drinks beer not wine.

   There's a beer in the fridge if you want one.

4 *time, space, room*

   I won't have time to finish my essay today.

   We had a really good time on holiday.

   We haven't got space for any more people I'm afraid.

   Fill in the spaces with a suitable word.

   There's room for a small table in the corner.

   I'd like a double room for three nights.

Determiners used with countable and uncountable nouns

Before countable nouns, we can use:

a/an, few(er), a few, many, a great many, not many, several

Before uncountable nouns, we can use:

(very) little, a little, much, not much, a great deal of, a small/large amount of

Before both countable and uncountable nouns, we can use:

some, any, (quite) a lot of, lots of, plenty of, a lack of

1 *few/a few* and *little/a little*

   Use *few/a few* with plural countable nouns and *little/a little* with uncountable nouns.

   A *a few* (for countables) and *a little* (for uncountables) are used to talk about positive ideas. A *few* means 'some but not many' and *a little* means 'some but not much'.

   I went out for dinner with a few friends.

   There's a little cake left.

   B *few* (for countables) and *little* (for uncountables) are used to talk about negative ideas. *Few /little* are generally used to mean 'not enough'/'almost none'.

   Few people are interested in coming to the meeting.

   Little money was collected for the new roof appeal.

2 *many/much*

   Use *many* with plural countable nouns and *much* with uncountable nouns.

   How many dogs have you got?

   There are many places we could go on holiday.

   I haven't got much money left.

   How much pasta is in that packet?

3 Some determiners can be used with both plural countable nouns and uncountable nouns.

   *I've got **some** paper in my bag if you want to borrow some.*

   *The library has got **some** new computers.*

   ***A lot of** equipment was stolen from the school.*

   *They've got **a lot of** relatives who live in South Africa.*

4 *a slice, a lump, a piece,* etc.

   Use specific words to make uncountable nouns countable. The most common ones are:

   a slice of bread, toast, cheese, ham, meat

   a loaf of bread

   a carton of milk, juice

   a joint of meat

   a bar of chocolate

   a lump of sugar, cheese

   a tube of toothpaste

   an item of news

   a stroke of luck

   a fit of temper

   a state of emergency

   a breath of fresh air

Articles

The definite article: *the*

Use the definite article *the* to talk about the following:

inventions: *When was **the** jet engine invented?*

species of animal: ***The** tiger is now an endangered species.*

oceans and seas: *We went on holiday to an island in **the** Aegean Sea.*

mountain ranges: *Which are higher: **the** Andes or **the** Dolomites?*

island groups: *I'd love to go to **the** Seychelles.*

areas: *She comes from **the** north of England.*

rivers: *We took a boat along **the** River Thames to the London Eye.*

deserts: ***The** Sahara Desert is growing every year.*

hotels: *We spent a week staying at **the** Hilton in New York.*

cinemas: *That new Brad Pitt film is on at **the** Odeon.*

theatres: *I saw Shakespeare's 'Macbeth' at **the** Globe Theatre in London.*

newspapers: *I usually read **the** 'Guardian' during the week and **the** Observer on Sundays.*

national groups: ***The** British are known for being rather reserved.*

Also:

With superlatives.

*She's **the kindest** friend I've ever had.*

When there is only one thing.

*Don't forget to take some sun cream as **the** sun is really hot today.*

To talk about particular nouns when it is clear what we are referring to.

*Do you mind looking after **the** cat while I'm away?*

To talk about previously mentioned things.

*Take one egg, a small onion and a bunch of parsley. Break **the** egg into a bowl.*

The indefinite article: *a/an*

Use the indefinite article *a/an*:

With (singular) jobs, etc.

*She's **an** architect.*

With singular countable nouns (mentioned for the first time or when it doesn't matter which one).

*Don't forget to bring **a** pen.*

With these numbers: 100, 1,000, 1,000,000.

*There were over **a** hundred people at the party.*

In exclamations about singular countable nouns.

*What **a** lovely jacket!*

The zero article

Use no article (the zero article) to talk about:

continents: *They're travelling across Africa on foot.*
countries: *Have you been to Brazil?*
mountains: *They have reached the summit of Mount Everest.*
lakes: *What country is Lake Tanganyika in?*
villages, towns, cities: *Zahara is a village just along the coast from here. I was born in Milan.*
streets, roads, etc.: *Oxford Street and Tottenham Court Road are very busy shopping streets in London.*
magazines: *I usually read 'Hello' magazine when I go to the hairdresser.*
illnesses: *I had chickenpox and measles when I was a child.* (But: *I've got a headache.*)

uncountable, plural and abstract nouns used in their general sense:

People who drop litter really make me angry.
I always buy fruit and vegetables at the local greengrocer's.

Also use no article in the following expressions:

to/at/from school/university/college

in/to class
to/in/into/from church
to/in/into/out of prison/hospital/bed
to/at/from work
for/at/to breakfast/lunch/dinner
by car/bus/bicycle/plane/train/tube/boat
on foot

Unit 09

Participle clauses

Participle clauses can be used to express condition, reason, result, etc. They are often quite formal.

***Maintained regularly**, this dishwasher should last for many years.* (If it is maintained regularly …)

***Hearing a noise in the garden**, I went out to investigate.* (After hearing …)

***Having been left some money by an old uncle**, I decided to go travelling.* (As a result of having been left …)

Expressing purpose

1 We can use the infinitive to talk about purpose with *to*, *in order to* and *so as to*. *To* is the least formal.

*John is coming over tonight **to** talk about the holiday.*

In order to and *so as to* are normal before negative infinitives.

*I'm putting on lots of suntan lotion **so as not to** get burnt.*

2 *So that* and *in order that* are often followed by auxiliary verbs, e.g. *can* and *will*. *So that* is more informal.

*I'd like to do a part-time degree **so that** I'll have a better chance of getting promoted.*

In an informal style, *that* can be dropped after *so*.

*I want to go back to the CD shop **so** I can get a refund for the CD I bought yesterday.*

3 *In case* is used to talk about being prepared for things or taking precautions. To talk about the future, we use a present tense after *in case*.

*You should take your swimming trunks **in case** you decide to go swimming.*

Unit 10

Adverbs

We use adverbs to modify verbs, adjectives, other adverbs and sometimes whole sentences.

Adverbs and adverbial phrases – different types:

1 Adverbs of manner describe how someone does something, e.g. *angrily*, *in a friendly way*.

2 Adverbs of place describe where something happens, e.g. *here, in the corner.*

3 Adverbs of time describe when something happens, e.g. *tomorrow, soon*.

4 Adverbs of frequency describe how often something happens, e.g. *usually, once a week*.

5 Adverbs of certainty describe how certain something is, e.g. *perhaps, certainly*.

6 Adverbs of completeness (or degree) describe how much or how strongly something happens, e.g. *nearly, quite*.

7 Emphasising adverbs emphasise the following word, e.g. *very, extremely*.

8 Connecting adverbs join a clause to what came before, e.g. *next, however*.

9 Comment adverbs give the speaker's opinion of an action, e.g. *surprisingly, stupidly*.

How to form adverbs
We form most adverbs by adding *-ly* to the adjective:

slow > slowly; beautiful > beautifully

Exceptions:

1 Adjectives ending in *-le* form adverbs by changing *-le* to *-ly*.
simple > simply

2 Adjectives ending in *-y* form adverbs by changing *-y* to *-ily*.
easy > easily

3 Adjectives ending in *-ic* form adverbs by adding *-ally*.
automatic > automatically

4 Some adverbs which end in *-ly* come from nouns.
day > daily; week > weekly

5 We cannot add *-ly* to adjectives which end in *-ly*. In these cases, we use an adverbial phrase (*in a ... way/manner/ fashion*).
friendly > in a friendly way; silly > in a silly manner; lonely > in a lonely fashion.

6 There are other exceptions which do not fit the rules.
fast > fast; hard > hard; still > still; good > well; full > fully; true > truly; public > publicly

Position of adverbs (and adverbial phrases)
Different types of adverbs go in different positions in a sentence. There are general rules about this (and some exceptions).

1 We do not usually put adverbs between a verb and its object.
She speaks English well.
~~*She speaks well English.*~~

2 There are three normal positions for adverbs:
A Front position (at the beginning of a clause).
   ***Suddenly**, someone ran through the door.*
B Mid position (before the main verb).
   *I've **never** been so upset.*
C End position (at the end of a clause).
   *Shall we go to the cinema **tomorrow**?*

3 There are common positions for the different types of adverbs.
Adverbs of manner usually go in end position. (Adverbs ending in *-ly* can also go in mid position if the adverb is not the main focus of the sentence.)

Adverbs of place usually go in end position (but can also go in front position – especially if the adverb is not the main focus of the sentence).

Adverbs of time usually go in end position (but can also go in front position – especially if the adverb is not the main focus of the sentence). *Soon* can go in mid position.

Adverbs of frequency such as *usually, normally, often, frequently, sometimes* and *occasionally* are most common in mid position. (They can also go in front position or end position if they are the main message of the sentence.)
Always, ever, rarely, seldom and *never* cannot normally go in front or end position.

Adverbs of certainty – *maybe* and *perhaps* usually go in front position. Other adverbs of certainty (e.g. *probably, definitely*) usually go in mid position.

Adverbs of completeness (or degree) usually go in mid position.

Emphasising adverbs go directly before the word they are emphasising.

Connecting adverbs usually go in front position (but can also go in mid position and end position).

Comment adverbs usually go in front position (but can also go in mid position).

4 When there are adverbs of manner, place and time in one sentence, they normally go in that order.
He sat quietly in the corner of the room for hours.

Causative *have* and *get*

1 *Have/get* + object + past participle is used to talk about when somebody else does something for you (often when you arrange and pay them to do so). (*Get* in this case is sometimes considered slightly more informal.)
*We're **having the house painted**.*
*I must **get my watch repaired**.*
*I'm going to **get my hair cut** this afternoon.*

2 *Have/get* + object + past participle is used to talk about an 'experience' or something that happens to you (often something which you have no control over). (*Get* in this case is sometimes considered slightly more informal.)
*We **got our roof blown off** in the storm last week.*
*I've just **had my first article published.***

3 *Get* + object + past participle is used to talk about completing work on something. (We cannot use *have* in this case.)
*I'll **get the washing up done** and then I'll help you in the garden.*

4 *Get* + object + *to*-infinitive is used to talk about when you make (or persuade) somebody/something do something (often with the idea of difficulty). (We cannot use *have* in this case.)
*You could **get Jim to help** us.*
*I tried to **get someone to listen** to our complaint.*

Unit 11

Relative clauses and pronouns

Relative pronouns

The most common relative pronouns are:

who, whom: to refer to people
which: to refer to things
that: to refer to people or things
whose: the possessive of *who* and *which*
when: used after nouns referring to time
where: used after nouns referring to place
why: used to refer to reasons

Defining relative clauses

1 The relative clause defines or identifies the person, thing, time, place or reason.
   *Kate is the woman **who told me about the new job**.*
   *That's the street **where John's just bought a flat**.*

2 *That* can be used instead of *who* and *which*.
   *The man **that** (who) is doing the project with me isn't here today.*
   *The room **that** (which) is booked for the meeting is locked.*

3 The relative pronoun can be omitted when the clause defines the object of the clause.
   The place (where/that) we're going on holiday is supposed to be lovely.
   The reason (why/that) I'm late is that the traffic was awful.

4 No commas are used before and after the relative clause.

Non-defining relative clauses

In non-defining relative clauses the relative clause gives extra information which can be left out. Commas are used before and after the relative clause.
David, whose brother already lives in New York, is about to move to the States.
My computer, which I only got two months ago, keeps crashing.

Prepositions in relative clauses

Prepositions can come before the relative pronoun or at the end of the relative clause depending on whether the sentence is formal or informal.
The person to whom you need to speak is not available. (formal)
Stella, who you need to give the money to, will be back later. (informal)

if structures

Linking words in *if* structures

Some common conditional linking words are:

if, when, as/so long as, until, unless , even if, no matter how/who/what/where/when, provided (that)

Punctuation in *if* structures

When the clause with the conditional linking word (*if, unless,* etc.) is at the beginning of the sentence, there is a comma. When the main clause begins the sentence, there is no comma.
If I see her, I'll give her the money back.
I'll give her the money back when I see her.
I won't lend her any money unless she promises to pay me back.
As long as you pay me back by Friday, I'll lend you some money.

Different types of *if* structures

A

   FORM
   if + present simple + present simple in the main clause

   USE
   To talk about something which is always true or describe what always happens. (Sometimes called the **zero conditional**.)
   If you stroke our cat, she purrs.
   Ice melts if you heat it.

B

   FORM
   if + present simple/present continuous/present perfect + future/present continuous or imperative in the main clause

   USE
   To talk about something that is a real possibility in the future. (Sometimes called the **first conditional**.)
   If she passes her exam, she'll be really pleased with herself.
   Unless you phone me, I won't know you're coming.
   Tell Penny to ring me if you see her.
   As long as you've eaten enough breakfast, you won't need to take any food with you.

C

   FORM
   if + past simple/continuous + conditional in the main clause

   USE
   To talk about something:
   1 That is impossible and just imagined.
   2 Which is very unlikely to happen in the future (Sometimes called the **second conditional**.) Also, this form is often used to give advice.
   If she was a bit taller, she'd look really good in that dress.
   I wouldn't go parachuting even if you paid me.
   If I were you, I'd have an early night.

D

   FORM
   if + past perfect + *would have* + past participle in the main clause

USE

To talk about something in the past that could have happened, but didn't, or something that shouldn't have happened, but did. (Sometimes called the **third conditional**.)

I wouldn't have put any meat in if I'd known he was vegetarian.

If you'd asked me earlier, I would've given you a lift.

E

FORM

an *if*-clause referring to the past with a main clause referring to the present or the future

USE

To talk about if something had been different in the past, the present (or future) would be different. (Sometimes called a **mixed conditional**.)

If she'd had more practice, she'd feel a lot more confident about passing her test today.

I'd be a wealthy man if I'd got that job I applied for.

F

FORM

an *if*-clause referring to the present or future with a main clause referring to the past

USE

To talk about if something in the present (or in general time) were different, the past would have been different. (Also sometimes called a **mixed conditional**.)

If I knew him better, I would have invited him to the party.

She wouldn't have ordered spaghetti if she didn't like pasta.

Modals in *if* structures

Modal verbs (*may, might, could,* etc.) can be used in all *if* structures, except those expressing general truth (in **A** above).

I might go to the cinema if I'm not too tired.

If she studied harder, she could pass the exam.

If they had told me what the course involved, I might never have signed up for it.

Polite expressions using *if, would* and *should*

Would can be used after *if* in polite expressions.

If you wouldn't mind waiting for a moment, the manager will see you shortly.

Should is used in the *if*-clause to make it even less likely. This is common in formal letters.

If you should require any further information, please do not hesitate to contact us.

Should can replace *if* in formal letters.

Should you wish to contact me, I can be reached at the above address.

Unit 12

Direct speech

This is when we report the exact words that someone says or writes.

'Are you going to call the police?' she asked.

In her email she said, 'I need to see Jo urgently.'

Reported speech

This is when we report something that has been said or written. If the report is after the time the thing was said or written, the verb form generally changes as follows:

Direct speech	Reported speech
1 Present simple/continuous	Past simple/continuous
'I am living with my brother,' she said.	*She said she was living with her brother.*
2 Past simple/continuous	Past simple/continuous or past perfect simple/continuous
'We arrested Mr Brown this morning,' a police spokesperson said.	*A police spokesperson said that they arrested/had arrested Mr Brown that morning.*
3 Present perfect simple/continuous	Past perfect simple/continuous
'I have played the guitar since I was seven,' he said.	*He told me (that) he had played the guitar since he was seven.*
4 *will*	*would*
'I'll answer the door,' she said.	*She said she would answer the door.*
5 *must* (obligation)	*had to*
'You must tell the police everything you know,' Becky insisted.	*Becky insisted that I had to tell the police everything I knew.*
6 *can*	*could*
'I can do a handstand,' said Peter.	*Peter said he could do a handstand.*

The verb form does not need to change when:

The thing being reported is still true.

'The Sun is approximately ninety-three million miles from the Earth,' the teacher told us.

The teacher told us that the Sun is approximately ninety-three million miles from the Earth.

'The bus leaves at 4.00 p.m.,' said the woman at the ticket office.

The woman at the ticket office told us that the bus leaves at 4.00 p.m.

The thing reported contains the modals *would, could, might, ought to* and *should* as well as *must* for logical deduction.

'You ought to revise for your exam this weekend,' she said.

She said I ought to revise for my exam this weekend.

'We might not be free on Friday night,' she said.

She said they might not be free on Friday night.

'I think she must be working late,' Tim said.

Tim said he thought she must be working late.

The thing being reported contains the past perfect.

'He had been helping the police with their enquiries,' she said.

She said he had been helping the police with their enquiries.

The changes that occur in reported speech are:

Direct speech	Reported speech
tomorrow	the next day, the day after, the following day
yesterday	the day before, the previous day
last week	the week before
here	there
this/that	the
this morning	that morning
today	that day
next Friday	the following Friday
ago	before

Reported statements

FORM

verb (+ *that*) + clause

'I stole the car,' she admitted

She admitted (that) she had stolen the car.

'He sleeps during most of the day and then goes out clubbing all night' she said.

She said (that) he slept during most of the day and then went out clubbing all night.

Reported questions

Reported *Yes/No* questions

FORM

When there is no question word in the direct speech question, we use *if/whether*. Word order is the same as in the statement. The verb tense and other changes are the same as for other types of reported speech.

'Are you going to arrest him?' she asked.

She asked if/whether they were going to arrest him.

'Do you like dogs?' he asked.

He asked us if/whether we liked dogs.

Reported *wh-* questions

FORM

When *wh-* question words are used, the *wh-* word is followed by statement word order, that is the subject followed by the verb.

All the tense and other changes are the same as for other types of reported speech.

'Why isn't John here?' she asked.

She asked why John wasn't there.

'Where do you usually have lunch?' he asked her.

He asked her where she usually had lunch.

Reported orders

FORM

verb + (*that*) + clause or verb + object + infinitive with *to*

'Go back to college,' his father said.

His father recommended (that) he go back to college.

'Bring in the washing, will you?' she said.

She told me to bring in the washing.

Reported suggestions

FORM

suggest + *-ing*

suggest + *that* + *should* + infinitive without *to*

suggest + past simple

'Let's make a picnic and take it to the beach,' she said.

She suggested making a picnic and taking it to the beach.

She suggested that we should make a picnic and take it to the beach.

She suggested we made a picnic and took it to the beach.

Note: we cannot say ~~She suggested to have a party for Mario~~.

Reporting verbs

1   Verb + object + infinitive

   They asked us to stay.

   Other verbs with the same pattern are:
   advise, beg, encourage, invite, order, persuade, remind, warn

2   Verb (+ *that*) + clause

   He says (that) he is very angry with you.

   Other verbs with the same pattern are:
   claim, admit, explain, promise

3   Verb + object (+ *that*) + clause

   We told him (that) we had just moved to Manchester.

   Other verbs with the same pattern are:
   remind, warn

4   Verb + gerund

   He admitted taking the shoes without paying for them.

   Other verbs with the same pattern are:
   deny, recommend, suggest

   Note: Verbs in groups 2, 3 and 4 can also be used with *that* + clause.

   He admitted that he had taken the shoes without paying for them.

5 Verb + preposition + gerund
She apologised for lying to me.
She discouraged me from leaving school early.

Other verbs with the same pattern are:
accuse (of), blame (for), congratulate (on), insist (on)

6 Verb + infinitive
We agreed to write to each other as often as we could.

Other verbs with the same pattern are:
decide, offer, promise, refuse, threaten

Unit 13

Possibility and certainty

Factual possibility – *could, may and might (not)*
We use *could, may* and *might (not)*:

1 To say that something is possibly true at the moment of speaking.

FORM
might/may/could + infinitive
She might be angry about something you said.
He may be back earlier than expected.
That number couldn't be wrong – I've used it before.

Note: We don't use *can* in this case (to talk about possibility in the present): ~~She can be Italian but I'm not sure~~.

2 To talk about the possibility that past events happened.

FORM
could/may/might + *have* + past participle
They may have decided to stay the night there.
He might not have met her before.
She could have talked to him yesterday.

3 To say there is a chance that something might happen in the future.

FORM
might/may/could + infinitive
We may go to Australia next Christmas.
It could snow tonight.
She might not come and see us after all.

Theoretical possibility – *can*
We use *can*:

1 To ask, speculate or guess about past events.
   Note: This is only in questions.

FORM
(*Wh-* word +) *can* + subject + *have* + past participle
Can he have thought we'd left already?
Where can they have gone?

2 To say that things are possible in the future (without saying what chance there is that they will happen).

FORM
can + infinitive
Anyone can learn to use a word processor.

1 Talk about typical behaviour of people or things.

FORM
can + infinitive
Dogs can be jealous of small babies.

Certainty – *must*
We use *must*:

1 To talk about something which is certain or highly probable to be true, or for which we have excellent evidence for believing to be true in the present or future.

FORM
must + infinitive
You must be exhausted after all that running.

2 To express conclusions about things that happened in the past when we are certain, or it is highly probable, something was true, or for which we have excellent evidence for believing to have been true.

FORM
must + *have* + past participle
He must have overslept this morning – he's never usually this late.

Certainty – *can't*
We use *can't*:

1 To talk about something which is certain or highly probable NOT to be true, or for which we have excellent evidence for believing NOT to be true in the present or future.

FORM
can't + infinitive
That can't be Michael at the door – he's on holiday at the moment.

2 To express conclusions about things that happened in the past when we are certain, or it is highly probable, something was NOT true, or for which we have excellent evidence for believing NOT to have been true.

FORM
can't + *have* + past participle
She can't have understood what you meant.

Note: We can also use *couldn't* in this case (to talk about certainty):
That couldn't be Michael at the door – he's on holiday at the moment.
She couldn't have understood what you meant.

We don't use *mustn't* in this case (to talk about certainty): ~~He mustn't have liked the film because he left halfway through it.~~

-ing forms and infinitives

Certain grammatical constructions and certain verbs are followed by:

1 The infinitive without *to* (e.g. *do*).
2 The infinitive with *to* (e.g. *to do*).
3 The *-ing* form (e.g. *doing*).

Grammatical constructions/patterns

1 Use the infinitive without *to* (e.g. *do*):

after modal verbs
*You **must take** all the medicine.*

after *make* and *let*
*She **let me borrow** the DVD.*

after *I'd better* and *I'd rather*
***I'd better phone** Michael soon.*

2 Use the infinitive with *to* (e.g. *to do*):

after certain adjectives
*I'm really **pleased to be** here.*

after the construction *too ... to ...*
*It's **too cold to swim** in the river at the moment.*

to express purpose
*I go to dance classes **to keep fit**.*

3 Use the *-ing* form (e.g. *doing*):

after prepositions
*He accused me **of taking** his pen.*

when an action (not a noun) is the subject or object of a sentence
***Smoking** is not permitted inside the building.*

With certain verbs:

1 Verbs followed by the *-ing* form (gerund).
Here are some common verbs which are followed by the *-ing* form:
admit, appreciate, can't help, can't stand, consider, delay, deny, detest, dislike, enjoy, escape, excuse, face, feel like, finish, forgive, give up, imagine, involve, mention, mind, miss, postpone, practise, put off, resent, risk, suggest, understand
*He **admitted taking** part in the robbery.*

2 Verbs followed by an object + the infinitive without *to*.
Here are some common verbs which are followed by an object and the infinitive without *to*:
know, hear, feel, help
*Would you **help me finish** tidying this room?*

In passive sentences these verbs are followed by an infinitive with *to*.
*Young children were **helped to board** the boat safely.*

3 Verbs followed by an infinitive with *to*.
Here are some common verbs which are followed by an infinitive with *to*:
afford, agree, appear, arrange, ask, attempt, bear, begin, care, choose, consent, decide, determine, expect, fail, forget, happen, hate, help, hesitate, hope, intend, learn, like, love, manage, mean, offer, prefer, prepare, pretend, promise, propose, refuse, regret, remember, seem, start, swear, trouble, try, want, wish
*We **arranged to meet** the following week.*

4 Verbs followed by object + infinitive with *to*.
Here are some common verbs which are followed by an object and the infinitive with *to*:
advise, allow, ask, cause, command, encourage, expect, forbid, force, get, hate, help, instruct, intend, invite, leave, like, mean, need, oblige, order, permit, persuade, prefer, press, recommend, request, remind, teach, tell, tempt, trouble, want, warn, wish
*He **encouraged me to make** an appointment.*

5 Verbs followed by a gerund or an infinitive with a difference in meaning.
remember, forget, stop, try
remember: the gerund is used when the action happens before the remembering; the infinitive refers to an action that happens after.
*I **remember seeing** someone behaving strangely at the bus stop.*
*Did **you remember to get** some more bread?*

forget: when used with the gerund this means 'forget what you have done'; when used with the infinitive with *to*, this means 'forget what you have to do'.
*I had completely **forgotten putting** that book on the shelf.*
*I **forgot to post** the letter you gave me.*

stop: when used with the gerund, this means 'stop something you do'; when used with the infinitive with *to*, this means 'stop in order to do something'.
*I **stopped drinking** coffee because I couldn't sleep.*
*We **stopped to have** a coffee on our way into town.*

try: when used with the gerund this means 'make an experiment' – doing the action may not be successful; when used with the infinitive this means 'make an effort' – the action may be difficult or impossible to do.
*Try **drinking** some warm milk before going to bed.*
*Try **to listen** to English radio for at least half an hour a day.*

can't bear/stand, hate, like, love, prefer
When these verbs are used with the infinitive they refer to more specific situations. When they are used with the gerund they refer to more general situations. The difference in meaning is very slight.
*I **prefer to go** to school by bus.*
*I **can't bear getting up** so early, but I have to.*

Grammar Reference

Unit 14

Passives

FORM

appropriate tense of *be* + past participle

Present simple: All notebooks **are kept** in the cupboard by the window.

Present continuous: My computer **is being looked at** just now by someone from the IT department.

Past simple: We **were** all **given** the day off yesterday.

Past continuous: The last time I saw Tim, he **was being shown** how to use a new design program by one of the designers.

Present perfect: **Have you been told** about the cutbacks in staff they are planning?

Past perfect: We **had been asked** to meet in the boardroom by 10.00 a.m.

Future *will*: You**'ll be told** about all your duties when you start work on Monday morning.

Future perfect: These **will have been** completely **redesigned** by the time we move in.

going to: The meeting **is going to be chaired** by Philip.

Modals: The file **must have been put back** in the filing cabinet.

Passive gerund: Emily hates **being patronised**.

Note:

1 Verbs that do not take an object (e.g. *ache, arrive, sit down*) do not have passive forms. It is not possible to say: ~~I was arrived~~.

2 Stative verbs like *have, fit, suit* are not used in the passive with the same meanings.

Do you have an iPod? (have = *own*)

They've only given us £5 change. We've been had. (have = *deceived*)

Those jeans don't fit you any more. (fit = *be the right size*)

My new flat is being fitted with all the latest TV and hi-fi equipment. (fit = *installed*)

That jacket suits you. (suit = *look nice*)

Tina and Jerry are really suited to each other. (suit = *are compatible*)

USE

The passive is used for the following reasons:

To talk about actions, events and processes when the action, event or process is seen as more important than the agent. This is often the case in scientific writing.

The Eiffel Tower was built in 1889.

The subjects in the experiment were given three of the pills every four hours.

To put new information later in the sentence.

This photo was taken by my uncle.

To put longer expressions at the end of the sentence.

I was very surprised by the way she seemed to blame me for what had happened.

by + agent

When we are interested in the agent, we use the preposition *by*.

*The idea for our new advertising slogan was suggested **by** my secretary.*

*These documents were found **by** the evening cleaner.*

Ability

1 *can*

We use *can* to talk about present ability.

Can you speak any Arabic?

We use *can* to talk about future actions which we will be able to do because of present ability, present circumstances, etc.

I can go to next week's meeting in New York.

In other cases, we use other structures, e.g. *will be able to*.

Next year we will be able to give all our employees a 7% pay increase.

2 *could*

We use *could* to talk about general past ability.

I could ride a horse quite well by the time I was thirteen.

We do not normally use *could* to say that somebody did something on one occasion. Instead, we use other expressions.

*We **succeeded in** our aim of opening three more branches last year.*

*We **managed to** double our advertising revenue last year.*

*Were you **able to** speak to the managing director?*

Unit 15

Hypothetical meaning

wish

We use *wish* + past simple to express a wish that has not come true in the present. We also use *wish* + past simple to talk about wishes that might come true in the future.

I wish I had a dog.

Don't you wish you had your own flat?

If the verb is *be*, we can use the past simple (*I/he/she/it was; you/we/they were*) or *were* with all persons (*I/you/he/she/it/we/they were*).

We all wish the weather wasn't/weren't so awful.

I wish she wasn't/weren't quite so hard up.

We use *wish* + *would* and *could* to refer to general wishes for the future.

I wish I could see you tonight but I have to work late.

I wish she would be a bit more friendly.

Wish + would is often used to talk about other people's irritating habits. This form is not often used with *I* or *we*. To talk about our own irritating habits we use *could*.

I wish you would stop humming. It's very irritating.

Don't you wish she wouldn't be so patronising?

I wish I could improve my tennis.

We use *wish + past perfect* to refer to things we are sorry about in the past.

I wish I hadn't lost my temper.

She wishes she hadn't resigned from her job.

if only

If only is used with the same verb forms as *wish*, and is used when your feelings are stronger. It is often used with an exclamation mark (!). It is used very commonly with *would/wouldn't* to criticise someone else's behaviour.

If only I could speak Spanish well!

If only I had more time to be with my children.

If only she hadn't read my diary.

If only you wouldn't criticise Tania all the time.

it's time

It's time is used with the past simple to talk about the present or future. We mean that the action should have been done before. We can also say *It's about time* and *It's high time*.

It's time you had a break. You've been working on those spreadsheets for hours.

It's about time we painted the spare room. It's looking very shabby.

It's high time she got a job. She finished her college course months ago.

I'd rather (would rather)

We use *I'd rather* + past simple when we want to say what we want someone or something else to do in the present or future.

I'd rather you came and picked me up from the airport.

Would you rather go to the cinema next week?

We use *I'd rather* + past perfect when we want to say what we wanted to happen in the past.

I'd rather you hadn't told them about our engagement.

I'd rather she had asked us before borrowing the car.

I'd rather + infinitive without *to* is used to talk about our preferences or other people's preferences in the present or future.

I'd rather stay at home than go out tonight.

We'd rather get a takeaway pizza.

suppose

Suppose means 'What if …?'. It is used with:

The present simple to describe something that may possibly happen or may have happened.

Suppose Jane tells someone about what you did.

Suppose someone saw you using Mr Green's computer.

The past simple to talk about something that is just imagination or which is unlikely to happen in the future.

Suppose he asked you to marry him. What would you do?

Suppose they offered you a job in the USA. Would you go?

The past perfect to talk about something that could have happened but didn't in the past.

Suppose we had known each other when we were teenagers. How well do you think we would have got on?

Suppose you had stayed in Australia. Do you think you would have been happy there?

Verb–subject agreement

Most words ending in -ics (e.g. *politics, mathematics, athletics*) are normally singular uncountable and have no plural use.

Mathematics was my favourite subject at school.

Some singular uncountable nouns end in -s. These have no plurals, e.g. *news, billiards, measles*.

I'm afraid the news about your father isn't very good.

Singular words which refer to groups of people (e.g. *family, team, government*) can have either singular or plural verbs and pronouns.

Our team is/are going to play this afternoon.

Police is a plural word used to talk collectively. (*Staff* and *crew* are used in the same way.)

The police are hunting a thirty-five-year-old man last seen running from the bank.

Trousers, jeans, scissors, glasses and the names of many similar divided objects are plural and have no singular forms.

Do you know where my glasses are?

Plural names of countries usually have singular verbs and pronouns.

The United States is represented today by Mr William O'Donnell.

Sums of money, periods of time, distance, etc. are seen as one thing, so we use a singular verb.

Two hours is a long time to have to travel to and from work each day.

Writing Reference

Review

(For work on reviews, see pages 10 and 94.)

1 Task

> Your teacher has asked you to write a review of a book you have read recently.
>
> You should include information on the author and type of book it is. You should also say what you liked/disliked about the book and whether you would recommend it to other people.
>
> Write your **review**. (You should write between **120** and **180** words.

2 Model answer

DO give some details of personal interest to catch your reader's attention.

I saw the musical of 'The Phantom of the Opera' and wondered if the book would be as good. The novel was written about 100 years ago by Frenchman Gaston Leroux. He was fascinated by the Opera House in Paris and decided it would be a perfect setting for a detective story.

DO use specific vocabulary about the CD/book/film/play, etc. that you are reviewing

DON'T only describe the CD/book/film/play, etc., but make sure you give your opinion.

The book starts with a death and the sighting of a ghost in the Opera House in Paris and continues in the style of a detective novel. It is well-written and the plot was extremely gripping. One of the other strengths of the book is the description of one of the main characters, Erik. He is a complex character because, although he is very talented, he has a terribly deformed face and is therefore rejected by society.

DO organise your review into clear paragraphs.

DON'T give away the ending or spoil any surprises in the book/film/play.

I would highly recommend this book. Even if you don't usually like detective stories, do not be put off. The various parts of the story are expertly put together and it is very easy to read. Personally, I couldn't put it down!

DO end your review with a recommendation (briefly summarising the reasons for your opinion).

(171 words)

USEFUL LANGUAGE

Giving information (about the CD, book, film or play/musical)

The album was released in 2006 and went straight to number one.

It's a huge production with a cast of about sixty singers and dancers.

This film is produced by the same company that made Toy Story and The Incredibles.

The novel describes the author's childhood in Scotland in the 1960s.

Giving your opinion (about the CD, book, film or play/musical)

One of the strongest things about the book is the plot, which is exciting and unusual.

The acting is very good, especially the main character, who is played by …

My favourite track is …

The song is very lively and has interesting lyrics.

The only negative thing I would say about the … is …

Giving a recommendation

I would definitely recommend buying/seeing/reading it.

It's an easy read and I would say it's perfect for taking on holiday.

If you get a chance, then go and see it as soon as you can.

I would say try to see it at the cinema (not just on DVD) to make the most of the special effects.

3 Sample task, answers and comments

Task

> You have seen this advertisement in an English-speaking magazine.
>
> **See it again! Read it again!**
>
> Write a review of a film or book that you would like to see/read again. Include information about the type of film or book it is. You should also say what you liked/disliked about it and whether you would recommend it to other people.
>
> The writer of the best review will win £500 in cash.

> Write your **review**. (You should write between **120** and **180** words.)

Answer A

Always I've thought that I was very good detective so always I enjoy reading detective stories. One of the best ones I've read recently is *Sherlock Holmes Short Stories* by famous English writer Arthur Conan Doyle.

In this book, there are seven different stories. In each ones Sherlock Holmes and his friend Doctor Watson try to solved the mystery and get to the truth of what happened. The plots are always clever and interesting and I like trying work out the end.

I know what happens and I already enjoyed reading this book more than once. The stories are situated in interesting places like in Baker Street in London and the characters are fun. And I also like the details in the stories.

I would definitely recommend reading this book. It is easy to read especially because they are short stories.

Comments

There is good organisation of paragraphs with a clear introduction which includes personal details, creating interest for the reader.

There are some good expressions (e.g. *One of the best ones I've read …* and *… get to the truth of what happened.*) But there are also some inaccuracies of grammar (e.g. word order – *Always I've thought …* and missing articles – *I was very good detective … / … by famous English writer.*)

There is quite a good range of topic-related vocabulary (e.g. *detective stories, plots, characters*).

There are not many linkers, however, and sometimes the sentence construction is too simple and repetitive.

The style is appropriate and the task is achieved. It has a positive effect on the reader.

Band 4

Answer B

I'm sure that everyone would agree with me that the *Lord of the Rings* films are fantastic. The three films are based on the books by Tolkien and the stories are full of drama and excitement. In my opinion, they are the best fantasy films ever.

I have seen each film three times and I don't get tired with watching them. If you get a chance, then go and see them as soon as you can possible. You won't be disappointed.

Although the story is quite complicated and has many parts, the films aren't confusing or dull. Each of the films is quite long but the director, Peter Jackson, manages to keep the excitement going throughout them all. The action and the fight senes are so spectacular and I think that the special effects are amazing. Sometimes you can hardly believe what you are watching. The cast is very large and the acting is very good, especially one of the main characters, Frodo Baggins, who is played by Elijah Wood.

Comments

This is a full and effective answer to the task, using an appropriate style.

Vocabulary is appropriate (e.g. *based on, director, cast*) and there is a good range of expression (e.g. *… manages to keep the excitement going throughout them all*); *Sometimes you can hardly believe …*

There are only a couple of small mistakes (e.g. collocation – *I don't get tired ~~with~~ of watching …* and spelling – *~~senes~~ – scenes*) but these don't impede communication.

The paragraph organisation is rather weak, but the overall answer would have a positive effect on the reader.

Band 4

Writing Reference

Informal Letter

(For work on informal letters, see pages 25 and 84.)

(For work on informal letters, see pages 25 and 84.)

1 Task

You have received a letter from your penfriend inviting you for a visit in July. Write a letter to your penfriend, accepting the invitation, suggesting something you would like to do and asking what you should bring with you.

Write your **letter**. Do not write any postal addresses. (You should write between **120** and **180** words.)

USEFUL LANGUAGE

Beginning the letter

Many thanks for your letter (– it was really nice to hear from you again).

I thought I'd better write (and give you some more details about ...)

It's been such a long time since we wrote to each other.

How are you and your family?

How are things with you?

How was (your holiday)?

Introducing the topic

I know you're longing to hear all about (my holiday).

You remember I told you in my last letter (that I was going to ...)

Ending the letter

Once again, (thanks very much for all your help).

Give my love/regards to (your family).

Please write/drop me a line soon.

I look forward to (meeting up again soon).

---

2 Model answer

Dear Carla,

DO mention a letter you have received from the person you are writing to, or refer to a shared experience.

Thanks for your letter – it was great to hear from you. I'm sorry I haven't written for ages, but I've been really busy preparing for my exams. It's really good news that you've passed your driving test. Congratulations!

DO invent a name. Don't write *Dear Penfriend.*

DO say what you've been doing recently.

Thank you so much for your invitation to stay with you for a week in July – I'd love to come. I know that you have a wonderful beach near your house, and I'd really enjoy spending some time there. I expect that the weather will be hot, so I hope we can go swimming.

DO think of some specific details to include in each paragraph – this will make your letter more interesting.

You said that I don't need to bring much with me. What sort of clothes should I pack? Casual or formal? Would you like me to bring anything for you? I would like to bring something special for you and your family from my country.

I'd better stop now and get on with my studying. I hope you're enjoying driving your car, and I'm looking forward to seeing you in July! Thanks again for the invitation.

DO mention the next time you will see the person you are writing to.

DO use an appropriate informal phrase to end your letter, e.g. *Love, All the best, Best wishes.* DON'T finish your letter with *Yours sincerely/ faithfully.*

All the best,

Irene

---

3 Sample task, answers and comments

Task

You have received a letter from a penfriend who is planning to visit you in July. Write a letter to your penfriend, describing the activities you have planned for his/her visit. Give advice on what to bring and ask about any special requests.

Write your **letter**. Do not write any postal addresses. (You should write between **120** and **180** words.)

Answer A

Dear Carria,

Nice to hear from you. I'm so surprised that you are on your way to come here this summer. I have to say that you've made a good decision.

First of all, I would like to recommend you some places where you shouldn't miss such as Sentosa island. You can have different activities there. For example, if you would like having sunbathing. I think 'Sun World' is the best choice to relax. Don't forget to bring swimwear. I don't think Bird Park is a good place to visit. It's quite boring I have to be honest to say that. However if you are really interesting in visiting there I could show you around.

Secondly, it's the best time come here if you enjoy the shopping. We have big on sale in July. Therefore, I can arrange the shopping table for you. I will be very please to show you how interesting on big sale in here!

I don't think you need to bring any special stuff. That's because you can buy them here. Don't forget to prepare some more empty suitcase for your shopping.

If you have any question just ask me. I'll do my best to solve them.

I'm looking forward to hearing from you again!

Best wishes,

Carel

Comments

This is a full answer to the question, with a fairly good range of grammar, but there are quite a few grammatical problems (e.g. *recommend you some places where you* instead of *recommend some places to you which; interesting in* instead of *interested in*). Vocabulary problems sometimes make the meaning unclear (e.g. *I can arrange the shopping table for you*).

Paragraphs and connecting words are well used and the style is generally suitable for a letter from a friend.

It has a satisfactory effect on the reader.

Band 3

Answer B

Dear Diego,

Hi! How are you? Thank you for your letter! I'm very happy about your plan!

OK! If you let me know your arrival time, I will come to you, at Narita airport. I've thought about our plan in Japan. I know you really like football! So, how about visiting stadiums of the World Cup? You can visit a locker room in Yokohama International Stadium where the final was held, and you can see autographs of Brazilian national team members.

In July, Japan is very hot, but sometimes there is a heavy rain so you have to bring an umbrella. And there are lots of mosquitoes, you must bring a medical cream to protect yourself against them.

Do you have any special requests? If you have any, please let me know. I'll try to do it!

I'm looking forward to your reply and to meeting you in July!

Lots of love,

Yuka

Comments

All parts of the question are dealt with, in an informal style. There are some grammatical mistakes (e.g. *there is a̶ heavy rain*) and problems in pronoun use (e.g. *I'll try to do t̶h̶e̶m̶!*) but the student uses tenses accurately and shows a good range of vocabulary, and the paragraphs are clear and well constructed. The letter has a positive effect on the reader.

Band 4

Writing Reference

Essay

(For work on essays, see pages 35 and 129.)

1 Task

You have been doing a class project on technology. Your teacher has asked you to write a composition giving your opinion on the following statement:

People in the modern world depend too much on computers.

Write your **essay**. (You should write between **120** and **180** words.)

USEFUL LANGUAGE

I think/believe that …

Some people claim that (your teenage years are the best years of your life).

It is often said that (TV is a bad influence on young people).

However, in my view/opinion, …

Firstly it is clear that (money cannot buy happiness).

While it is true that (computer games are stimulating, they may not be good for you in the long term).

From my point of view, (job satisfaction is more important than a large salary).

Finally, it is important to remember that …

On balance then, I feel that …

To sum up/In conclusion, it seems to me that …

2 Model answer

DO restate the question in your first sentence.

In today's world, nearly every aspect of life is affected by computer technology. Computers are used for business, public services, education and entertainment.

DON'T start by saying I agree with this – your essay should present your own argument.

Some people are concerned by this development. They fear that vital skills are being lost as computer technology replaces traditional ways of working in a wide variety of areas, from art and design to banking and commerce. They point out the chaos that can occur when computer systems fail, leading to the breakdown of essential services such as transport, law and order.

DO include supporting detail for the points in each paragraph.

DO use linking expressions to introduce points.

However, people could not continue to enjoy their present standard of living without computer technology. There are now far more people in the world than there were a generation ago. The fact that there is enough food for them, that they can travel safely from one place to another, and that they can be provided with medical care, is largely due to computer technology.

In my opinion, therefore, we have to accept our dependence on computers, but at the same time we should work to find ways of making this dependence less dangerous.

DON'T forget to express your opinion in the conclusion.

3 Sample task, answers and comments

Task

You have had a class discussion on what people do in their free time. Your teacher has now asked you to write an essay, giving your opinions on the following statement:

Shopping has little value as a leisure activity.

Write your **essay**. (You should write between **120** and **180** words.)

Answer A

I believe that shopping can be one of the important things people do, like eating and sleeping, and for some shopping is their chance to do their favourite things like walking and meeting friends.

On the one hand, I think that is true that shopping has no value in some lifestyles. People think of shopping only as a chance to do whatever they want, and then it is an escape from doing things they should do. I mean people go shopping instead of do work.

However, others think of it as a chance to meet some friends who you only see from time to time. In addition, it is useful time to discuss every day problems – for example, if you have got some problems, in that shopping time you might listen to others problems and think that yours are nothing compared to theirs. It can make a break from every day work pressure and so it is valuable for some who have a hard job and lifestyle.

In conclusion, it's true that buying things has little value, but people are different, which means that shopping will be priceless for some.

Comments

This answers the question clearly and uses a wide range of vocabulary and some good expressions (e.g. *think that yours are nothing compared to theirs*).

However, there are grammatical mistakes (e.g. *instead of do work*).

The style is appropriate. The conclusion clearly returns to the question and gives a nice summary of the writer's opinion.

It has a positive effect on the reader.

Band 4

Answer B

Does shopping have little value as a leisure activity? I think most people are really keen on shopping but is it really useful?

For example, if we ask students what they're going to do in a big city, the answers are almost always 'shopping', and they don't think about going to museums and sight-seeing. Most tourists go shopping sometime instead of to see the famous places and so they don't learn about places they visit.

However, people who enjoy shopping like every stage about shopping, from window shopping, trying clothes on, thinking if they should buy or not, to buying. The final stage is to be satisfied with seeing what they have bought in their house or wearing it in front of their mirror like a fashion show.

This activity is proved to be a complete leisure activity. Indeed, I read an article in a newspaper called 'Shopping is a way to relax'. We should all use this nice relaxation and not feel guilty. Don't you think so?

Comments

This has clear organisation, with paragraphs giving points for and against the statement.

However, the first sentence just repeats the task.

There are some good expressions (e.g. *if we ask … the answers are almost always 'shopping'*) but also some grammatical mistakes (e.g. *go shopping sometime instead of to see*).

There is quite a good range of topic-related vocabulary, but the style is too informal in places (e.g. *Don't you think so?*).

It has a positive effect on the reader.

Band 4

Writing Reference

Story

(For work on stories, see pages 44 and 138.)

1 Task

Your teacher has asked you to write a story for the school's English language magazine. It must begin with the following words:

I wanted to do my best, but more than that I wanted the team to win.

Write your **story**. (You should write between **120** and **180** words.)

2 Model answer

DO use phrases to show when things happened in your story (e.g. *It was the last football game of the season. When the second half started …*). DON'T make mistakes with narrative tenses.	*I wanted to do my best, but more than that I wanted the team to win. It was the last football game of the season, and if we won, we would be the champions. As we ran onto the pitch, I couldn't help feeling nervous. The crowd was cheering, but the opposition looked strong. It wasn't going to be easy.*	DON'T write about a topic if you don't know some specific vocabulary related to it (e.g. *score, goalkeeper, goal, pitch*).
	The game started. I got the ball and raced towards the goal. 'Go on!' roared the crowd, but I kicked it straight into the hands of the goalkeeper. 'Never mind,' yelled my team-mate Joe. 'Good try!' We played hard, but at half-time the score was 0–0.	DO use interesting vocabulary (e.g. *raced, roared*). DO use direct speech because it makes the story more interesting to read.
DO add extra detail to add to the atmosphere of the story.	*When the second half started, it was raining heavily. Our chance of winning the championship was slipping away. We struggled to get the ball through the defence, but time after time they stopped us. Now there were only two minutes left. Suddenly I had the ball. I passed it to Joe, who headed it straight into the goal, just as the referee blew his whistle. The crowd went crazy. We were the champions!*	DO try to create some suspense. DO try to have a dramatic end.

USEFUL LANGUAGE

We had been (talking about John) just before (he phoned).

It wasn't until (I read the letter) that (I realised how dangerous the situation was).

While (I was waiting for my friends, I saw someone go into the house opposite).

As soon as (my friends arrived, we went to have a look).

I was just about to (open the door), when (I heard a noise downstairs).

By the time (I got back to the house, there was no one to be seen).

After waiting (for a few minutes, I decided to climb in through the window).

A few seconds later, (the lights went out).

Eventually/After a while, (my friends arrived).

At last (I knew what I had to do).

3 Sample task, answers and comments

Task

Your teacher has asked you to write a short story for the school's English language magazine. Your story must begin with the following words:

It was not easy, but Carol knew she had to do it.

Write your **story**. (You should write between **120** and **180** words.)

Answer A

It was not easy, but Carol knew she had to do it. In front of her there was this big river, with water that was running very fast, and this rubber dinghy. Behind her she could hear the guide explaining that the water is only about 8°C warm. Furthermore, he told to Carol's group that there are some dangerous places, where they have to take special care. After that, the guide smiled and cried: 'Let's go!' For one moment, Carol was thinking of an escape. But this river-rafting tour was her birthday present from her friends, and they were all there. She was the last one who got into the boat, and sat down at the back of it. She tried to smile and join the others pleasure, however, she wasn't very successful. She closed her eyes and the boat set off. After a while, Carol began to enjoy the trip. In fact, it was great fun, and at the end, when they arrived, Carol decided to book a next trip two weeks later.

Comments

This answers the question and gives some detail, and there is a clear beginning, middle and end.

There is some good accurate use of language (*Behind her she could hear the guide explaining; After a while, Carol began to enjoy the trip*) but there are several mistakes with reported speech (e.g. *he told to Carol's group that there are some dangerous places*) and other mistakes (e.g. *an escape; a next trip*).

There is some use of direct speech to add interest and there is quite a good range of vocabulary, but the student has not divided the story into paragraphs.

It has a positive effect on the reader.
Band 4

Answer B

It was not easy, but Carol knew she had to do it. She was in Trieste, Italy. She came there to visit her friend. His name is Stefano who she met in their language school in England. Actually she didn't know about Italy until she met him. So she couldn't speak Italian, was not good at Italian geography.

As the first mistake, she thought that Trieste was close to his house, but it was his fault. He lived in Trento, near Verona. She should have used a different airport. Trieste airport was quite small. She wasn't able to find a person who can speak English.

As the biggest mistake, she couldn't call him! She usually contacted with him by emails, so she didn't know how to call.

She tried to communicated with Italian people with body language many times. She didn't give up. If she gave up, she couldn't meet him. One hour past … and she learnt how to call him!! Eventually she was able to talk with him.

Three hours later Stefano come to her at the airport. She shouted for joy " Stefano!! I missed you!!"

Comments

This is a lively story. There are quite a lot of grammar mistakes (e.g. *who she met* instead of *and she had met him; she tried to communicated with*).

However, the student also uses a range of structures accurately (e.g. *She should have used; She didn't give up.*)

There are some mistakes in vocabulary so that the meaning is not always clear (e.g. *it was his fault* instead of *He'd made a mistake; she learnt how* instead of *she found out how*). Linking of ideas and sentences is not always clear.

However, there is good use of direct speech and a strong ending which has a positive effect on the reader.
Band 4 (Low)

Writing Reference

Report

(For work on reports, see pages 55 and 101.)

(1) Task

The school where you study English has decided to spend some money on either buying more computers or improving the library. You have been asked to write a report for the school director describing the benefits to the school of both these things, and saying which one you think should be chosen and why.

Write your **report**. (You should write between **120** and **180** words.)

USEFUL LANGUAGE

Introduction
The aim of this report is to ...
This report is intended to ...

Reporting results
Most people seem to feel that ...
Several people said/told me/suggested/thought that ...

Presenting a list
They gave/suggested the following reasons:
They made the following points:
1 ...
2 ...

Making recommendations
I would therefore recommend (that we expand the library/ installing a new coffee machine).
It would seem that (banning mobile phones) is the best idea.

(2) Model answer

DO use headings because this makes it easier for the reader to find the main information.

DO say how you collected the information.

DO use a range of specific vocabulary or set phrases, e.g. Some thought this was a good idea ..., other students said they preferred ..., but DON'T use lots of adjectives and dramatic language as you do in a story. A report gives factual information.

DO use numbering or bullet points to highlight main points.

DO express opinions impersonally. DON'T express recommendations or opinions until the conclusion.

Use of money for school improvements

Introduction

The aim of this report is to compare the advantages of additional computers and of improving the library, and to suggest which of these would be best. I interviewed a number of students to find out their views.

Buying more computers

Some of the students thought that this was a good idea, saying computers were useful for:

* *practising writing;*
* *using the Internet;*
* *playing games.*

However, other students said that they preferred to use their own computers at home.

Improving the library

Most of the students preferred this suggestion, giving the following reasons:

1 Many students do not have a quiet place to study at home. The library would be a good place for private study, but at present there are not enough tables and chairs there.

2 They feel that up-to-date dictionaries and reference books are needed.

3 They want to be able to read modern books written for young people.

Recommendations

Both ideas have benefits, but the majority of students felt that improving the library would be more useful. I would therefore recommend this.

DON'T begin and end your report with Dear Sir/Madam as you would in a letter.

DO include two or three points under each heading.

DON'T include irrelevant details or description.

DO use formal language.

3 Sample task, answer and comments

Task

> The owner of the school where you study English has decided to make some changes to the school classrooms. He has asked for ideas from students about what should be done to make the classrooms better places to study in. Write a report making suggestions for how the classrooms could be improved.
>
> Write your **report**. (You should write between **120** and **180** words.)

Answer

Introduction

This report is to suggest what we need to make the classrooms better in our school. I asked students for their ideas.

Background situation

What it's need to be inside a good school classrooms is that they all have all the equipment students might need starting from the essential things like chair, blackboards, finishing with accessories like televisions.

Suggestions

I certainly believe that two things need to start our plan to improve the school classrooms, they are money and good management. My idea of improving the classrooms is to start with what we have and see what needs to be repared and what has to be thrown away and replaced with a new equipment and some computers that the students might need also having a massive liberrary is one of the more important things that students request. Heating and air conditioning are necessary to make the atmosphere in the classrooms cosy.

Personal opinion

In conclusion, the chance of having a good classrooms looks easy from a distance, in fact it isn't, and that we must try to find the balance between having a very good school and not spending too much.

Comments

This report makes some relevant points, but the style is more suitable for an essay than a report. It would be much better in bullet points.

It is not easy to identify the main suggestions because of problems with sentence linking and punctuation. *My idea of … is to start with what we have* is good. The problem is the sentence is too long and needs splitting up, e.g. *My idea of improving the classrooms is to start with what we have. Then we can see … .*

There are some problems with passive forms (e.g. *what it's need* instead of *what is needed*), but also some good expressions (e.g. *to start with what we have; we must try to find the balance between*).

The student has a good range of vocabulary although this is not always appropriately used (e.g. *massive, cosy*) and there are some spelling mistakes (e.g. *repared, liberrary*). It has a satisfactory effect on the reader.

Band 3

Writing Reference

Letter/email

(For work on Part 1 letters/emails, see pages 85 and 146.)

1 Task

You recently had a short holiday in a large city which you booked through a company called Citibreaks. You were very disappointed with the holiday. Read the Citibreaks advertisement for the holiday you booked and the notes you have made. Then write a letter to Citibreaks, explaining what the problems were and telling them what you want them to do.

> **Citibreaks**
>
> Enjoy a short holiday in the capital city.
>
> We offer two nights' accommodation in a four-star hotel in a central location. — *View not river – only car park*
>
> *Not central – long way out!* All rooms have their own bathrooms, and a view of the river.
>
> *Dinner cost extra* The price of £150 per person includes all meals as well as a ticket for a show of your choice in one of the city's leading theatres. — *Refund – half cost?* — *No choice of show*
>
> This will be a real holiday to remember!

Write a **letter/email** of between **120** and **150** words in an appropriate style. Do not write any postal addresses.

2 Model answer

Dear Sir,

I am writing to complain about a short holiday I had recently, which was organised by Citibreaks. I was dissatisfied with several things.

DO begin by saying why you are writing. DON'T begin by saying who you are.

First, your advertisement promised a hotel in a central location, whereas in fact the hotel was a long way from the city centre. You also said that all the rooms would have a river view, but my window just looked over the car park, which was very noisy. I also had to pay extra for dinner, although the advertisement had stated that it was included in the price. To make matters worse, I had no choice of which show to go to. I had wanted to go to a new musical, but the only ticket offered to me was for one which I had seen already.

DO make a clear connection between your letter/email and the task input. DON'T repeat the exact words in the task input.

DO list your complaints clearly, using linking words to connect your actual complaint with the details.

I had been looking forward to my holiday very much, but it was completely ruined by these problems. I therefore feel that you should refund half the cost of the holiday in compensation for my disappointment.

I look forward to hearing from you soon.

Yours faithfully,

Ursine Schmidt

Ursine Schmidt

If you begin your letter/email Dear Sir/Madam, DO end with Yours faithfully. If you begin Dear Ms (or Mr, Mrs, Miss) Jones, etc., DO end with Yours sincerely.

If you expect a reply to your letter/email, DO finish with this sentence on a separate line.

DO sign and print your full name.

USEFUL LANGUAGE

Complaining

I am writing to you about (several problems related to my city break in June).

I have been waiting for (two weeks for a reply to my letter).

To make matters worse, (we were informed that there was no record of our cheque being cashed).

I would be grateful if you could (refund my deposit as soon as possible).

Requesting information

I am writing in response to (your advertisement in 'The Daily Standard' on July 20th).

I would be grateful if you could (send me further details about the position).

I am writing to enquire whether (you could let me have further details about the holiday).

I would like to know more about (the arrangements for the evening meal).

Giving information/responding to requests for information

In response to your query, I would like to inform you that (I passed the FCE in June).

With reference to your letter of … (I enclose details of my qualifications).

You asked me to tell you about (my travel plans and I enclose further details).

3 Sample task, answer and comments

Task

You recently entered a competition for learners of English, and have just received a letter from the organisers of the competition. You have made some notes on the letter.

Congratulations! You have won first prize in our competition – a two-week trip to Vancouver or San Francisco.   *Direct flight?*

Your prize includes: *Hours?*

*FREE return flight to the city of your choice   *Morning/afternoon?*

*FREE two-week course at the Vancouver or San Francisco School of International English   *Distance from school? Meals?*

*Two weeks' FREE accommodation with a family

We need to know your choice of city, your preferred dates, and if you would like us to make any special arrangements for you.   *Stay an extra week?*

We look forward to hearing from you. Once we have the information we will send you your tickets and further details.

Yours sincerely

Jacky Thompson

Jacky Thompson

Competition Manager

Write a **letter/email** of between **120** and **150** words in an appropriate style. Do not write any postal addresses.

Answer

Dear Mrs Thompson,

Thank you very much for the letter which I've received yesterday. I am very pleased that I've won the prize. I would like to go to San Francisco because I never have been to the USA before. However, there are several questions I would like to ask.

First of all, I would like to know whether the return flight is a direct flight or not. I would like to book a direct flight because it is much more comfortable.

Secondly, I would like to know how long we are being teached every day and if there are classes in the morning or the afternoon.

You wrote about a free accommodation with a family. Are the meals included and/or do I have the opportunity to cook by myself?

Finally, I would like to ask you if it is possible to stay at school for an extra week. If it is possible please let me know the price I have to pay concerning this point.

I like to thank you in advance for your assistance and I look forward to hearing from you soon.

Yours sincerely,

Lennart Moser

Comments

This is rather long, but there is no irrelevant information and the student answers all parts of the question.

There are some grammatical mistakes (e.g. *which I've received*, *I never have been*, *we are being teached*), but these don't cause major problems in understanding the meaning.

He uses quite a wide range of structures, although he tends to repeat *'I would like to know'* too much. Vocabulary is generally appropriate although the style is sometimes too formal (e.g. *concerning this point*). The ideas are organised in clear paragraphs and the letter would have a positive effect on the reader.

Band 3

Writing Reference

Article

(For work on articles, see pages 76 and 156.)

1 Task

You see this advertisement in a local English-language newspaper.

> *Hey!* magazine is looking for articles about celebrations around the world. Write us an article about a celebration that is important in your country, explaining why the celebration is important and describing what people do. If your article is chosen for the magazine, you will win a weekend in a city of your choice.

Write your **article**. (You should write between **120** and **180** words.)

2 Model answer

DO think of an interesting title.

DO try to involve your readers, e.g. by using a question.

Olinda's carnival – something for everyone

When most people think of Carnival, they think of Rio de Janeiro. But Rio isn't the only city in Brazil that knows how to have parties. I live in Olinda, a lovely city in the north-east of Brazil. What can we say about the carnival at Olinda? Just that it's the best in the world!

Carnival has its origins in ancient Egyptian and Roman festivals. It was introduced to Brazil by the Portuguese, and was influenced by African rhythms and Indian costumes. Now it's a big national celebration.

Once Carnival starts, the whole town goes crazy! Everyone's singing and dancing. Parades of people wearing costumes typical of our north-eastern folklore dance through the streets. I love the giant street dolls, both the traditional ones such as 'the man of midnight' and the new ones that appear each year.

DO finish your article by summarising your main point and giving your opinion or expressing your feelings.

The best thing about our carnival is that no one has to pay and there are no big stars. Everyone takes part, rich and poor, old and young, residents and tourists. If you come, I promise you'll never forget it!

DON'T start and finish your article in the same way as a letter.

DO use informal language to involve the reader.

DON'T forget to express your opinion.

USEFUL LANGUAGE

Involving the reader

Are you thinking of (getting married in the near future)?

I'm sure you'll agree (it was a great idea).

Developing your points

Let's start with (why it is so important to take plenty of exercise).

Another advantage (of using a computer is that ...)

On top of that, ...

Giving your own opinion

I think that/In my opinion (traditional celebrations are very important).

It seems to me that (people are much more aware of the importance of a good diet nowadays).

3 Sample task, answer and comments

Task

You have seen this advertisement in a magazine for young people.

> *I'd love to have ...*
>
> Write an article about something you would like to have, saying why you would like to have it and what difference it would make to your life. The writer of the best article will win a lap-top computer.

Write your **article**. (You should write between **120** and **180** words.)

Answer

I'd love to have a lot of money although I think money is not a perfect solution. Of course not! However, if I had enough money, I could do a plenty of things which I want to do.

Above all, I want to study in other countries, because. It is a good chance to develop my abilities. In this case, I don't need to worry about the fee of education in my life. I can only concentrate on studying as long as I do my best.

Secondly, I would like to prepare a lovely house for my parents. Although they didn't say to me at all, I think the work of electric services is so hard to continue at their ages within ten years. Therefore, I hope that I could make them relax and enjoy their life.

On the other hand, I can help the other people who are suffering from lack of food, illness and so on. When I saw a TV programme which announced those people's stories, I thought if I were them I would get really depressed.

Sometimes, money can be used in a bad way, but if I am a rich person, I will spend them on not only for me, but I also give an opportunity to others.

Comments

This answer gives relevant information and answers the question. There is quite a good range of structures and vocabulary but these are not always used very accurately (e.g. *If I am a rich person, I will spend them on not only for me* instead of *If I were rich, I wouldn't just spend the money on myself*).

It is also difficult to understand exactly what she wants to say about her parents in the line *Although they didn't say to me at all, I think … .*

The paragraphs are well planned but there are mistakes with linking words (e.g. *On the other hand* instead of, e.g. *As well as that*) and with punctuation.

There is a mixture of informal language (e.g. *Of course not!*) and formal language (e.g. *Therefore*).

It has a satisfactory effect on the reader.
Band 3

Writing Reference

Letter of application

(For work on writing applications, see pages 66 and 146.)

1 Task

You see this advertisement in a local English-language newspaper.

> We are looking for students of English to spend two mornings a week helping in the local tourist office.
>
> *Good pay and conditions for the right applicants.*
>
> Write to us, giving information about your level of English, and explaining why you would be suitable for the job.

Write your **application**. Do not write any postal addresses. (You should write between **120** and **180** words.)

2 Model answer

DO say which job you are applying for and where and when you saw it advertised. You can invent a newspaper and date if you need to.

DO organise your application so that you mention each of the areas in the advertisement.

DO say when and how you can be contacted.

Dear Sir/Madam,

I am writing to apply for one of the positions helping in the local tourist office which were advertised in 'Kent Weekly' on August 23rd.

I am nineteen years old and come from Switzerland. German is my mother tongue and I have been learning English and French for five years at a comprehensive school. At the moment I'm a student at English International, studying for the FCE.

I have always been interested in working with people. As I have already spent three months in England, I know the local tourist attractions quite well. I would also say that I have a good knowledge of history and old places because I have read a lot about the subject recently. In the near future, I would like to continue studying English, and so the job in your tourist office would be a great opportunity for me to improve my speaking.

I am available for interview at any time. I can be contacted on 0795 51 32 41 after 6 p.m. every evening.

Thank you for considering my application. I look forward to hearing from you.

Yours faithfully,

Gabriella Daniels

DON'T start and finish your article in the same way as a letter.

DON'T make mistakes with time expressions and tenses.

DON'T forget to mention why you think you are suitable.

DO begin and end your letter as you would other formal letters.

3 Sample task, answer and comments

Task

You recently saw this notice in an international magazine.

> We are looking for ten people from different countries to walk with us to the Base Camp of Mount Everest to raise money for charity. We guarantee it will be the experience of a lifetime! You just need to be fit, be free for two weeks in April and have a reasonable level of English.
>
> Write and tell us why you are one of the people we are looking for and why you would like to be part of this adventure.

Write your **letter of application**. (You should write between **120** and **180** words).

Answer

Dear Sirs or Madams,

I am writing in reply to advertisement I was seen in international magazine last week. I would like to apply to be part of the group that walks to the Base Camp of Mount Everest.

I play tenis and football a lot and go to my gym two times in every week. So, I am a quite fit person. My level of English is upper-intermediate and I will take my First Certificate in English exam in June. My teacher thinks I will succeed! I am on holidays for most April but it depend on the dates of the voyage. I think raise money for charity is a very good way to spend holidays.

I can be contact by phone on 07945 392 693. If I don't answer your call, please leave message and I will phone you after.

I look forward to hearing from you.

Yours faithfully,

Pietro Sampras

Comments

This is an adequate response to the task. It is organised appropriately and includes all the necessary information.

There are some mistakes of grammar (e.g. *I was seen, I can be contact*) and vocabulary (e.g. *succeed, voyage*) but they don't cause significant problems in understanding the meaning.

The range of structures and vocabulary used is limited but sufficient for the task. The target reader would have all the information they asked for and a reasonable impression of the applicant.

Band 3

Punctuation

Full stops (.), question marks (?) and exclamation marks (!) are used to finish sentences. After these a new sentence has a capital letter.

Mark got all 'A' grades in his final exams! He's going to Manchester University to study law.

Capital letters are used to start sentences, for names and with *I*.
We like Angela. She's very friendly.
I worked in Kenya for a year.

Commas (,) usually reflect a pause in speech. They are often used to separate items in a list (but not before *and*) and add information.
In the end we went to Peru, Chile, Ecuador and Brazil.
That's my oldest sister, who now lives in Paris.

Colons (:) usually introduce an explanation or a list.
I decided to resign from my job: it no longer gave me any real satisfaction.
I played lots of different sports at school: rugby, cricket, tennis, hockey and squash.

Semi-colons (;) can be used to separate items in lists of phrases.
Before you leave the house, please remember to do what I asked: shut all the windows; leave a light on in the living room; water the plants and put some food out for the cat.

Quotation marks can be single ('…') or double ("…"). They are also called 'inverted commas'. We use them (single or double) when we quote direct speech. We also use single quotation marks when a word is used in a special way.
"Get out of the way," she cried.
Pete said he found my brother 'interesting'. Unfortunately I have no idea what he meant!

Apostrophes (') show where letters have been left out or are used to indicate possession.
I'm sorry I'm late.
This is Simon's coat.

Set book

In Question 5 of the Cambridge FCE exam, you may answer one of two questions based on your reading of one of the set books. You may be asked to write an article, an essay, a report or a letter. You do not have to answer Question 5. If you do, make sure that you know the book well enough to be able to answer the question properly. Here is a suggested procedure for writing about the set text.

1 Read the book all the way through to get a general idea of the story and the characters – and to enjoy it!

2 Read the book again, this time more carefully. Make notes under the following headings.
   Plot: include the main events and the order they occur.
   Characters: include information about what they are like and how important they are in the story.
   Relationships: include information about who likes/dislikes who, and the things that affect their relationships.
   Places: include descriptions of the most important places.
   Your own reactions: write down your feelings about the book, with some reasons for your opinion.

3 Make a list of the kind of questions you might be asked to write about, and discuss them with other students. Here are some ideas:
   • What makes the book interesting/exciting? Describe an exciting or memorable moment in the book.
   • Choose the most interesting character. Describe him/her. Is this your favourite character?
   • Is the title a good one for the book? Why?
   • Does the book have a good ending? Why/Why not.
   • Do you think the book would make a good film? Explain your reasons.
   • Would you recommend the book? Why/Why not.

1 Task

> *Great Expectations* – Charles Dickens
> Ambition and self-improvement are central themes in the book. Write an essay describing in what ways they are important to the character of Pip.

2 Model answer

> Pip is the key character of 'Great Expectations' and he is an idealist; whenever he sees that something can be better than it already is, he immediately wants to make that improvement. The themes of ambition and self-improvement take three forms – moral, social and educational.

DO answer the question directly. DON'T just tell the story of the book.

> First, Pip desires moral self-improvement. He is very hard on himself when, for example, he acts badly towards Joe and Biddy. He feels a terrible sense of guilt which makes him want to act better in the future. Second, Pip wishes to improve his social position. In love with Estella, he desperately wants to become a gentleman and a member of her social class. Third, Pip wants educational improvement. This desire is, in fact, deeply connected to his social ambition and longing to marry Estella. While he remains an ignorant country boy, he has no hope of social advancement.

DO make links between paragraphs clear.

DO give examples (where relevant) from the book.

DO use a good range of vocabulary and grammar.

> Ultimately, however, through the examples of Joe, Biddy and Magwitch, Pip learns that ambition and self-improvement are irrelevant to the true value of a person and that conscience and affection are much more important.

USEFUL LANGUAGE

The book is really exciting because (it starts with a murder).
The best moment is when (the murderer is revealed).
The book tells the story of (a family who have been separated).
The first thing that happens is (Sarah leaves home).
The main character, (Marian, is a teenager who …).
The most interesting character is (Joe, the young man who lives …).
The title is really good, because (it is mysterious and it makes you want to find out what it really means).

The story takes place in (the South of France).
Events revolve around (a robbery).
The ending is very exciting because (it is completely unexpected).
It would make (a really good film), because (it is such an exciting story).
The best thing about the book is that (the characters are so interesting).
I would recommend this book because (it is easy to read).

3 Sample task, answer and comments

Task

George Orwell – *Animal Farm*

Old Major is a key character in the development of the story of Animal Farm. Write an **essay** describing his particular strengths and weaknesses. (You should write between **120** and **180** words).

Answer

Old Major is introduced to us on the very first page of the story. He appears a very wise and important caracter and the other animals clearly respect him. He seems to have a special ability to make persueing speeches which have a big effect on the rest of the farm. In the speech we hear at the begining of the book he convinces the other animals to share his anger at the way they have all been treated by Man. He explains all of man's crimes and this makes the other animals to plan the rebellion. His power to persuede also happens when he starts the singing of "Beasts of England" Afterwards the animals sing it five more times on their own. The main weakness in old Major's ideas is that he gives all the blame to Man for all the animals problems. According to him, once they get rid with Man, hunger and overwork will be disappear. Old Major seems to believe that Man is only capable of doing harm and that animals are only capable of doing good. The story of Animal Farm shows how this view is too simple and, in fact, by the end of the book Napoleon and the other pigs are exactly like there human masters.

Comments

This essay is a full and direct response to the task. A good range of grammar and vocabulary is used with only a few minor spelling and punctuation mistakes.

An appropriate style has been used with some appropriate linking phrases.

The essay, however, has not been organised into paragraphs appropriately making it slightly more difficult to read. It is also a little too long.

Band 4

Band descriptions

When assessing written work, examiners look for these features at each grade.

Band 5

The writing has the right effect on the reader.
The question is fully answered.
The ideas are organised well in appropriate paragraphs.
A variety of linking words/phrases is used.
A wide range of grammar and vocabulary is used.
Very few errors.
The style of the writing is appropriate.

Band 4

The writing has the right effect on the reader.
The question is fully answered.
The ideas are organised well in appropriate paragraphs.
Appropriate linking words/phrases are used.
A good range of grammar and vocabulary is used.
Not many errors.
The style of the writing is generally appropriate.

Band 3

The writing mainly has the right effect on the reader.
The question is fully answered.
The ideas are organised adequately in paragraphs.
Simple linking words/phrases are used.
An adequate range of grammar and vocabulary is used.
The errors that occur do not prevent communication.
A reasonable, but not always successful, attempt at a style of writing that is appropriate.

Band 2

The writing may not clearly communicate the message to the reader.
Some points required are not adequately covered or are missed out.
Ideas are inadequately organised.
Very few, if any, linking words/phrases are used.
The range of grammar and vocabulary is quite limited.
Errors distract the reader and may obstruct communication.
Attempts at an appropriate style of writing are unsuccessful or inconsistent.

Band 1

The writing has a very negative effect on the reader.
A number of important points required are missed out.
A noticeable lack of organisation and linking words/phrases.
Very narrow range of grammar and vocabulary.
Frequent errors.
Little or no awareness of the appropriate style of writing.

Band 0

For a Band 0 to be awarded, there is either too little language for assessment (fewer than fifty words) or the candidate's writing is totally irrelevant or totally illegible.

Pearson Education Limited
Edinburgh Gate
Harlow
Essex CM20 2JE
England
and Associated Companies throughout the world.

www.longman.com/exams

© Pearson Education Limited 2008

The right of Richard Acklam and Araminta Crace to be identified as authors of this Work has been asserted by them in accordance with the Copyright, Designs and Patents Act 1988.

First published 2008

Designed by James Hall

Picture Research by: Frances Topp, Sandra Hilsdon

ISBN 978-1-4058-4917-3

Set in Cronos Pro Light 10.5/11.5

Printed in Spain by Graficas Estella.

Acknowledgements

The publishers and authors would like to thank the following people and institutions for their feedback and comments during the development of the material: Will Moreton, Spain; Tina Zaharopoulou, Greece; Dorota Adaszewska, Poland; Sarah Ellis, Italy; Steven Miller, Mayfair School of English, London, UK; Paula Kler, Malvern House, London, UK; Kate Leigh, Spain

Araminta Crace would like to thank Ian Wood, Helena Gomm, Yolanda Durham, James Hall, Ann Oakley and everyone else on the team at Pearson Education for all their hard work and professionalism and for making this project run as smoothly as it possibly could. On a more personal note, my thanks again go to my lovely daughters Petra and Lola for being themselves, and to my mum Gay for just about everything.

We are grateful to the following for permission to reproduce copyright material: Agatha Christie Limited for material from *Agatha Christie, an Autobiography* copyright © 1977 Agatha Christie Limited (a Chorion company) all rights reserved; Susan Aldridge for an extract adapted from "Be happy" by Susan Aldridge published in *BBC Focus Magazine* December 2005 copyright © Susan Aldridge; Atlantic Syndication for an extract adapted from "Book of The Week (*A Short History of Nearly Everything* by Bill Bryson) by Craig Brown published in *The Mail on Sunday* 22nd June 2003 copyright © Atlantic Syndication 2003; The BBC for extracts from "I will if you will" published on www.bbc.co.uk 14th June 2005, "The Carnivore, Nairobi, Kenya" published on www.bbc.co.uk 29th March 2001, "Pompeii: Portents of Disaster" by Professor Andrew Wallace-Hadrill published on www.bbc.co.uk 23rd September 2003, "Free enterprise" by Duncan Walker published on www.bbc.co.uk 20th June 2005, "The million-dollar student" by Tom Geoghegan published on www.bbc.co.uk, and "Head for Heights required" by Duncan Walker published on www.bbc.co.uk 22nd August 2005 copyright © www.BBC.co.uk; Bloomsbury Publishing plc for an extract adapted from *The Kite Runner* by Khaled Hosseini copyright © 2003; Delaware North Companies Travel Hospitality Services, Inc for information about LA Encounter Restaurant; Dennis Publishing for an extract adapted from "Tortoise befriends baby hippo" published in *The Week* 15th January 2005 copyright © The Week 2005; Deutsche Welle for an extract adapted from "Modern-Day Robin Hoods have Hamburg Cops Baffled" by Nicholas David Amies published on http://www.dw-world.de/english 8th May 2006 copyright © 2006 Deutsche Bank AG-Koln; Guardian News & Media Ltd for extracts from "2050 and immortality is within our grasp" by David Smith published in *The Observer* 22nd May 2005, "Gambian toad hitches life" by Patrick Barkham published in *The Guardian* 3rd January 2006 and "A merry band" by Luke Harding published in *The Guardian* 17th May 2006 copyright © The Guardian 2005, 2006; A.M. Heath and Bill Hamilton as the Literary Executor of the Estate of the Late Sonia Brownell Orwell and Secker & Warburg Ltd for an extract from *Animal Farm* by George Orwell copyright © George Orwell 1945; The Independent News & Media Ltd for extracts from "The 50 Best: Put the excitement back in your life" by Alister Morgan published in *The Independent* 24-30th April 1999 copyright © The Independent 1999; Little, Brown Book Group for a review of *Long Way Round* by Ewan McGregor and Charley Boorman published by Time Warner Books copyright © 2004; Music Sales Limited & Warner/Chappell Music Ltd for the lyric reproduction of "Talk" Words & Music by Guy Berryman, Chris Martin, Karl Bartos, Jon Buckland, Will Champion, Emil Schult & Ralf Hütter copyright © 2005 Sony/ATV Music Publishing (UK) Limited; Edition Positive Songs, Kling Klang Music, R Huetter, F Scheider, Esleben & BMG Music Publishing Ltd. Used by permission. All Rights Reserved. International Copyright Secured; Profile Books Ltd for an extract from *Talk to the Hand* by Lynne Truss copyright © 2005; Radio Times for an extract adapted from "The Lost World" by Jenny Eden published in *Radio Times Magazine* 29th April 2006; Random House for an extract adapted from *If on a Winters Night a traveller* by Italo Calvino; and Telegraph Media Group Limited for an extract from "I think the Captains dead" by Julia Llewellyn-Smith published in *The Telegraph* 5th February 2005 copyright © The Telegraph 2005.

In some instances we have been unable to trace the owners of copyright material and we would appreciate any information that would enable us to do so.

The publisher would like to thank the ollowing for their kind permission to reproduce their photographs: (Key: b-bottom; c-centre; l-left; r-right; t-top) akg-images Ltd: Ullstein Bild 110tl; Alamy Images: Alan Dawson 159tl; Andre Jenny 27tl; Bildagentur Schapowalow 117tr; Bobbie Lerryn 32r; Chad Ehlers 59tr; Charlie Newham 98bl; Chuck Pefley 85r; David South 141br; David Young-Wolff 159tr; DRPics 27l; Imagebroker 55tr; Jan Stromme 137b; Janine Wiedel Photolibrary 73t; Jeff Greenberg 34l; Mark Harmel 137l; Mark Zylber 89tr; Mary Evans Picture Library 131br; mediacolor's 79tr; Photofusion Picture Library 58bl; Powerhouse Digital Photography Ltd. 86l; Profimedia International 106c; Rob Bartee 110bl; Rob Walls 55tl; Ron Buskirk 28tr; Simon Grosset 60tr; Aquarius Collection: 40c, 42r, 78b; Arenapal: Joan Marcus 9b; Artothek: Blauel/Gnamm 7br; BAA Aviation Photo Library: David Hares 25b; BBC Photo Library: 99c; BBC Picture Publicity: 42l; Blackpool Gazette: Martin Bostock 30b; Bridgeman Art Library Ltd: 90t, 135r, 151c; Collection of Mr and Mrs John Hay Whitney, New York, USA 120tr; Corbis: 58tl, 84t; Armando Babani 17tl; Christie's Images 12br; David Trilling 52l; Douglas Kirkland 40tl; Geoff Caddick 120tl; Helen Atkinson 7tr; Henrik Trygg 46bl; Hulton-Deutsch Collection 111br; Image Source 140b; Issei Kato / Reuters 59c; John Noble 36bl; Justin Lane 99br; Louie Psihoyos 36t; Marcos Delgado 89br; Michael Busselle 78bl; Ramin Talaie 47br; Randy Faris 12t, 17bl; Rick Gayle 71t; Samir Soudah 136l; Serge Krouglikoff 15b; Shaun Best 47c; Simon Jarratt 159bl; Simon Marcus 12bl; Digital Vision: 78tl; Education Photos: John Walmsley 63; Erik Aeder: 60br; FLPA Images of Nature: Ariadne Van Zandbergen 80br; Chris Mattison 32bl; Fritz Polking 94l; Terry Whittaker 40b; Wendy Dennis 17c; Future is Wild: 88tl; Getty Images: 147r; AFP 92l; Ami Vitale 60l; Image Bank 30t; Jacques Collet/AFP 153b; Kareem Black 141c; Larry Marano 119r; Manchan 151br; Marko Georglev 89cl; Peter Adams 26bl; Photonica 117tl; Stone 99tr; Taxi 37l; The Image Bank / Ron Levine 20b; Ronald Grant Archive: 121c, 130bl; Bad Robot / Touchstone Television 132bl; Jupiterimages: 59br; Workbook Stock 55br; LAWA: J. Berkowitz/LAWA 81br; Michael Stuber: Photographers Direct 83r; mytinygarden.com: Jay Dykes 28tl; NHPA Ltd / Photoshot Holdings: 80bl, 81bc, 81c; PA Photos: Chris Young 159br; John Walton 60c; Liam Creedon 142b; Yarish / Zuma 17tr; Photofusion Picture Library: Don Gray 32bl; Ute Klaphake 18tl; Photolibrary.com: Brandx Pictures 111c; Stockbyte 98tl; Yadid Levy 124l; PunchStock: Moodboard; 2b (Exam Reviser); BananaStock 7c; Digital Vision 28c, 55bl; Dynamic Graphics 140tl; GlowImages 129br; ImageSource 27tr; Purestock 147l; Redferns Music Picture Library: GAB Archives 8tl; Rex Features: 20thC.Fox/Everett / Rex Features 17br; 8tr, 18tr, 40cr, 100t; Action Press 11t; Andre Csillag 8br; Brian Rasic 7tl; CBS/Everett 121tr; David Fisher 8bl; Debra Rothenberg 131c; Eddie Mulholland 70c; Everett / ABC Inc 133b; ITV 121l; Photosport International 49b; Sipa Press 36tl, 46tl, 79br, 155b; Walt Disney/Everett 7bl; Science Photo Library Ltd: Coneyl Jay 74t; DAavid Mack 69br; GustoImages 69tl; James King-Holmes 73b; Jerry Mason 112tl; Mel Lindstrom 69tr; NASA 68bl; Neil Borden 150bl; Peter Ginter 69bl; Scott Sinklier 68tl; Spot Image 91b; Stephen Donovan : 47tr; SuperStock: 79c, 111tr, 140bl, 141tr; Casey Kelbaugh 96l; Raga Jose Fuste 37tr; Ron Dahlquist 37br; Tiger Aspect: 121br; Tom Steinberg: 33c; Elizabeth Whiting & Associates: Tony Timmington 27br

All other images © Pearson Education

Every effort has been made to trace the copyright holders and we apologise in advance for any unintentional omissions. We would be pleased to insert the appropriate acknowledgement in any subsequent edition of this publication.

Illustrated by Coburn pgs93, 95, 100, 102, 103, 107, 114, 124, 126, 128; Martina Farrow pgs38, 123; Otto Steininger pgs18, 19, 151(tr); Jurgen Ziewe pgs131, 151(tl)

Cover images © Arenapal: Joan Marcus br; Corbis: Henrik Trygg bl; Issei Kato / Reuters tr; PunchStock: tl; Science Photo Library Ltd: Peter Ginter cr; SuperStock: Raga Jose Fuste cl